The Principles of Buddhist Psychology

SUNY Series in Buddhist Studies
Kenneth K. Inada, Editor

The Principles of Buddhist Psychology

David J. Kalupahana

State University of New York Press

Published by
State University of New York Press, Albany

Printed in the United States of America

For information, address State University of New York Press, State University Plaza, Albany, N.Y., 12246

Library of Congress Cataloging in Publication Data

Kalupahana, David J., 1933–
The principles of Buddhist psychology.

(SUNY series in Buddhist studies)
Bibliography: p.
Includes index.
1. Buddhism—Psychology. I. Title. II. Series.
BQ4570.P76K35 1987 150'.882943 86-14583
ISBN 0-88706-404-3
ISBN 0-88706-403-5 (pbk.)

10 9 8 7 6 5 4 3 2 1

To Professor Stanley Weinstein,
teacher and friend
and Yogācāra enthusiast.

Contents

Abbreviations

A	*Anguttara-nikāya*, ed. R. Morris and E. Hardy, 5 volumes, London: PTS, 1885–1900.
AD	*Abhidharmadīpa*, see *Adv*.
Adv	*Abhidharmadīpa with Vibhāṣāprabhāvṛtti*, ed. P. S. Jaini, Patna: K. P. Jayaswal Research Institute, 1959.
AK	*Abhidharmakośa*, see *Akb*.
Akb	*Abhidharmakośa-bhāṣya*, ed. Pralhad Pradhan, Patna: K. P. Jayaswal Research Institute, 1967.
D	*Dīgha-nikāya*, ed. T. W. Rhys Davids and J. E. Carpenter, 3 volumes, London: PTS, 1890–1911.
DH	*Dhammapada*, ed. V. Fausbøll, London: Luzac, 1900.
DhsA	*Atthasalinī, Dhammasaṅganī-aṭṭhakathā*, ed. E. Müller, London: PTS, 1897.
ERE	William James, *Essays in Radical Empiricism*, ed. Frederick Burkhardt, Cambridge, Mass.: Harvard University Press, 1976.
ERM	William James, *Essays in Religion and Morality*, ed. Frederick Burkhardt, Cambridge, Mass.: Harvard University Press, 1982.
It	*Itivuttaka*, ed. E. Windish, London: PTS, 1889.
J	*The Jātaka*, ed. V. Fausbøll, London: PTS, 1962–1964.
Kārikā	*Mūlamadhyamakakārikā*, see *MKV*.
Kp	*Kāśyapaparivarta of the Ratnakūṭa-sūtra*, ed. A. Stael-Holstein, Shanghai: Commercial Press, 1926.
Kvu	*Kathāvatthu*, ed. A. C. Taylor, 2 volumes, London: PTS, 1894–1897.
M	*Majjhima-nikāya*, ed. V. Trenckner and R. Chalmers, 3 volumes, London: PTS, 1887–1901.
MKV	*Mādhyamikavṛtti* (*Madhyamakakārikās*), ed. L. de la Vallee Poussin, *Bibliotheca Buddhica*, 4, St. Petersburg: The Imperial Academy of Sciences, 1903–1913.
MV	*Madhyāntavibhāga*, see *MVB*.

MVB	*Madhyāntavibhāga-bhāṣya*, ed. Gadjin M. Nagao, Tokyo: Suzuki Research Foundation, 1964.
MVBT	*Madhyāntavibhāga-ṭīkā*, ed. S. Yamaguchi, Nagoya: Heijinkaku, 1934.
PEW	*Philosophy East and West*, ed. Eliot Deutsch, Honolulu: The University Press of Hawaii.
PP	William James, *The Principles of Psychology*, ed. Frederick Burkhardt, Cambridge, Mass.: Harvard University Press, 1981. (References in parenthesis are to the original editions, New York: Henry Holt, 1908.)
PTS	The Pali Text Society, London.
S	*Saṃyutta-nikāya*, ed. L. Feer, 5 volumes, London: PTS, 1884–1904.
Sakv	*Sphuṭārthābhidharmakośa-vyākhyā*, ed. U. Wogihara, Tokyo: The Publication Association of Abhidharmakośavyākhyā, 1932–1936.
Sdmp	*Saddharmapuṇḍarīka-sūtra*, ed. H. Kern and B. Nanjio, St. Petersburg: The Imperial Academy of Sciences, 1912.
Sn	*Sutta-nipāta*, ed. D. Anderson and H. Smith, London: PTS, 1913.
SPP	William James, *Some Problems of Philosophy*, ed. Frederick Burkhardt, Cambridge, Mass.: Harvard, 1979.
Triṃś	*Triṃśikā Vijñaptimātratāsiddhi*, see *Viṃś*.
Ud	*Udāna*, ed. P. Steinthal, London: PTS, 1948.
VbhA	*Sammohavinodanī, Vibhaṅgaṭṭhakathā*, ed. A. P. Buddhadatta, London, PTS, 1923.
Vin	*Vinaya Piṭaka*, ed. H. Oldenberg, 5 volumes, London: PTS, 1879–1883.
Viṃś	*Viṃśatikā Vijñaptimātratāsiddhi*, ed. S. Levi, Paris: Libraire Ancienne Honore Champion, 1925.
Vism	*The Visuddhi-magga of Buddhaghosa*, ed. C. A. F. Rhys Davids, London: PTS, 1975.
VRE	*The Varieties of Religious Experience*, ed. Frederick Burkhardt, Cambridge, Mass.: Harvard University Press, 1985.
WB	William James, *The Will to Believe*, ed. Frederick Burkhardt, Cambridge, Mass.: Harvard University Press, 1985.

Preface

Several books dealing with Buddhist psychology have appeared since Mrs. C. A. F. Rhys Davids highlighted the importance of psychological analysis in the Buddha's teachings (see *Buddhist Psychology*, London: G. Bell and Sons, 1914). More recently, the Buddha's psychological speculations have been compared with those of modern psychologists and psychoanalysts (see M. W. Padmasiri de Silva, *Buddhist and Freudian Psychology*, Colombo: Lake House Investments, 1978). Even a world-renowned psychoanalyst got heavily involved in the study of Buddhist psychology (see D. T. Suzuki, Erich Fromm and Robert De Martino, *Zen Buddhism and Psychoanalysis*, New York: Grove Press, 1960). While it would be grossly unfair to say that these studies have no contribution to make, there is no denying that most of them labor under the old cliché that the goal of Buddhist psychological analysis is to reveal the hidden mysteries in the human mind and thereby facilitate the development of a transcendental state of consciousness beyond the reach of linguistic expression (see Thomas A. Kochumuttom, *A Buddhist Doctrine of Experience*, Delhi: Motilal Banarsidass, 1982). The Buddha's statements, as well as the statements of some of his faithful disciples throughout the centuries, have therefore been looked upon as enigmatic utterances or *koans* with no directly implied meanings. *Experiences not described by the Buddha or his more enlightened disciples are being constantly discussed, while those that are described and "laid bare"* (*uttānī-kata*, as the Buddha himself would characterize them) *are ignored.*

Even though the Buddha's ideas were totally opposed to those expressed in India during his day, their influence on mankind has remained pervasive. They spread rapidly both in India and beyond her boundaries to gain a lasting hold in the lives of countless millions throughout the centuries in South, South-East and East Asia. Yet soon they were to disappear from the country in which they were first promulgated. This disappearance was due mostly to the way in which the Brahmanical tradition reasserted itself by emphasizing transcendence in the spheres of psychology, metaphysics, ethics and religious experience, as is evident from a careful study of the *Bhagavadgītā*.

Buddhism, it has been said, is "the last of the great Asiatic schools of thought to reach American shores," and "has been moving ever deeper into the very substratum of American philosophy, . . ." (*Buddhism and American Thinkers*, ed. Kenneth K. Inada and N. P. Jacobson, Albany: The State University of New York Press, 1984, p. vii). Yet, considering the manner in which Buddhism is being presented in the Western world, one can raise questions regarding its fate in this country, which in a way may not be very different from the Indian senario.

If the techniques of Buddhist psychology were to reveal an "ineffable" ultimate reality, then it would have nothing to do with philosophy which, according to James, is very talkative. Thus, Buddhist psychology not only becomes mystical or spiritualist, but also loses its claim to be a genuine philosophy. Under these circumstances, neither the psychologists nor the philosophers, however restricted the parameters of their respective fields of inquiry are, could be blamed for not recognizing Buddhism as embodying a genuine psychological analysis or a viable philosophical method. While Buddhism loses its passport to the sacred domains of both psychology and philosophy, its appeal to the so-called students of religion also dwindles the moment it is described as a form of non-absolutism, for religion becomes almost meaningless for most people unless it recognizes an Absolute or Ultimate Reality. Buddhism thereby becomes an enigma.

In my previous writings, I have constantly struggled to explain the early Buddhist tradition as one based upon an extremely sophisticated empiricist foundation. In considering it to be a form of empiricism I was not making an equation between Buddhism and the British form of empiricism, especially the Humean version, primarily because the Buddha looked upon relations to be part and parcel of the events, hence they are as real as the events themselves and not merely products of human imagination. In a more recent publication I have provided evidence in favor of a similarly empiricist interpretation of even the philosophy of Nāgārjuna, who has generally been regarded as a champion of the mystical and the transcendental. Yet it seems that one of the major obstacles to accepting such an interpretation of either the Buddha or Nāgārjuna is the present understanding of the nature of Buddhist psychology.

The present volume is devoted to an examination of the basic principles of Buddhist psychology. Contrary to most interpretations, it will be argued that there is no need to assume any form of transcendence or absolutism in reading the Buddhist texts. A non-absolutist or non-transcendentalist interpretation of the later forms of Buddhism would not only align some of the leading philosophers of that period with the Buddha himself, but also prevent the fate that befell Buddhism in India being repeated in the modern Western world, where it has come to be studied with some enthusiasm. In the process of examining the principles of Buddhist psychology every effort would be made to show how the Buddha's psychological analysis is subservient to his philosophical discourse. When he decided to speak about his freedom and explain it to the world he was donning the cloak of a philosopher. His interest in distinguishing between a right view (*sammā-diṭṭhi*) and a confused view (*micchā-diṭṭhi*) and, his claim that he avoids empty or false statements (*tuccha, musā*) and confines himself to true and well-founded statements (*taccha, bhūta*)[1] makes him a genuine philospher, even according to the most restricted definition of philosophy. However, his philosophical enterprise is closely wedded to his psychological speculations and, as may be shown in the course of the following discussions, this relationship has engendered a rather unique philosophical outlook, namely, a thorough-going non-substantialism, non-absolutism, and anti-essentialism.

This particular philosophical outlook in Buddhism renders any comparison of the Buddha with many of the leading philosophers of the Western world a difficult task, except in a rather piecemeal way. Yet the situation is not hopeless. Since the Buddha appears to have combined the vocations of a psychologist and a philosopher, what is needed is to look for someone in the Western world who also combined in himself these two vocations. The obvious choice is William James. Furthermore, such a comparison is justified by the fact that William James, after he compiled the *magnum opus* on religion, perceived a close relationship between his ideas and those of Buddhism (see section on "Epistemology and Psychology"). The comparison between Buddhist and Jamesean psychology is undertaken with a view to showing the possible similarities in their outlook, not their identity. After all, James was a medical man who had the oportunity to dissect and analyse the physical structure of the human brain. Yet his explanation of human consciousness had to depend upon introspection and observation, the latter being confined to the testimony and behavior of other conscious human beings. The Buddha, on the contrary, was strictly confined to introspection and observation without the benefit of brain surgery. If their approaches to understanding the nature of human consciousness are comparable, then their speculations regarding the nature of existence, of moral phenomena, etc., may also turn out to be equally comparable. Thus, the present work is only a prolegomenon to a more detailed examination of Buddhism and the Jamesean version of American pragmatism.

In presenting James in the way I have done, I am not claiming any originality in interpretation. All that I am attempting to do here is to utilize the Jamesean psychological ideas and concepts in order to clarify the ideas expressed by a this-worldly-minded yogin of the sixth century B. C. and which are enveloped in darkness due to the intricacies of the classical languages in which they are preserved. After years of neglect, since Ralph Barton Perry's detailed treatment of James' work, the last two decades witnessed a resurgence of interest in James, leading especially to the publication of a definitive set of editions of his writings under the title: *The Works of William James*, with introductions that place James in the Western philosophical background even though James seems to have been familiar with even the non-Western philosophical traditions. The availability of such a definitive edition of James' works will facilitate a more detailed comparative study of James' pragmatism with similar pragmatic movements in other parts of the world.

The first part of the present work is devoted to an outlining of the principles of psychology that can be traced back to the Buddha himself, with detailed comparisons with James'. The second part deals with the understanding of these principles by the later disciples of the Buddha. In contrast to the generally held view that Buddhist thought gradually evolved from small beginnings to elaborate systems, like a lotus bud blooming forth into a multi-petalled lotus, I have tried to show that revisions were made by some of the scholastics and that there was a continued and persistent effort to resurrect the teachings of the Buddha by disciples like Moggalīputtatissa, Nāgārjuna, and Vasubandhu. Such a reading of Nāgārjuna will be found in my *Nāgārjuna. The Philosophy of the Middle Way* (1986). Similar analyses of Maitreya's *Madhyāntavibhāga* and the Vasubandhu's *Vijñaptimātratāsiddhi* are appended to this volume.

It is my sincere hope that this brief comparison of the psychological reflections of some of our great ancestors will lead to more comprehensive and fruitful comparative studies in philosophy and culture.

David J. Kalupahana

Department of Philosophy
University of Hawaii

Part One: The Buddha's Psychological Reflections

Chapter One
History of Buddhist Philosophy — An Interpretation

T. R. V. Murti's *Central Philosophy of Buddhism* (1956) examined the philosophy of Nāgārjuna in great depth and provided an explanation of one era in Buddhist thought, an explanation that is completely dominated by his Vedāntic temperament. His basic theme was that early Buddhism, with a semi-metaphysical system presented by the Buddha in the form of a "theory of elements" (*dharma*)[1] which, when placed in the Mādhyamika combustion chamber and ignited, produced the more sophisticated system of "emptiness" that brought about a "Copernican revolution" in Buddhism. For nearly thirty years, this interpretation of Nāgārjuna's philosophy has dominated modern scholarship, providing justification for an age-old sectarian conflict between Theravāda and Mahāyāna. Indeed, the final victim was the Buddha himself, who is presented not only as a metaphysician whose ideas had to be improved upon by his later disciples, but also as one who did not have the capacity to instruct his immediate disciples in the truth he had discovered.

Our most recent work on Nāgārjuna[2] has provided sufficient evidence to indicate that he, instead of improving upon the Buddha's teaching, made a determined attempt to clean up the weeds of substantialist metaphysics that had grown around it. We have also shown how, in this endeavor, Nāgārjuna was preceded by another less-known Buddhist philosopher, Moggalīputta-tissa.[3]

The next most important tradition in Buddhism is Yogācāra. Asok Kumar Chatterjee, following the tradition of his teacher, Murti, has produced one of the few detailed and significant treatments of Yogācāra. His work, *The Yogācāra Idealism*[4] has not, unfortunately, enjoyed the same publicity as his teacher's work. Yet, it is in no way second to Murti's treatment of Mādhyamika philosophy. This does not mean that his presentation of the most prominent philosopher in the Yogācāra tradition, namely, Vasubandhu, is accurate. In fact, the perspective in which Murti looked at early Buddhism and Nāgārjuna is here adopted in examining early Buddhism and Vasubandhu. Two important factors seem to have influenced the perspectives of Murti and Chatterjee. The first is the rather superficial treatment of the history of Buddhist thought by classical historicans like Vaśumitra,[5] who tried to justify a theory of evolution of Buddhist thought from small beginnings to sophisticated systems. The second seems to be the difficulties both Murti and Chatterjee experienced in uprooting themselves from their own philosophical tradition, namely, Advaita Vedānta, when examining a tradition that is philosophically different. For these reasons, a fresh look at the work of Vasubandhu, the most prominent philosopher of the so-called Yogācāra, seems appropriate. Vasubandhu's *Vijñaptimātratāsiddhi* represents the *locus classicus* of the Yogācāra tradition, in the same way as Nāgārjuna's *Mūlamadhyamakakārikā* served as the fundamental treatise of the Mādhyamika school.

In presenting Nāgārjuna's philosophy, we have depended heavily on the doctrines embodied in the early discourses. His *Kārikā* was analysed not only in relation to the early discourses, but also in the background of the two most metaphysical schools of Buddhism, Sarvāstivāda and Sautrāntika. That same methodology will be adopted in the present translation and annotation of Vasubandhu's treatise.

In doing so, we are brought face to face with the gigantic task of dealing with the historical interpretation of Buddhism referred to by classical Buddhist historians as "The Three Revolutions of the Wheel of Dharma" (*tri-dharma-cakra-pravarttana*). These three revolutions were understood and interpreted long after the so-called revolutions took place. For example, the medieval Mahāyāna historians like Buston would look upon the Abhidharma, the Mādhyamika and the Yogācāra as the three revolutions. Yet, the philosophical character of these three revolutions were never clearly examined or defined. The modern interpretation that takes the three revolutions as representing the *realistic*, *critical* and *idealistic* phases of Buddhism stems from Stcherbatsky's explanation of the conception of *dharma*, adopted enthusiastically by most scholars. Chatterjee, having complimented Stcherbatsky for the fine exposition of the conception of *dharma*, proceeds to explain the three revolutions as follows:

> Buddhism is thus not one system but a matrix of systems, comprising as it does three great philosophies along with their satellites, viz., realism, criticism and idealism.[6]

This interpretation seems to be based on the model of development of thought in the Western world familiar to Stcherbatsky, than on a careful examination of the history of Buddhist thought. In the first place, the characterization of early Buddhism as realism is based upon a mistaken and extremely superficial identification of Sarvāstivāda and Sautrāntika metaphysics with the teachings of the Buddha. The source of Stcherbatsky's definition of *dharma* is Vasubandhu's *Abhidharmakośa* and not the early discourses. This mistaken identification has been noted in our exposition of the Buddha's conception of "dependent arising."[7]

We have also provided sufficient evidence to indicate that the so-called criticial philosophy of Nāgārjuna applies to the Sarvāstivāda and Sautrāntika metaphysics only and that, contrary to most existing interpretations of Nāgārjuna, his philosophy represents a re-statement of the Buddha's own middle way. The comparison of the ideas embodied in the early discourses, some of the early Prajñāpāramitā texts and the canonical Abhidharma has convinced us that Nāgārjuna's philosophy is in no way a "Copernican revolution" in the history of Buddhist thought. Instead, it turns out to be a resurrection of the Buddha's doctrine. Thus the interpretation of the first two phases of Buddhist thought as realistic and critical rests upon mistaken identities and assumptions.

As we did in the case of Nāgārjuna, we propose to show in the present analysis of Buddhist psychology that even the great Vasubandhu was not an innovator but a faithful interpreter of the Buddha's teachings as originally expounded. Thus, the *re-volutions* are not changes, as they are generally understood, but *re-turnings* to the original message. Such returning is not only the work of Nāgārjuna and Vasubandhu, but also of Moggalīputtatissa, who preceded them. Whatever the sectarian prejudices of the so-called Theravāda or Mahāyāna, prejudices that are being perpetuated by most modern scholars, an inquiry into the history of Buddhist philosophical thought can provide sufficient evidence in favor of the view that the three revolutions are three major attempts to resurrect the teachings of the Buddha and that these three attempts are embodied in the *Kathāvatthu*, the *Mūlamadhyamakakārikā* and the *Vijñaptimātratāsiddhi*.

A comprehensive treatment of Yogācāra literature is available in Chatterjee's work. The present Introduction will, therefore, be confined to an analysis of the history of Buddhist psychology beginning with the Buddha until the time of Vasubandhu.

Chapter Two
Epistemology and Psychology

The Buddha is looked upon as one of the foremost spiritual leaders who walked the surface of this earth. For countless millions of people over many centuries he was the greatest symbol of moral and spiritual perfection, and this continues to be the case today. Yet, from the very beginning of his career, he was also involved in a pursuit that has generally become the vocation of a philosopher, namely, the attempt to distinguish a true view from a false one, a right view from a wrong one.

One function of epistemology is said to consist in the clarification of 'truth' or 'true propositions' or 'true statements' so that these could be distinguished from 'untruth' or false propositions and statements. As a result, through centuries of development, the sciences of logic, linguistics and semantics have reached a high level of sophistication utilizing a whole mass of complicated arguments, theorems and propositional calculi. Conceptual analysis has been looked upon as the revealer of constant relations among the various components of a statement—subject, object, predicate, etc.—on the basis of which true statements could be distinguished from false ones. Having recognized that there are many realms of reality which mutually interpenetrate, the conceptual systems formulated in mathematics and logic are applied in the realms of aesthetics and ethics. The key word in all these discussions is 'structure.' The knowledge of such 'structures' makes the philospher's vocation an exalted one.

Considered in the light of such tantalizing discoveries and developments in logic, mathematics and semantics, it is hardly possible to call the Buddha a 'philosopher' in the 'true' sense of the term. The fact that he abandoned this very system of philosophizing at the very outset would make him a non-philosopher according to the above criterion. For example, placing the philosophic enterprise referred to above, which he calls "reflection on form" (*ākāra-parivitakka*), in the same category as faith (*saddhā*), preference (*ruci*), revelation (*anussava*) and acceptance of solidified views (*diṭṭhinijjhānakkhanti*), he has the following to say:

> . . . even if I know something on the basis of the profoundest reflection on form, that may be empty, hollow and false, while what I do not know on the basis of the profoundest reflection on form may be factual, true and not otherwise. It is not proper for an intelligent person, safeguarding the truth, to come categorically to the conclusion in this matter that this alone is true and whatever else is false.[8]

Ironically, this statement was made by a person who had renounced princely comfort and devoted six long years to the practice of meditation or reflection on the form or nature of existence. This is in contrast to others whose 'meditations' led them to the recognition of massive structures providing a foundation for the unity of experience, experience that comes to us in unpredictable variety and novelty. Foremost among these are the Upaniṣadic thinkers in India who propounded a notion of an eternal self (*ātman*) which prefigured the speculations of both Descartes and Kant in the Western world. As is well known, the Cartesian *cogito* is a sort of "self-perceiving consciousness," while Kant's "transcendental apperception" is a primordial unifying condition of all forms of experience and conception. While the Cartesian view has been subjected to much criticism as a "ghost in the machine," Kant's theory has gained respectability among most rationalists as a necessary condition for knowledge. Describing "transcendental apperception," Kant has the following to say:

> This original and transcendental condition is no other than the *transcendental apperception*. Consciousness of self according to the determinations of our state in inner perception is merely empirical, and always changing. No fixed and abiding self can present itself in this flux of inner appearances. Such consciousness is usually named *inner sense* or *empirical apperception*. What has *necessarily* to be represented as numerically identical cannot be thought as such through empirical data. To render such a transcendental presupposition valid, there must be a condition which precedes all experience, and which makes experience itself possible.
>
> There can be in us no modes of knowlege, no connectoin or unity of one mode of knowledge with another, without that unity of consciousness which precedes all data of intuitions, and by relation to which representation of objects is alone possible. This pure original unchangeable consciousness I shall name *transcendental apperception*.[9]

This transcendental apperception is also "the original and necessary consciousness of the *identity* of the self"[10] and, as such, should involve some kind of self-consciousness.[11] This structure, which is a pre-requisite of all experience and knowledge, is then followed by other structures such as forms and categories of our ordinary empirical judgments.

According to this analysis, our knowledge or experience of things is possible only under certain conditions and these conditions are always the same. They are the *a priori* structures such as the transcendental apperception, the forms of sensibility and the categories of understanding. Apart from these conditions, sense data would not represent objects. For Kant, this apperception and these forms and categories are essential because without them "the existence of things outside us (from which we derive our whole material of knowlege, even for our inner sense) must be accepted merely on *faith*, . . . "[12]

A situation is thus created where we either recognize the extrenal world by accepting the validity of *a priori* strucutres or abandon our knowledge of the external world as a mere hallucination (unless we are prepared to make a supreme being responsible for our having such knowledge). There seems to be no middle ground between *a priori* categories and empirical knowledge.

Whether the so-called structures of *a priori* forms and categories (*ākāra*) provide us with any element of certainty about the external world is a question raised by the Buddha in the passage quoted earlier. What is the basis of this *a priori* knowledge? Is it any different from the knowledge based upon *faith* (from which Kant expects to distinguish *a priori* knowledge) or preference or revelation or dogmatically accepted views? Even though looking at the psychological *idealism* that was prevalent during his day or that preceded him, Kant found it to be "a scandal to philosophy,"[13] yet the structures of knowledge that Kant himself was recommending are not easily accepted unless there were to be excessive faith (*saddhā*) or some kind of revelation (*anussava*) or even some sort of preference (*ruci*). Unfortunately, Kant did not have the benefit of a psychologist of the calibre of William James, with a strong background in medical science, in order to instruct him on the way the human mind functions, especially in formulating concepts about man and the world. While Hume was advertantly or inadvertantly falling back upon the associationist psychology that dominated Britain during his day, Kant was living in an environment where psychology was from beginning to end structuralist in temper, reaching its culmination in the writings of both Freud and Jung. Between these two dominant trends in Western psycholgy, James' *The Principles of Psychology* (1890) comes as a breath of new and fresh air and, without being "a scandal to philosophy," provides an enduring explanation as to what experience is, how conceptual structures are formed, how likes and dislikes are generated and, above all, how human beings become enslaved in their own creations. In this work James laid the foundation of what he later called "radical empiricism" which, in its turn was to color his version of pragmatism (1898 California Lecture: "The Philosophical Conceptions and Practical Results,") respectfully borrowed from C. S. Peirce. Peirce, as an outstanding mathematician and logician, remained more faithful to the Anglo-European philosophical tradition[14] thereby earning the respect of his contemporaries across the Atlantic. He made an enormous effort to dissolve the realist-nominalist conflict by giving more validity to inductive reasoning (when Russell was looking upon them as "a mere method of making possible guesses[15]) and underscoring the importance of what he called abduction, thereby allowing a measure of truth to the "general" compared with the "concrete." However, probably haunted by the Kantian edict that psychology is a "scandal to philosophy," Peirce seems to have tipped the scale in favor of the "Outer World . . . full of irresistible compulsions" to the neglect of the "Inner World . . . of comparatively slight compulsion upon us."[16] On the contrary, James followed a more moderate path in treating the objective and subjective worlds as being equally important and relevant to philosophical discourse and utilized the pragmatic method to banish metaphysics from both psychology and philosophy. Peirce once remarked: "Wright, James, and I were men of science, rather scrutinizing the doctrines of metaphysicians on their scientific side than regarding them as very momentous spirituality. The type of our thought was decidedly British. I, alone of the number, had come upon the threshing-floor of philosophy through the door-way of Kant, and even my ideas were acquiring the English accent."[17] Even though Peirce characterizes James as decidedly a "British" philosopher, recent studies of James' philosophy has revealed that it represents a definite break away from traditional Anglo-European throught.[18] Thus, James' psychological speculations, which eventually led him to formulate his radical empiricism, checked and balanced by his pragmatic method, served as a basis for his moral reflections and religious thought. His anti-substantialist and anti-essentialist attitude is clearly reflected in his analysis of experience relating to the subject as well as the object. It pervades every aspect of his thought, whether it pertains to epistemology, psychology, ontology, ethics or religion. It is precisely in this respect that he can be said to have abandoned much of the Anglo-European philosophical tradition.

Yet, almost two and half millenia before that revolution, a similar phenomenon occurred in India with the Buddha, and, as will be shown below, that revolution came in the face of similarly rigid substantialist and essentialist modes of thinking. The parallels between the Buddha's non-substantialist philosophy and that of William James are so many that one begins to wonder about the extent to which the latter may have been influenced by the former. In his early writings James refers to the Buddha's doctrines, sometimes with understanding and sometimes without. The doctrines of "no-self" (*anatta*) and the conception of a "middle way" (*majjhimā paṭipadā*) were generally well known to him. However, most of the Buddha's teachings, especially his conception of freedom (*nibbāna*) were available to him through the filtered versions provided either by the European scholars or by Vedāntins like Swāmi Vivekananda, and therefore, extremely substantialist. However, after he compiled his Gifford Lectures published under the title of *The Varieties of Religious Experience* (1902), James felt that what he was presenting was in some way closer to the teachings of the Buddha. In a postscript to this work, James makes the following statement:

> I am ignorant of Buddhism and speak under correction, and merely in order the better to describe my general point of view; but as I apprehend the Buddhistic doctrine of Karma, I agree in principle with that. All supernaturalists admit that facts are under the judgment of higher law; but for Buddhism as I interpret it, and for religion generally so far as it remains unweakened by transcendentalistic metaphysics the word "judgment" here means no such bare academic verdict of platonic appreciation as it means in Vedāntic or modern absolutist systems; it carries, on the contrary, *execution* with it, is *in rebus* as well as *post rem*, and operates "causally" as partial factor in the total fact. The universe becomes a gnosticism pure and simple on any other terms. But this view that judgment and execution go together is the crasser supernaturalist way of thinking, so the present volume must on the whole be classed with the other expression of that creed.[19]

It is interesting that this statement appears in a postscript, not in the lectures. During the year that James' appointment to the Gifford Lectureship was proposed (1896, actual appointment was made in 1898), T. W. Rhys Davids, the founder of the Pali Text Society of London which opened up the study of the early discourses of the Buddha to the West, published his *American Lectures on the History of Religions* (First Series—1884-1885) under the title, *Buddhism. Its History and Literature* (New York and London, 1896). James' lectures were not put into finished written form until 1900. Yet James does not refer to Rhys Davids' work, even though the basic teachings of the Buddha were presented in this work in the most accurate form. It is, therefore, possible that when James published his lectures, he realized the close affinity between Buddhism (as presented by Rhys Davids) and his own philosophical reflections. Hence his observation in the postscript, an observation that has failed to attract the attention of most modern treatises on James.

The present volume is primarily an attempt to outline the *psychological* speculations of the Buddha and his followers. These psychological speculations are at the very root of Buddhist philosophical and religious thought. We have already referred to James' conclusions regarding his own reflections on religion. If James' and the Buddha's views regarding the nature of religious phenomena could be so compatible, there could be strong resemblences between their psychological theories as well. Therefore, as a first step in the direction of a more detailed comparative study of Buddhism and James, the examination of Buddhist psychology is here presented in relation to ideas of William James. Whatever be the motivations of the Buddha or James when they first undertook an examination of human psychology, it will become clear that when they made psychology the foundation of their philosophical reflections, without considering it a scandal, they were able to abandon substantialism, essentialism or even "structuralism," allowing the discipline of philosophy to take a totally different direction. Their psychological speculations enabled them to reconsider some of the epistemological theories accepted during their day, thereby freeing themselves from blind faith, preference, revelation, and reflection on form as well as dogmatic acceptance of views.

Chapter Three
The Indian Background

The Indian philosophical background, with a strongly substantialist metaphysic and a rigid social, political and moral structure founded upon that metaphysic, provided the Buddha with an opportunity to reflect seriously upon the questions regarding human experience and understanding. The substantialist metaphysic was presented as follows:

> In the beginning, this [world] was only the self (*ātman*) in the form of a person. Looking around he saw nothing else than the self. He first said 'I am.' Therefore, arose the name of 'I.' Therefore, even to this day when one is addressed he says that 'This is I' and then speaks whatever other names he may have.[20]

The self (*ātman*), so conceived, is the permanent and eternal reality unsmeared by all the change and fluctuations that take place in the world of experience. In fact, it is the basis of the unity of empirical experience of variety and multiplicity, of change and mutability, of past, present and future. The real self and the unreal or mutable self, the transcendental apperception and empirical consciousness are graphically presented with the parable of the "two birds" perched on one branch, the one simply watching and the other enjoying the fruit.[21]

The self-same *ātman* is next presented as *brahman*. This time it is not a simple *a priori* fact, but also the *a priori* value on the basis of which all other values in the world are to be judged. The passage reads as follows:

> Verily, in the beginning this [world] was *brahma*, one only. Being one, he was not developed. He created a still superior form, the *kṣatra*, even those who are *kṣatra* among gods: Indra, Varuṇa, Soma, Rudra, Parjanya, Yama, Mṛtyu, Iśāna. Therefore, at the *rājaśūya* ceremony, the *brahman* sits below the *kṣatriya*. Upon *kṣatra* alone does he confer this honor. This same thing, namely, *brahma*, is the source of the *kṣatra*. Therefore, even if the king attains supremacy, he rests finally

> upon *brahma* as his own source. Whosoever injures him [i.e., *brahman*], he attacks his own source. He fares worse in proportion as he injures one who is better.
>
> ... ...
>
> He was not yet developed. He created a still superior form, *dharma*. This is the power of the *kṣatriya* class, namely, law. Therefore, there is nothing superior than law. So a weak man controls a stronger man by law, just as if by a king. Verily, that which is law is truth (*satya*). Therefore, they say of a man who speaks the truth: "He speaks the law," or of a man who speaks the law: "He speaks the truth." Verily, both are the same.[22]

Having stated the law (*dharma*) and its absolute validity or truth (*satya*), and identifying both with the brahman class as the standard of value judgment, the passage goes on to explain the evolution of the two other classes in society, the *vaisya* and *śūdra*. There could be little doubt as to the implication of this passage. The source of the value-system is *brahman* and, as the source of everything else, it is inviolable. The fourfold caste system and the values attached to it are inviolable and irrevocable. A person's duty as a human being is determined by the nature of the caste to which he is born. Whatever other things he may do are subordinate to this primary duty. It is pre-ordained. That duty is to be performed whatever the consequences are. This is the notion of duty that came to be inculcated in the *Bhagavadgītā*, which made the reluctant Arjuna go to war. In other words, by performing that duty Arjuna was acting according to his 'conscience,' and as such, even if he were to destroy another human being, he would be free from any form of guilt.

The unity of *ātman* and *brahman* represents the wedlock between "consciousness of self" and "conscience," between the "starry heavens above" and the "moral law within." Even though presented in a very crude form, the implications and intentions of this theory are no more different from those of the elaborate system propounded by Kant.

The Buddha's teachings are embodied in the discourses included in the Pali Nikāyas and the Chinese Āgamas. Even some of the later Buddhists, who had questions regarding the nature of the teachings, openly admitted that these represented the original sources for the study of the Buddha's message. What is extremely significant is that among the doctrines taken up for criticism in these discourses, the concepts of *ātman* and caste are the most prominent, especially considering the frequency with which they are taken up for analysis and refutation by the Buddha. The former being the foundation of the latter, the Buddha spared no pains in refuting it, devoting more time to its negation than to a presentation of his own positive thesis, namely, "dependent arising" (*paṭiccasamuppāda*).

Chapter Four
The Buddha's Conception of Personhood

While the Buddha utilized a variety of sophisticated arguments and methods to reject the conception of an *ātman* or a "transcendental apperception," the most significant among these is the description of a human being as a "psychophysical personality" (*nāmarūpa*) and its further analysis into five aggregates (*pañcakkhandha*) or six elements (*cha-dhātu*). In this process he explained the nature and function of the so-called "transcendental apperception" and, instead of considering it as an indispendable foundation of epistemology, criticized it as the source of bondage and suffering.

The Psychophysical Personality

The first step toward rejecting the metaphysical self is the recognition of a psychophysical personality, generally referred to as *nāmarūpa*. In order to avoid the metaphysical problems that arise as a result of analysing the personality into two distinct entities or substances as mind and matter, the Buddha carefully refrained from speaking of two entities as *nāma* and *rūpa*. He was not prepared to assume that mind (*nāma*) can have independent status or existence. It is always associated with a body or a physical personality. There could be no consciousness or mental activity unless it is located in such a personality.

The almost universal tendency to look upon mind and matter as two distinct entities, with matter existing on its own and mind, whenever it is present, reflecting such matter, was abandoned by the Buddha. He did not succumb to the "philosophic faith, bred like most faiths from an aesthetic demand," that is, the faith that "mental and physical events are, on all hands, admitted to present the strongest contrast in the entire field of being."[23] He was probably anticipating such reactions as those of the so-called scientific minds, referred to by James: "It is time for scientific men to protest against the recognition of any such thing as consciousness in a scientific investigation."[24] Yet, in explaining both mind and matter, he was prepared to recognize such things as contact and sensation as the "unscientific half" of existence, leaving himself with the problem of dealing with emotion later on. For this reason, when the question regarding the nature of mind (*nāma*) and matter (*rūpa*) was raised, he responded by saying that the so-called matter is "contact with resistence" (*paṭigha-samphassa*) and what is called mind is "contact with concepts" (*adhivacana-samphassa*).[25] In so doing, he was reducing both mind and matter to contact (*samphassa*) and, therefore, processes of experience rather that any kind of material-stuff or mind-stuff.

Such an explanation of both mind and matter avoids the so-called "automaton-theory" as well as the idea of "ghost in the machine." With it, the Buddha relinquishes any search for a mysterious *something* that determines the physical laws as well as the laws of thought. In short, it is an abandoning of all metaphysical criticisms that make all causes and conditions obscure. This is clearly expressed in the following statement of the Buddha:

> In this case, monk, it occurs to someone: "What was certainly mine is certainly not mine (now); what might certainly be mine, there is certainly no chance of my getting." He grieves, mourns, laments, beats his breast, and falls into disillusionment. Even so, monk, does there come to be *anxiety* (*paritassanā*) about something objective that does not exist.
>
> . . . . . .
>
> In this case, monk, the view occurs to someone: "This world is this self; after dying I will become permanent, lasting, eternal, not liable to change, I will stand fast like unto the eternal." He hears the doctrine as it is being taught by the Tathāgata or by a disciple of the Tathāgata for rooting out all resolve for, bias, tendency and addiction to the determination and conditioning of views, for the appeasement of all views, for the appeasement of all dispositions, for the relinquishing of all attachment, for the waning of craving, absence of lust, cessation, and freedom. It occurs to him thus: "I will surely be annihilated, I will surely be destroyed, I will surely not be." He grieves, mourns, laments, beats his breast, and falls into disillusionment. Thus, monk, there comes to be *anxiety* about something subjective that does not exist.[26]

For the Buddha, the dissatisfaction with what is given and the search for *something* hidden in or behind experience, even though leading to metaphysical theories, is good evidence for the creativity of man when responding to experience whether that be subjective or objective. It also supports the view that a human being is not merely a hapless object swayed to and fro by the irresistible force of the "Outer World," but also one who is able to exert similarly irresistible force upon that outer world and bring about changes in it. Just as much as the world is dependently arisen (*paṭiccasamuppanna*), it is also dispositionally conditioned (*sankhata*). The realization that the world is dispositionally conditioned as well prompted him to admit consciousness as a significant part of the human personality, not a mere "epi-phenomenon." As will be shown later, the Buddha would have no difficulty agreeing with William James, who defined consciousness as "at all times primarily a *selecting agency*. Whether it is in the lowest sphere of sense, or in the highest of intellection, we find it always doing one thing, choosing one out of several of the materials so presented to its notice, emphasizing and accentuating that and suppressing as far as possible all the rest. The item emphasized is always in connection with some interest felt by consciousness to be paramount at the time."[27]

This view of consciousness, as will be shown later, leads to the recognition of the efficacy of consciousness even in the matter of dealing with the physical world. Thus, the psychophysical personality admitted by the Buddha emphasizes the dependence of consciousness on the physical personality as well as the capacity on the part of the former to mould the latter without being a mere receptacle of impressions.

The Five Aggregates (pañcakkhandha)

The next most popular description of the human personality is in terms of the five aggregates or constituents. These are referred to as "aggregates of grasping" (*upādānakkhandha*), for it is these aggregates that a person clings to as his personality. The five constituents are as follows:

(1) *Rūpa* or material form. Whether it stands for one's own physical body or whether it implies the experience of material objects, the definition of it provided by the Buddha makes it a function rather than an entity. It is so called because of the way in which (a person) is affected (*ruppatīti kho rūpaṃ*).[28] For example, the experience of cold or warmth, of wind and heat, of various forms of insect bites, etc., are listed as the way in which one is affected. In other words, unless the experience of such phenomena are available, it is meaningless to speak of material form. Neither is it appropriate to assume that such experiences are mere imaginations. It may be noted that Hume's "bundle of perceptions," in terms of which he was explaining away the belief in self, included such experiences as cold and warmth. Thus, earth (*paṭhavi*) represents solidity or roughness, water (*āpa*)

fluidity, etc.[29] Apart from such experiences, the Buddha was reluctant to speak of any material elements.

Furthermore, "material form" (*rūpa*) as part of a human personality, becomes extremely important as a way of identifying that personality. While there are instances where the Buddha would speak of mental states or states of meditation which are immaterial (*arūpa*), it is difficult to come across any reference by him to a human person who is without a body or material form (*rūpa*).

(2) *Vedanā* or feeling or sensation is another important aspect or constituent of the personality. It accounts for emotions which are an inalienable part of a living person, whether he be in bondage or has attained freedom (*nibbāna*). Feeling consists of three types: the pleasant or the pleasurable (*manāpa, sukha*), the unpleasant or the painful (*amanāpa, dukkha*) and neutral (*adukkhamasukha*). Except in the meditative trance where all perceptions and feelings (or more specifically, "what has been felt") are made to cease (temporarily) and which, therefore, represents a non-cognitive state, feelings are inevitable in experience. However, the human responses to such feeling can always be restrained, for these responses consist of continous yearning or thirsting for the feelings. Thus, a living person is expected to eliminate lust (*rāga*) or craving (*taṇhā*) that arise on the basis of pleasurable feelings.

(3) *Saññā* or perception stands for the function of perceiving (*sañjānātīti saññā*). It is not a percept that can be separated or isolated from other activities. Instead, it is a continous process of perception, with flights as well as perchings, the latter being determined mostly by interest. Thus, we may continually return to our perchings ignoring the flights so much so that we carve out discrete objects out of the flux of experience and assume that they are the same objects existing independently of all experience.

As in the case of feelings, the perceptions are also related to all other constituents of the human personality. Thus, they are not atomic impressions that are compounded into complex entitites as a result of the activities of mind such as imagination. Each one of our perceptions constitutes a mixed bag of memories, concepts, and dispositions as well as the material elements or the functions referred to by *rūpa*. A pure percept undiluted by such conditions is *not* recognized by the Buddha or any subsequent Buddhist psychologist who has remained faithful to the Buddha. A pure percept is as metaphysical as a pure *a priori* category.

(4) *Saṅkhārā* or dispositions explain why there cannot be pure percepts. In the Buddha's perspective, this is *the* factor that contributes to the individuation of a person, and therefore, of his perceptions. Almost everything including physical phenomena, come under the strong in-

fluence of this most potent cause of evolution of the human personality as well as its surroundings. Hence the Buddha's definition of disposition as "that which processes material form, feeling, perception, disposition [itself] and consciousness into their particular forms."[30]

What the Buddha was attempting to explain on the basis of dispositions, which is part of the conscious process, is what James endeavored to describe in relation to consciousness itself. Refuting the "automaton-theory," so popular with modern-day biologists, James argues that evolution is not a strictly physiological process. He says:

> Survival can enter into a purely physiological discussion only as an *hypothesis made by an onlooker* about the future. But the moment you bring in a consciousness into the midst, survival ceases to be a mere hypothesis. . . . *Real* ends appear for the first time now upon the world's stage. The conception of consciousness as a purely cognitive form of being, which is the pet way of regarding it in many idealistic-modern as well as ancient schools, is thoroughly anti-psychological, as the remainder of this book will show. Every actually existing consciousness seems to itself at any rate to be a *fighter for ends*, of which many, but for its presence, would not be ends at all. Its powers of cognition are mainly subservient to these ends, discerning which facts further them and which do not.[31]

For very valid reasons (to be explained later), the Buddha attributes such evolution to dispositions, rather than to consciousness in general. Indeed, the dispositions are responsible not only for the manner in which we groom our physical personality once we are in possession of it, but also in partly[32] determining the nature of a new personality that we may come to possess in the future. It is not merely the human personality that is moulded or processed by dispositions. Our physical surroundings, even our amenities of life, housing, clothing, utensils, and in a major way, our towns, cities, etc., our art and architecture, our culture and civilization, and in the modern world, even outer space come to be dominated by our dispositions. Karl Popper calls this the World Three.[33] For this very reason, the Buddha, when describing the grandeur in which a universal monarch lived, with palaces, elaborate pleasure gardens and all other physical comforts, referred to all of them as dispositions (*saṅkhārā*).[34]

Epistemologically, the dispositions are an extremely valuable means by which human beings can deal with the world of experience. In the absence of any capacity to know everything presented to the senses, dispositional tendencies function in the form of interest, in selecting material from the "big blooming buzzing confusion"[35] in order to formulate one's understanding of the world.

(5) *Viññāṇa* or consciousness is intended to explain the continuity in the person who is individuated by dispositions (*saṅkhārā*). Like the other constituents, consciousness depends upon them for existence as well as nourishment. It is not a permanent and eternal substance or a series of discrete momentary acts of conscious life united by a mysterious self. Thus, consciousness separated from the other aggregates, especially material form (*rūpa*), cannot function. It is said to act with other aggregates if thoughts were to occur.

The theory of aggregates provides an interesting parallel to the relationship between mind and body envisaged by James:

> The consciousness, which is itself an integral thing not made of parts, 'corresponds' to the entire activity of the brain, whatever that may be, at the moment. This is a way of expressing the relation of mind and brain from which I shall not depart during the remainder of the book, because it expresses the bare phenomenal fact with no hypothesis, and is exposed to no such logical objections as we have found to cling to the theory of ideas in combination.[36]

When consciousness is so explained, it is natural for someone to conclude that it is a substantial entity. This was the manner in which the substantialists responded to both the Buddha and William James, and as may be seen later, to Vasubandhu himself. Buddha's response was that consciousness is nothing more than the act of being conscious (*vijānātīti-viññāṇaṃ*).[37] So did William James assert when he insisted:

> To deny plumply that 'consciousness' exists seems so absurd on the face of it—for undeniably 'thoughts' do exist—that I fear some readers would follow me no further. Let me then immediately explain that I mean only to deny that the word stands for an entity, but to insist most emphatically that it does stand for a function.[38]

Thus, the analysis of the human personality into five aggregates is intended to show the absence of a psychic self (an *ātman*). James was literally agreeing with the Buddhas *anātma*-view when he underscored the non-substantiality of this phenomenal fact:

> *The bare* PHENOMENON, *however, the* IMMEDIATELY KNOWN *thing which on the mental side is in opposition with the entire brain-process is the state of consciousness and not the soul itself.*[39]

These five aggregates are not intended as the ultimately irreducible elements (*dharma*) of existence. Instead, they illustrate some of the most prominent functions that are involved whenever the human personality is the subject of discussion. At least four basic functions are represented by them. *Rūpa* or material form accounts for the function of identification; *vedanā* or feeling and *saññā* or perception represent the function of experience, emotive as well as cognitive; *saṅkhārā* or disposition stands for the function of individuation; *viññāṇa* or consciousness explains the function of continuity in experience. After denying a permanent and eternal self underlying or embodying these functions, the Buddha felt the need to explain the continuity in human experience. This leads him to the recognition of the "stream of consciousness" (*viññāṇa-sota*).

Chapter Five
Stream of Consciousness and the Consciousness of Self

Strange as it may seem, confusing as it may appear, the Buddha who spent a good part of his philosophical discourses on the negation of self (*atta*) should continue to use terms like 'I' (*ahaṃ*), 'mine' (*mama*), 'you' (*tumhe*), 'yours' (*tumhākaṃ*) and, above all, the very term 'self' (*atta*). This apparently strange and confusing situation has led most scholars to assume that while he rejected an empirical self identical with the five aggregates, he was indeed recognizing a self that transcends ordinary experience and, as such, he was merely re-stating the position of the Upaniṣadic thinkers who preceded him.[40] Very often the denial of the so-called self can leave the impression that it is a mere convention or a mental fabrication without any reality.[41] While the former interpretation can give the impression that the Buddha's view is comparable to that of Kant, the latter interpretation makes his teachings similar to that of Hume. Both these interpretations seem to arise as a result of a logical analysis of experience into discrete, if not momentary events. Experience defined as nothing more or less than discrete atomic impressions paved the way for the Humean view of self as a mere mental fabrication. The rationalist Kant, who was not satisfied with Hume's view of self, desired a more substantial process of unification of the discrete impressions and arrived at the transcendental unity of apperception. To explain the Buddha's teachings in the light of the ideas expressed either by Hume or by Kant would be a gross mistake, especially if the problems they were trying to solve with these theories of self were created by their own views on the nature of the process of experience. The Buddha did not analyse experience into discrete entities or momentary impressions and then try to find a way of unifying them. Such an enterprise was undertaken by his misguided disciples a few centuries later, namely, the Sarvāstivādins and the Sautrāntikas. These two schools were the first to explain the Buddha's conception of change (*pariṇāma*) and impermanence (*anicca*) in terms of a metaphysical theory of momentary (*kṣaṇika*) impressions. Taking the speculations of these schools as a faithful representation of the Buddha-word, the Brahmanical philosophers attributed statements like "All that exists is momentary" (*yat sat tat kṣaṇikaṃ*) to the Buddha himself,[42] when no such statement is found anywhere in the early discourses or in the canonical texts of the Abhidharma or even in the works of later Buddhist philosophers like Nāgārjuna and Vasubandhu. Thus, for the Brahmanical thinkers, the Buddha turned out to be an advocate not only of momentariness but also of absolute distinctions in experienced phenomena. By criticizing Buddhism in general (and not merely the Sarvāstivāda or Sautrāntika schools) for upholding such views, the Brahmanical philosophers, especially those belonging to the Advaita Vedānta, were able to formulate the conception of "ultimate reality" as something beyhond linguistic description and definition. Enamored with this transcendentalism of Advaita Vedānta, many modern-day scholars have favored a similar interpretation of the Buddha's teachings. Thus, one can often read about the Buddha's "middle path" being described as a third alternative to Hume's and Kant's, namely, the self as being neither existent nor non-existent but something beyond all linguistic description.

It seems that none of these explanations are necessary if human experience had not been analysed into discrete events in the first place. The Buddha's approach to the philosophical problem of self may better the "Copernican revolution" in that it does not merely abandon a one-way treatment of experience as impressions left on a *tabula rasa*, but also rejects permanent and eternal structures of mind through which experience is supposed to be modified. Thus, instead of finding solutions to an artificial philosophical problem, the Buddha avoided creating the problem. Kant's epistemology is a "Copernican revolution" only in the background of Hume's analysis of experience into discrete momentary events and Locke's treatment of mind as a *tabula rasa*. Relinquishing the Lockean and Humean explanations of experience, which are more passive, Kant's mental structures become superfluous. Neither absolute identity nor absolute difference need to be brought into the philosophical discussion.

By avoiding the extremes of metaphysical or absolute idenity (*ekatta*, Sk. *ekatva*) and difference (*puthutta*, Sk. *pṛthaktva*)[43] the Buddha laid the foundation for a non-metaphysical explanation of experience. It is this avoidance of metaphysical extremes that constituted the "middle way" (*majjhimā paṭipadā*), and not transcendence of ordinary experience either soaring up to the heights of reason or taking refuge in a pure "impression" or huddling up in a non-sensuous intutiton.

After negating such metaphysics, the Buddha explained experience as a stream of thought or consciousness (*viññāṇasota*)[44] or a stream of becoming (*bhavasota*).[45]

This notion of a stream of consciousness or stream of becoming was of great importance to the Buddha. In the development of retrocognition (*pubbenivāsānussati-ñāṇa*), consciousness functions in the wake of memory (*satānusāri-viññāṇam*).[46] Such retrocognition is not confined to the present life alone. In fact, it is retrocognition extending beyond the present life that induced him to admit the possibility of survival or rebirth (*punabbhava*), an idea not emphasized by James. For the Buddha, the survival of a human being was more of a phenomenal fact than the creation by a supreme being. Such survival is due to the uninterrupted flow or flux of consciousness (*viññāṇasota*). Indeed, it is rather ironical that some modern philosophers, who constantly seek refuge in unperceived structures of thought or language, could consider the statements about past lives based upon retrocognition to be metaphysical and, therefore, meaningless.

Moreover, the stream of consciousness coupled with dispositions (*saṅkhāra*) provided a more realistic explanation of the notion of human progress or development. Substantialist thinkers of the Brahmanical tradition believed that the "self" (*ātman*) is pure by nature and that its association with the corruptible psychophysical personality produced bondage. For the Buddha, who rejected such a metaphysical self, disposition and consciousness constituting the stream of becoming (*bhavasota*) provided a better means of explaining human progress or degradation.

Buddha's conception of the "stream of consciousness" (*viññāṇasota*) formulated twenty-five centuries ago finds detailed elaboration in a major treatises on psychology by William James who, in the eyes of the materialistically inclined philosophers of the modern world, turns out to be a metaphysician. Introducing this strange conception of the "stream of thought" to the Western world, James says:

> Consciousness, then, does not appear to itself chopped up in bits. Such words as 'chain' or train' do not describe it fitly as it presents itself in the first instance. It is nothing jointed; it flows. A 'river' or a 'stream' are the metaphors by which it is most naturally described. *In talking of it hereafter, let us call it the stream of thought, of consciousness, or of subjective life.*[47]

This lengthy chapter on "The Stream of Thought" is a modern version of the Buddha's theory of consciousness presented in his statements scattered all over the discourses, with the difference that the Buddha, on the basis of his experiments in yoga (see section on "Analytical Yoga") was not the least reluctant to extend that stream into the past beyond the confines of the present life.

The stream of thought or experience or consciousness is not a "pure experience." The recognition that it is always conditioned by dispositions (*saṅkhārapaccayā viññāṇaṃ*) means that there could be no *actus purus* of thought, intellect or reason. Neither pure sensation nor pure reason would be possible. In order for pure sensation to occur, it must occur without any relation to anything that had gone before. In order to achieve this, either a newly created brain or a nervous system (a *rūpa*) has to be implanted in the psychophysical personality or the conscious process has to be emptied of all its contents. Even though the former is an impossibility, many have asserted the possibility of achieving the latter. Thus, the stage of meditation characterized by the cessation of perception and what is felt (*sañña-vedayita-nirodha*) is sometimes misunderstood as reflecting a "pure experience," whereas it is a state in which one has no experience at all. Feeling or sensation is a cognitive state, not a non-cognitive one. When feelings occur, they bring along with them relations of all types. James has the following to say about them:

> If there be such things as feelings at all, *then so purely as relations between objects exist in rerum natura, so surely and more surely, do feelings exist to which these relations are known*. . . . When we speak objectively, it is the real relations that appear revealed; if we speak subjectively, it is the stream of consciousness that matches each of them by an inward coloring of its own. In either case, the relations are numberless, and no existing language is capable of doing justice to all these shades.[48]

A statement of the Buddha, supposed to have been made immediately after his enlightenment, expresses a similar view regarding experience:

> When phenomena appear to a noble one who is deeply concentrated and contemplating, his doubts disappear, as he understands their causal nature.[49]

This statement provides no support for the *sensationalist* who admits a "pure sensation" apart from any relations, or for the *intellectualist* who perceives the relations as belonging to an entirely different plane of existence. "As the brain-changes are continuous, so do all these consciousnesses melt into each other like dissolving views. Properly they are but one protracted consciousness, one unbroken stream."[50] The Buddha's use of the term *saṃsāra*, in the sense of "wandering," to refer to the life-process, further defined as the unbroken and continuous (*ubhayato abbocchinnaṃ*) stream of consciousness (*viññāṇasotaṃ*),[51] enabled him to free himself from the sensationalist and intellectualist metaphysics in explaining his insight into the nature of existence as "dependent arising" (*paṭiccasamuppāda*). Dependent arising is neither a mental fabrication that weaves together discrete sensations nor an *a priori* category of understanding through which experience comes to be filtered. It is an explanation of the experience of "dependently arisen phenomena" (*paṭiccasamuppannā dhammā*).[52] The Buddha was insistent that this stream of consciousness be understood as one that is "dependently arisen."[53] "Dependent arising" (*paṭiccasamuppāda*), being the insight that enabled him to attain freedom from suffering, was utilized by him to explain all experienced phenomena (*dhammā*) without falling into substantialist traps.

William James, however, did not live to complete his writings on causation.[54] Yet he utilized his conception of the stream of thought to justify a radical empiricism[55] which, when carefully examined, would be no more different form the experience on the basis of which the Buddha formulated his famous theory of "dependent arising."

Just as much as the stream of experience is not a pure experience, it cannot be considered an "unconscious process," even though such an interpretation seems to have emerged in the more metaphysical schools of Buddhism (see section on "Rationalist Psychology" below). So long as consciousness is defined as the act of being conscious (*vijānātīti viññāṇaṃ*), the idea of the "unconscious" should mean the absence of any form of consciousness. The disposition (*saṅkhāra*) are sometimes taken to mean the "unconscious," but this would imply that they could occur without consciousness. This is not supported by the Buddha's statements. Indeed, every stream of consciousness is a personal stream because of dispositions, feelings, memories and perceptions.

It may be said that on waking from sleep or rising from the state of cessation (*nirodha-samāpatti*), one can usually know that one has been "unconscious," and sometimes there can be an accurate judgment of how long.[56] This judgment is said to be an inference from sensible signs and long practice of such judgment accounts for the ease with which one can wake up from sleep or rise from a trance involving cessation by determining the length of time one wishes to remain in such states. Thus, as in the case of sleep, a person can enter the state of cessation and emerge from it on the basis of his own determination (*adhiṭṭhāna*) and without any external instigation.

This fact, like the interruption of the perception of external objects in time and space, may give rise to the notion of an underlying "unconscious process" that is brought to the surface with the help of objects, attention and consciousness of self. The Buddha, following the insight into dependent arising, and James relying upon his radical empiricism, did not require such a metaphysical theory of the unconscious. James explains this continuity in the stream of consciousness interrupted by sleep in the following manner:

> When Paul and Peter wake up in the same bed, and recognize that they have been asleep, each one of them mentally reaches back and makes the connection with but *one* of the two streams of thought which were broken up by the sleeping hours. As the current of an electrode buried in the ground unerringly finds its way to its own similarly buried mate, across no matter how much intervening earth; so Peter's present instantly finds out Peter's past, and never by mistake knits itself on to that of Paul. . . . He *remembers* his own states, while he only *conceives* Paul's. Remembrance is like direct feeling; its object is suffused with warmth and intimacy to which no object of mere conception ever attains.[57]

Such interruptions do not represent absolute breaks, nor are they united by an intrusive alien substance. The Buddha utilizes the conception of dependence to explain such continuity, the dependence involving both objective and subjective factors. Utilizing this notion of dependence, the Buddha was prepared to explain, not only the interruptions of consciousness within one life, but also between different lives. Thus, the so-called unbroken continuity between two lives is understood by a person who has developed the capacity for retrocognition or memory going beyond those with unconcentrated minds (*asamāhita citta*).

It is this personal stream of consciousness, with the totality of feelings, perceptions and dispositions, which receives the natural name of *myself*, *I* or *me*. It is the individuated stream of consciousness, thought, or experience that provides for the "feeling of oneself." It is neither an absolute fiction nor a necessary pre-condition for all forms of conscious activity. It is a river or a stream of thought or experience or subjective life that the Buddha referred to as *atta* or *ahaṃ*. It is not a permanent and eternal pure Ego that remains the same in spite of all experiences.

With this analysis of the stream of becoming (*bhavasota*), the Buddha was prepared to move on to the explanation of the rationalization that leads to the belief in a transcendental Self that is permanent and eternal, distinguished from the empirical self with its changing directions, either blooming into a morally perfect being or fading into oblivion.

Chapter Six Perception

The stream of thought, consciousness, or experience discussed above is intended by the Buddha as a means of avoiding the metaphysical notion of self (*ātman*) propounded by the Upaniṣadic thinkers. In fact, this metaphysical notion of self is based upon two similarly metaphysical assumptions: the first is the assumption that it is originally pure and that bondage represents its concealment by layers and layers of defilements produced by the perception of plurality, etc., and the second consists of the assertion that this pure mind or consciousness of self is the permanent and eternal agent or observer of everything that goes on in the fluctuating sensory experiences.

The view that the Buddha accepted the former assumption and rejected the latter has come to be generally admitted by some of the classical as well as modern scholars of Buddhism. This interpretation is based upon an explanation of an oft-quoted passage which reads: "Luminous is this thought, O monks, and it is defiled by adventitious defiling elements" (*pabhassaraṃ idaṃ bhikkhave cittaṃ, tañ ca kho āgantukehi upakkilesehi upakkiliṭṭhaṃ*).[58]

Analysing this passage independent of all other statements of the Buddha, it is easy for someone to conclude that this refers to a *tabula rasa* upon which experience does the actual writing. This is to read the metaphysics of Lockean empiricism into the teachings of the Buddha. In the first instance, "luminosity" (*pabhassara*) need not be taken in the sense of "original purity," for it can simply mean effulgence. It is only the reference to adventitious defilements that gives the wrong impression that this effulgence involves ultimate purity. Secondly, there is another statement that denies such luminosity (*na pabhassaraṃ*) and which compares thought with "gold-ore" (*jātarūpa*). As gold-ore needs to be washed and smelt in order to obtain gold (*suvaṇṇa*); even so this thought process requires purification in order to be luminous.[59]

Thus, when the Buddha proceeds to explain every act of sense experience, he begins with the statement "depending upon the visual organ and visible form arises visual consciousness," (*cakkhuñ ca paṭicca rūpe ca uppajjati cakkhuviññāṇaṃ*). Consciousness in this context could not be an "originally pure" thought if it were to occur in the human personality (*nāmarūpa*) or the stream of consciousness (*viññāṇasota*) or the stream of becoming (*bhavasota*) discussed earlier.

However, for the Buddha, the more menacing metaphysical issue was the *cogito* or the transcendental apperception of the rationalist, which was also implied in the Upaniṣadic notion of self (*ātman*). Utilizing an argument comparable to one used by Wittgenstein, the Buddha questioned the ability of the so-called independent self to dictate terms in the world of experience insisting upon what it wants and does not want to be.[60] In other words, if there were to be a self, that self could not be independent in the context of the world that is dependently arisen (*paṭiccasamuppanna*).

The most important method utilized by the Buddha in order to get rid of this metaphysical self is the analysis of the process of sense experience showing how this belief arises and what its consequences are. The briefer statement of the process of sense experience is embodied in the theory of the twelve spheres (*āyatana*). The term *āyatana* literally means the "gateway.' The gateway of experience is not only the sense organ but also the object of sense. These are listed in six pairs:

1. eye (*cakkhu*) and form (*rūpa*),
2. ear (*sota*) and sound (*sadda*),
3. nose (*ghāna*) and small (*gandha*),
4. tongue (*jivhā*) and taste (*rasa*),
5. body (*kāya*) and tangible (*phoṭṭhabba*),
6. mind (*mano*) and concepts (*dhammā*).[61]

The relationship between the five aggregates (*khandhā*) and the twelve spheres (*āyatana*) has not received much attention, even though an examination of this relationship could clarify many confusions regarding Buddhist psychology. While it is possible to locate the twelve spheres within the category of the five aggregates, these two categories are not identical in any way. It is possible to place the first five senses (eye, ear, nose, tongue and body) under the general category of the aggregate of form (*rūpakkhandha*), and the sixth sense mind, together with its object, namely, concepts, under the category of the aggregate of consciousness (*viññāṇakkhandha*). Yet, the spheres do not exhaust the aggregates, primarily because the aggregate of consciousness is not identical with the two spheres, *mano* and *dhammā*. *Mano* is a specific faculty with *dhammā* as its object, whereas *viññāṇa* represents experience based upon all six faculties and their six objects, hence the category of eighteen elements (*dhātu*).

Yet, *mano* has a very specific function which is not shared by any of the other faculties and, therefore, adds a special element to consciousness or experience. It consists of the ability to survey the fields (*gocara*) or the objects of the other senses, an ability not possessed by the latter, which are said to fall back upon (*paṭisaraṇa*) the faculty of *mano*.[62] Unfortunately, this statement is taken to mean that *mano* is the pre-condition or the foundation of all experience, a sort of *sensus communis* which, indeed, is an exaggeration of its function. In fact, its function is to assist in bringing back the impressions produced by the other sense faculties and, as such, constitutes a form of "reflection." *Mano*, therefore, has "concepts" (*dhammā*) as its objects, and these are generally considered substitutes for percepts (see section on "Conception" below). This reflective faculty is also the source of the sense of personal identity or the conception of self. The relationship between *mano* and *viññāṇa* can be illustrated as follows:

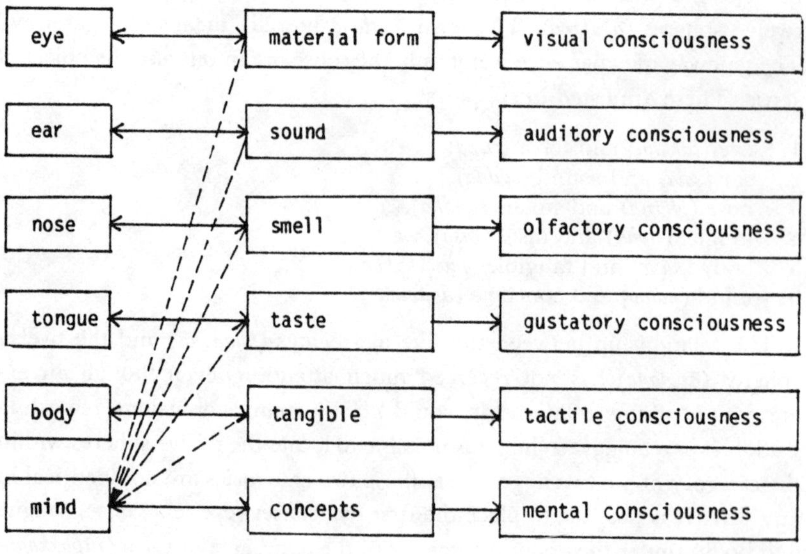

While *mano* is performing this special function, consciousness (*viññāṇa*) continues to flow uninterrupted like a stream fed by all the faculties including *mano*. In fact, the description of experience in terms of the eighteen elements (i.e., the six senses, the six objects and the six forms of consciousness) implies that *mano* is not the "original and transcendental condition" of all experience. It is merely one of the conditions and, according to the Buddha, a condition that gives rise to the belief in a permanent and eternal self and is also the cause of a great deal of suffering for the human beings.

The reference to *citta* (thought), *mano* (mind) and *viññāṇa* (consciousness) in one context, where they are contrasted with the physical body (*cātum-mahābhūtika kāya*) in relation to their change and fluctuation,[63] has left the wrong impression that these are synonymous. Yet, it may be noted that *mano* is never described as having continuity, while *viññāṇa* is sometimes referred to as an unbroken stream (*abbocchinnaṃ viññāṇasotaṃ*).[64] Even *citta* came to be looked upon as a continuous process (*santati*, *santāna*) in the later Buddhist tradition but not *mano*. The reason for this is obvious. The Buddha did not deny the function of *mano* in producing the "feeling of self," i.e., the so-called empirical self. Yet he was not prepared to make this self either the pre-condition for all experience or a permanent and eternal entity. For him, *mano* is one among six faculties that conditions consciousness. So long as the "feeling of self" produced by *mano* is understood in the same way as the feelings produced by the other senses, i.e., as being dependently arisen, impermanent and changing, the Buddha saw no great danger. Unfortunately, the faculty of *mano* and the feeling or consciousness produced by it (*mano-viññāṇa*) are susceptible to solidification more than any other faculty or consciousness, and this is the cause of the belief in a permanent and eternal self. Thus, the verb *maññati* (Sk. *manyate*) often expresses the activity that leads to such substantialist beliefs.[65] Such activities can dominate one's behavior and lead to harmful consequences. This seems to be the reason why the Buddha singled out *mano* as a pre-condition for all knowledge and experience.

The Buddha's reluctance to go beyond these twelve spheres (*āyatana*) of experience or consciousness to look for a permanent and eternal self or an immutable object is clearly and unequivocally expressed in the "Discourse on Everything" (*Sabba-sutta*).[67] For him, these constitute the totality (*sabbaṃ*) of human experience. Anything that does not come within these spheres is said to be beyond the sphere of experience (*avisaya*). As such, the importance of these twelve spheres of experience in the Buddha's epistemological investigations cannot be overemphasized.

The above explanation of the five aggregates (*khandhā*) and the twelve spheres (*āyatana*) can leave the impression that the Buddha actually replaced the Upaniṣadic conception of *ātman* with the notion of consciousness (*viññāṇa*). Such wrong impressions were formed even by some of the immediate disciples of the Buddha. For example, one of them named Sāti wrongly interpreted consciousness (*viññāṇa*) as being no different from the transmigrating, yet eternal, self.[68] The Buddha's immediate response was that this consciousness, which is part of the human personality, is conditioned by the sense and sense object.[69]

The Buddha's statement that consciousness depends upon the sense and sense object indicates that, while recognizing the impact of disposition on the stream of consciousness, he wanted to underscore the priority of sense and sense object in each act of veridical perception.

The category of eighteen elements (*dhātu*) explaining experience is no more than the twelve spheres plus the six types of consciousness (*viññāṇa*) that arises on occasions of sense experience.

With this understanding of the five aggregates (*khandhā*), the twelve spheres (*āyatana*) and the eighteen elements (*dhātu*), it would be possible to analyse the Buddha's description of sense perception in the most popular passage in the *Madhupiṇḍika-sutta*.[70] The passage reads thus:

> Depending upon the visual sense and the visible object, O brethren, arises visual consciousness; the coming together of these three is contact; depending upon contact arises feeling. What one feels one perceives; what one perceives, one reasons about. What one reasons about, one is obsessed with. Due to such obsessions, a person is assailed by obsessed perceptions and concepts in regard to visible objects cognizable by the visual organ, belonging to the past, the future and the present.

A description of sense experience comparable to this is rarely met with in the literature contemporary with the Buddha. If this statement is placed in the context of the five aggregates discussed above, the consciousness that arises depending upon the sense and object of sense cannot be an absolutely new and unrelated phenomenon. It is not an impression left by the sense and object on a *tabula rasa*. It is consciousness (*viññāṇa*) molded by the sense and object in the immediate situation as well as the dispositions (*saṅkhāra*) and consciousness (*viññāṇa*) which are constituents of the five aggregates or the psychophysical personality. In other words, each instance of sense experience is an occurrence conditioning and conditioned by the stream of becoming (*bhava-sota*).

The flux of experience, so conditioned, retains its individuality as a result of the dispositions (*saṅkhāra*).[17] Therefore, contact (*phassa*), which is the coming together (*saṅgati*) of the sense, the object and consciousness,[72] immediately becomes part of an individual flux of experience. Depending upon contact arises feeling (*vedanā*).[73] Feeling or sensation is broadly classified into three categories as pleasanṭ (*sukha*), unpleasant (*dukkha*) and neutral (*adukkhamasukha*).[74]

Until this stage, the dispositional tendencies (*saṅkhāra*) that were part of consciousness (*viññāṇa*) and which contributed to the individuation of the person even when perceiving an object shared by others as well functioned only in the form of "interest." However, at the time of the emergence of feeling (*vedanā*), these dispositions tend to increase in strength and, instead of manifesting themselves as "interest," they produce attachment to pleasant feelings, aversion towards unpleasant feelings and disinterest in neutral feelings. It is a time when the dispositional tendencies "solidify" (to use a phrase from James[75]) to such an extent that they not only individuate a person but go far beyond in producing metaphysical notions of self (*ātman*).

When the Buddha said that "depending upon contact arises feeling" (*phassapaccayā vedanā*), he was explaining a natural process. However, this could not be an entirely impersonal experience, as explained by Bhikkhu Ñāṇananda.[76] If it were to be a completely impersonal experience, the consciousness that preceded it should be a *tabula rasa*, with no dispositional tendencies (*saṅkhāra*) associated with it. This is not acceptable to early Buddhism. In the absence of such an unpolluted consciousness on occasions of sense experience, even if the sense organ were to be completely changed and the object of perception were to be something completely new, the perceiving consciousness will still bring back its old dispositions when experiencing that *feeling*.

Two important observations can be made at this point. The first is that all perceptions involve feeling or sensation. Feelings are either pleasant or unpleasant or neutral. This means that perceptions are invariably associated with an emotive element. Thus, neither the ordinary person nor an enlightened one is without emotion. The Buddha's claim that even a person who has attained freeom (*nibbāna*) continues to experience pleasant (*manāpa*) as well as unpleasant (*amanāpa*) sensations, so long as his sensory faculties remain,[77] is a clear indication that he is not a person without emotions.

Secondly, in addition to emotion, every act of perception includes some form of 'interest,' because it involves consciousness conditioned by disposition. Without such interest, it is not possible for a human being to deal with the sensory input. Omniscience (*sabbaññutā*), defined as the "knowledge of everything at the time of every act of experiencing" would be the only other means by which a human being can deal with the so-called "sensible muchness."[78] This latter possibility was, in fact, denied by the Buddha, not only with regard to ordinary unenlightened persons, but even in the case of enlightened ones.[79] The Buddha's explanation of even the threefold knowledge (*tevijjā*) relevant for enlightenment and freedom makes this very explicit. The threefold knowledge includes retrocognition, clairvoyance and knowledge of the waning of influxes. This last pertains to knowledge of oneself. However, with regard to retrocognition, which involves knowledge of one's own past, and clairvoyance, which relates to objective events, the Buddha was not willing to say that these are available all the time. He could develop such knowledge only when he needs them or is interested in them (*yāvad eva ākankhāmi*).[80] This means that even the enlightened one is left without any faculty that would enable him to instantly understand everything presented to him in sense experience every moment without resorting to some form of choice.

In the case of an ordinary person who is not freed from lust, hatred and confusion, at the moment when feeling occurs in the sensory process, he comes to be emotionally and intellectually involved. His emotions are converted to attachment or aversion. His interest becomes a dogmatic pursuit. It is an important change taking place in the causal process. This change in the perceptual process is expressed in an extremely sophisticated manner by the Buddha when he, instead of saying: "depending upon feeling arises perception" (*vedanāpaccayā saññā*), which would imply a normal or natural process of dependence, maintained that "what one feels, one perceives" (*yaṃ vedeti taṃ sañjānāti*). It is a sophisticated way of explaining the intrusion of the so-called pure Ego; sophisticated because it is done without interrupting the description in order to add a footnote. The uninterrupted description flows in such a way that by merely changing the linguistic expression, i.e., moving from "the language of dependence" to a "language of agency," the Buddha is able to express the most cruicial change taking place in the process of perception.

Having been involved with the pre-Buddhist meditative tradition for almost six years, it is possible that the Buddha came to understand how and why the yogins of that tradition were advocating the belief in a transcendental consciousness of self. In advocating the belief in such a self, these yogins were making the same mistake which James attributes to the modern-day psychologists. James calls it the "psychologist's fallacy."

> The psychologist, . . . stands outside of the mental state he speaks of. Both itself and its object are objects to him. Now when it is a *cognitive* state (percept, thought, concept, etc.), he ordinarily has no other way of naming it than as the thought, percept, etc. *of that object*. He himself, meanwhile, knowing the self-same object in *his* way, gets easily led to suppose that the thought, which is *of* it, knows it in the same way in which he knows it, although this is very far from the case.[81]

James thinks that the most fictitious puzzles have been introduced into the science of psychology by this means. Interestingly, the puzzles are appearing more in the context of philosophy, for example, in the controversies pertaining to presentative and representative theories of perception, nominalism and conceptualism, etc. James points out how this fallacy operates:

> Many philosophers, however, hold that the reflective consciousness of self is essential to the cognitive function of thought. They hold that a thought, in order to know a thing at all must expressly distinguish between a thing and its own self.[82]

In a footnote, James holds Kant responsible for this view. For the psychologist James, "This is a perfectly wanton assumption, and not the slightest shadow of reason exists for supposing it true."[83]

This is an unequivocal rejection of the conception of *sākṣin* ("the agent of perception") espoused so enthusiastically by the Brahmanical tradition. It seems that most yogins who came out of the meditative state and propounded a theory of *ātman* were committing a similar "psychologist's fallacy."

For the Buddha, as well as for James, the emergence of the belief in a pure Ego or the interpretation of the stream of experience leading to the "psychologist's fallacy" is in turn the result of an inappropriate understanding of the nature of sensation. The Buddha's statement explaining the process of perception (quoted above) clearly indicates that the *ātman* or the pure Ego is a result of the process of perception rather than its precondition. The fact that it occurs at the time of sensation, and not before, probably made the Buddha realize that it is futile to go elsewhere looking for an epistemological justification for it. If it were to emerge at the time of sensation, what needs to be done is to examine the nature of sensation without making the Ego an *a priori* condition for sensation itself. The substantialist search for truth and reality turns out to be the cause of the psychologist's fallacy.

However, substantialist search for truth and reality has sometimes left the philosopher with "pure sensation," often referred to as the "pure experience" undiluted by the cognitive function of thought. Such pure sensations go to make up the real world of experience, leaving room for the logician to discover specific and constant relations among them. The search for truth thus ends up with discrete pure entities and their logical relations. In such a context, the necessity for postulating a further metaphysical notion of a "pure Ego" is clearly stated by James:

> Take the pain called toothache for example. Again and again we feel it and greet it as the same real item in the universe. We must, therefore, it is supposed, have a distinct pocket for it in our mind into which it and nothing else will fit. This pocket, when filled, is the sensation of toothache; and must be filled or half-filled whenever and under whatever form toothache is present to our thought and whether much or little of the rest of the mind be fitted at the same time. Thereupon of course comes the paradox and the mystery. If the knowledge of the toothache is pent up in this separate mental pocket, how can it be known *cum alio* or brought into view with anything else? This pocket knows nothing else; no other part of mind knows the toothache. The knowing of the toothache *cum alio* must be a miracle. And the miracle must have an Agent. And the Agent must be a Subject or Ego "out of time."[84]

As in the pre-Buddhist tradition, the enjoyment of the fruit by one bird becomes a mystery unless there were to be another bird whose function is simply to watch. Separate the two birds, and the recriminations between the sensationalist and the spiritualist begin. For James, such "*a pure sensation is an abstraction.*."[85]

The emergence of the belief in a pure Ego at a time when sensation occurs makes a difference to the perception as well as the conception that follows. The search for *something* (*kiñci*, Sk. *kiṃcit*) in the subject is satisfied with the belief in the pure Ego. The self-same search for *something* is now directed towards the object of perception and terminates in an equally metaphysical notion of a self or substance in phenomena. This is clearly evident from the Upaniṣadic ontology, as described in the passage quoted earlier. According to that passage, the objective world turns out to be as real as the subjective world—the *ātman* pervading both. With perception thus providing the knowledge of an ultimately real object, intellectual activity begins. Such intellectual activity certainly needs the use of concepts that are now substituted for the percept. However, since the object is taken to be ultimately real, the substituted concept becomes either a mere name (*nāma-dheyam*) or be considered exactly equivalent to the object it denotes and, therefore, incorruptible.

Philosophical controversies engendered by such speculations have dominated human thinking for centuries. For the Buddha, the final result of such speculation is obsession (*papañca*) both with regard to the percept (*saññā*) and concept (*saṅkhā*), leading not only to conflict and strife (*kalaha*, *viggaha*), but also to frustration and suffering (*dukkha*) at not finding the subject and object remaining the same all the time as anticipated. The root cause of all this obsession, conflict and suffering is the belief in the self, the *cogito* or the transcendental apperception (*mantā asmi*, "thinker, I am").[86]

Chapter Seven The Selfless Self

The stream of experience or thought (*viññāṇasota*) discussed above is not a static entity. It is a changing stream of becoming (*bhavasota*) constantly fed by perceptions (*saññā*). Some perceptions could bring in new information, adding it to the mainstream and mixing it up with the rest, and some perceptions bring in practically the same information without adding anything new. Sometimes the so-called new information may be something that passed unnoticed because of a lack of interest. At other times it could be genuinely new data.

The dispositions (*saṅkhāra*) as well as memory (*sati*), as mentioned earlier, provide an individuality to this stream of becoming which is "blooming and buzzing" with life, with specific goals attained every now and then. The constituents of this self are the five aggregates (*pañcakkhandha*). In the context of these five aggregates, the Buddha was not reluctant to speak of 'I' or 'myself' (*ahaṃ*) or even the 'self' (*atta*). Without admitting a "ghost in the machine" or a transcendental apperception, the Buddha was willing to recognize the feeling of individuality, of self. It is a feeling that can contract and expand depending upon the context. It does not represent a static entity to which everything belongs.

Thus, we have the feeling of self confined to the physical personality. According to James, the body is the innermost part of the *material self* in each of us.[87] This feeling of self is extended to our clothes, to our immediate family—our parents, wife and children, our home and its surroundings. It can extend further to include our village, our country and our nation. Going beyond, we may have a feeling that makes us one of the human family or part of nature. Here again, the context comes to be of paramount importance.

There seems to be no justification for assuming that the Buddha encouraged the annihilation of this feeling of self. What was encouraged was the elimination of the belief in a permanent and eternal "ghost in the machine." Seclusion (*viveka*) or solitary confinement may have a therapeutic value in getting rid of the belief in such a metaphysical self, but may lead to disasterous consequences if it were to eliminate the feeling of the empirical self as well. Suicide, coupled with mass destruction of life, human as well as non-human, could result from an utter shrinkage of our personality, from a sort of conversion of ourselves into nothingness, which is a dangerous psychological phenomenon. "No-self" (*anatta*) or "emptiness" (*suññatā*), in their absolute forms, could be nihilistic (*uccheda*), encouraging not only a life of hedonism, but also acts of self-destruction, sometimes hailed as altruism. The Buddha's very first discourse condemned both forms of behavior; hedonism being viewed as vulgar (*gamma*) and extreme altruism as painful (*dukkha*), both being considered ignoble (*anariya*) and unfruitful (*anatthasaṃhita*).[88]

If "no-self" or non-substantiality (*anatta*) or "emptiness" (*suññatā*) were to be applied in a more restricted manner, that is, to imply the denial of a metaphysical self and/or eternal substance, one would not fall into the extremes mentioned above. Indeed, the reality of the feelings and emotions that occur in the stream of experience are relevant to an explanation of harmonious life, so long as these feelings and emotions are kept under restraint (*saṃvara*), without either annihilating them or allowing them to grow into monstrous proportions producing "pure Egos."

Thus, the Buddha spoke of 'I' or 'myself' (*ahaṃ*) and 'mine' (*mama*), but avoided and discouraged "I-making" (*ahaṃ-kāra*) or "mine-making" (*mamaṃ-kāra*), both terms implying egoism. This distinction should be kept in mind when interpreting the very popular statement by the Buddha in his admonition to his disciples asking them to consider the aggregates as "that is not mine; that person is not me; that person is not myself," (*n'etaṃ mama, n'eso ahaṃ, na m'eso attā*).[89] Here, the aggregates are *distinguished* from the self. The distinction that was made by the proponents of the metaphysical theory of self was foremost in the Buddha's mind. It is the distinction between the aggregates and the self—the former being impermanent (*anicca*) and the latter, permanent and eternal (*nicca sassata*). Thus, every time the Buddha negated the self with the above statement, it was preceded by the question as to whether the aggregates are impermanent or not. As soon as he received the obvious answer that the five aggregates are impermanent, he asserts the inappropriateness of the statement "that is mine; that person is me or that person is myself."[90]

The reluctance to make a distinction between the feeling of self or individuality and the knowledge of a permanent and eternal self has been the case of many a puzzle in the interpretation of the Buddha's teachings. Even the emergence of Absolutism founded upon absolute negation is the result of overlooking such a distinction. In other words, the recognition of the absolute necessity of a transcendental unity of apperception to account for the continuity in human experience, described by James as a "perfectly wanton assumption," without the faintest shadow of reason for believing it true, is the cause of this confusion regarding the conception of a person or self.

Attempts are sometimes made to explain the Buddha's negation of self as being absolute and that whenever he speaks of 'self' (*atta*) or 'I' (*ahaṃ*), he is using an empty concept, a mere name, as a useful device (*upāya*) to lead the ordinary unenlightened person to ultimate enlightenment and freedom. This would mean that the concepts of self (*atta*) and 'I' (*ahaṃ*), even if they were to imply a changing personality or a stream of becoming (*bhavasota*), would be false and yet possess pragmatic value. Unfortunately, such a theory of pragmatism would not be acceptable either to the Buddha or to James. In fact, it would be contradicted by the Buddha's refusal even to admit the possibility of statements that are false (*abhūta*, *ataccha*), yet useful (*atthasaṃhita*).[91]

It seems that human dispositions (*saṅkhāra*) tend to move the feeling of self in two different directions. The first is in the direction of absolute negation or shrinking it to the point of absolute nothingness. This, as mentioned before, could be utilized to advocate two totally different ways of life—either hedonism or absolute altruism. The other is in the direction of making it a permanent and eternal reality, which also can lead to the same extremes in behavior. For example, one who believes in such a permanent and eternal self can ignore the psychophysical personality to the point of mortifying it. On the contrary, it can lead to a form of "possessive individualism" and hedonism. For the Buddha, the "middle path" lies in avoiding both extremes of nihilism (*uccheda*) and eternalism (*sassata*).[92] Absolute self-negation as well as absolute self-assertion are not only morally repugnant, but also epistemologically unwarranted. The noble life enunciated in the very popular statement: "Taking oneself as an example for comparison, one should neither strike nor kill," (*attānaṃ upamaṃ katvā na haneyya na ghātaye*)[93] would make no sense at all in the context of the absolute negation or absolute assertion of self.

The feeling of self occurring in the stream of becoming thus turns out to be an important element in the affirmation of the relation of dependence (*paṭiccasamuppāda*) that exists between a person, his family, nation, humanity, as well as nature. The solidification of this feeling into a "pure Ego" can interrupt its extension at any level, confining it exclusively to the neglect of every other. As such it can lead to extreme selfishness, to tribalism, to nationalism or to pure altruism. For the Buddha, the so-called self-feeling is dependently arisen, and is therefore contextual, not absolute.

It is this empirical self that the Buddha admitted when he spoke of the "dominance of the self" (*attādhipateyya*).[94] Its contextual validity based upon its dependent arising makes it totally different from what is generally recognized as "conscience" in the absolutistic systems. It is significant to note that this notion of "conscience" had not attracted the attention of James when he wrote two extensive volumes on psychology. He refers to it occasionally,[95] but in all such instances he seems to use it in the sense of "sensibility." Hence, it would be very different from the use of the term "conscience" in an absolutistic system where one is expected to follow one's "conscience" irrespective of the consequences. Elsewhere, discussing "The Powers of Men," James condemns the popular notion of conscience.

> Conscience makes cowards of us all. Social conventions prevent us from telling the truth after the fashion of the heroes and heroines of Bernard Shaw. We all know persons who are models of excellence, but who belong to the extreme philistine type of mind. So deadly is their intellectual respectability that we can't converse about certain subjects at all, can't let our minds play over them, can't even mention them in their presence.[96]

Indeed, the transformation of Arjuna, the hero of the *Bhagavadgītā*, from being a questioning moralist to a man of unwavering faith in the social convention of his day, represents the triumph of this form of "conscience" condemned by James. Neither the background nor the context makes any difference to it. Neither the Buddha nor James had anything to do with it. Categorical imperatives based upon one's conscience had no place in their philosophical or ethical discussions.

After speaking of the "dominance of the self" (*attādhipateyya*), the Buddha also referred to the "dominance of the world" (*lokādhipateyya*). This latter would make no sense unless something like a "social self" comparable to what James recognized were to be accepted. James defines the social self as the recognition one gets from one's mates.

> We are not only gregarious animals, liking to be in sight of our fellows, but we have an innate propensity to get ourselves noticed, and noticed favorably, by our kind. No more fiendish punishment could be devised, were such a thing physically possible, than that one should be turned loosed in society and remain absolutely unnoticed by all the members thereof.[97]

He proceeds to identify this social self with "man's *fame*, good or bad, and his *honor* or dishonor." "It is his image in the eyes of his own 'set,' which exalts or condemns him as he conforms or not to certain requirements that may not be made of one in another walk of life."[98]

While the Buddha was prepared to criticize and condemn the social behavior of the Brahmanical thinkers dominated by the unreasonably rigid caste-system, he did not ignore the justified indignations on the part of the world to certain forms of behavior of his disciples. The discipline he recommended to them, as embodied in the *Vinaya Piṭaka*, often took into consideration the need to conform to custom and convention that did not interfere with his conception of community life. The justified protests, disappointments and indignations of people (*manussā ujjhāyanti khīyanti vipācenti*) served as a powerful incentive in the organization of the monastic rules.[99]

It is possible for someone to argue that one form of freedom that the Buddha admitted is the ability to remain unsmeared by "gain or loss, good repute or disrepute, praise or blame, happiness or suffering."[100] However, to remain unsmeared (*anupalitta*) does not mean to be utterly indifferent to everything that goes on around oneself. As a person with feelings and emotions, he does not not remain completely unaffected by the evils and suffering in the world. He could be justifiably indignant, but not revengeful. He could be compassionate, but not enamored. He was harsh on Ambaṭṭha who refused to listen to any arguments based upon experience or reason against the so-called superiority of the Brahman class.[100] He even allowed the indignation of the audience (metaphorically presented as the Demon Daṇḍapāni) to frighten the unrepentant advocate of caste-supremacy. In many instances like these, the Buddha was able to convert such people to accept a way of life that contributes to one's own welfare as well as to that of others.

And lastly, one can speak of the "moral or spiritual self." It would seem that the Buddha was speaking of such a self when he referred to the "dominance of *dhamma*" (*dhammādhipateyya*).[102] Referring to the spiritual self, James says:

> By the spiritual self, so far as it belongs to the Empirical Me, I mean a man's inner or subjective being, his psychic faculties or dispositions, taken concretely; not the bare principle of personal Unity, or 'pure' Ego, which remains still to be discussed. These psychic dispositions are the most enduring and intimate part of the self, that which we most verily seem to be.[103]

It was pointed out earlier that the dispositions, according to the Buddha, are responsible for the two different directions in which the stream of becoming can move. One is absolute negation of the self leading to the justification of two totally different ways of life: self-indulgence and self-immolation, and the other the absolute assertion of a permanent and eternal self providing justification for similar extremes of behavior. The appeasement of dispositions (*saṅkhāra-samatha*), instead of their complete elimination or solidification, was considered to be freedom. This appeasement of dispositions is the foundation of the so-called moral self. It is not only a psychological transformation of the individual, but also one that has objective relevance, for it leads to practical results in the objective world. The so-called emotivists may claim that good and bad are mere matters of feeling or taste. The Buddha, as a pragmatist having a totally different understanding of human emotions, will insist that this feeling or taste is not without practical consequences. No amount of pure reason would be able to deny the fact that a person with a nihilistic bent of mind or with a belief in a permanent and eternal self can bring untold suffering for humanity. It is these "appeased dispositions" that constitute the moral self. It is the moral principle that calls for a serious consideration of the context and the practical consequences. Hence it has been described as the "ultimate fruit" (*paramārtha*).[104] This ultimate fruit is not one to be achieved as a result of satisfying the exclusive interests of either the individual or the family or the society or the nation. Since the self as representing the individual, the family, the society or the nation is understood as being dependently arisen, such a moral self becomes inclusive rather than exclusive depending upon the context and consequences.

Chapter Eight
Emotions and the Foundation of the Moral Life

Buddhism clearly distinguishes between feeling or sensation (*vedanā*) and craving (*taṇhā*). Pleasant (*sukha*) or agreeable (*manāpa*) sensations as well as unpleasant (*dukkha*) and disagreeable (*amanāpa*) sensations do occur in all human beings whose sense faculties are functioning properly, whether it be an ordinary unenlightened person or an enlightened one.[105] They are absent only in a person who has attained the state of cessation (*nirodha-samāpatti*), when all sensory activities are cut off, hence described as the "state of cessation of perception and the felt" (*saññā-vedayita-nirodha*). In that state a person is not cognitive at all,[106] and the difference between such a person and a dead one was the subject of discussion in early Buddhism. However, emerging from that state, a person is said to experience bodily calm and relaxation. For this reason, when speaking of various forms of experience, the Buddha considered the state of cessation as one that is to be experienced by the body (*kāyena sacchikaraṇīyā-dhammā*).[107] It would be necessary to underscore the fact that such bodily calm or relaxation can be experienced only after one has emerged from that state, not during the time when a person is in it.

If pleasant, unpleasant and neutral sensations are inevitable parts of sense experience, they are not merely subjective attitudes, but bodily changes that follow directly the perception of the object. If the term *emotion* were to be used to refer to such sensations, as James does,[108] then it would not be possible to be "unemotional" so long as a person continues to have experience of the world. This would be contrary to the popularly held opinion that the mental perception of some fact excites the mental affection called the emotion, and that this latter state of mind gives rise to the bodily expression.[109]

The emotivists in the modern world, who confine moral discourse primarily to the sphere of emotion, denying its facutal validity, seem to follow a more popular notion about human emotions. An emotivist is uncomfortable with the emotions because he is not able to deal with them in the same way as he believes he can deal with facts. The variability in emotions, compared with the persistence of the so-called facts, seems to threaten him in his search for permanent and eternal truths. If the emotions are to be identified with bodily changes following directly upon the perception of the exciting fact, as James believes, then the emotivist's problem comes to be associated with the very act of perception which is the source material for his conception of truth and reality.

James was not unaware of the disbelief that his view of emotion would cause. Yet, rather bravely, he continues to explain his position:

> The various permutations and combinations of which these organic activities are susceptible make it abstractly possible that no shade of emotion, however slight, should be without a bodily reverberation as unique, when taken in its totality, as is the mental mood itself. The immense number of parts modified in each emotion is what makes it so difficult for us to reproduce in cold blood the total and integral expression of any one of them.[110]

Even though the Buddha recognized emotion as an inevitable part of human experience, he continued to emphasize its non-substantiality. Sensation (*vedanā*), whether it is pleasant or unpleasant, agreeable or disagreeable, is compared to a bubble (*bubbula*, Sk. *budbuda*).[111] Even though emotions are part of experience, they are not eternal but ephemeral. Any substantialist search for the ultimate content of emotion would lead to frustration. In a similar tone, James claims that the vital point of his whole theory of emotions is that "*If we fancy some strong emotion, and then try to abstract from our consciousness of it all the feelings of its bodily symptoms, we find that we have nothing left behind*, no 'mind-stuff' out of which the emotion can be constituted, and that a cold and neutral state of intellectual perception is all that remains."[112]

James insists that this is not a strictly materialistic view of emotion. Instead, he considers it a *sensationalist view*."[113] However, for the "platonizers in psychology" there is something peculiarly base about it. Between the two extremes, namely, the materialistic view of emotion and the so-called spiritualist view, James seem to consider his as a middle position and, as such, not "vile and materialistic."

The Buddha's explanation of *vedanā* as the result of contact (*phassa*) involving the harmony of the sense organ, the object of sense and consciousness, presents a straightforward sensationalist view. It was, indeed, the middle path that avoided the extremes of spiritualism and materialism, even though these latter were not presented in the same sophisticated way in which they were available to James in the modern world. For the Buddha, such sensations are dependently arisen (*paṭiccasamuppanna*). Their dependence is upon both material and conscious processes and, therefore, need not be strictly material or purely spiritual. James provides a similar account of emotion and proceeds to explain the reasons for the prevalence of chaotic variations, a phenomenon that has caused uneasiness among systematic philosophers with regard to their worth. According to James, "the moment the genesis of an emotion is accounted for, as the arousal by an object of a lot of reflex acts which are forthwith felt, *we immediately see why there is no limit to the number of possible different emotions which may exist, and why the emotions of different individuals may vary indefinitely*, both as to their constitution and as to objects which call them forth."[114] Discouraging any attempt on the part of the behaviorists, James insists that there is nothing "sacramental or eternally fixed in reflex action." Yet any classification of the emotion is seen to be true and as 'natural' as any other.

The Buddha's doctrine of non-substantiality (*anatta*) relating to sensation/emotion thus deprives the psychologist or the philosopher from discovering or positing any *structure* even in the crudest form of sensation that may be generated by the so-called material object.

The more subtle emotions pertain to moral, intellectual and aesthetic feelings. Most modern scholars in Buddhism have assumed that while the Buddha recognized, and even emphasized, the need to cultivate and promote moral feelings or emotions, he encouraged the annihilation of intellectual and aesthetic emotions. This unfortunate understanding of the Buddha's doctrine, which has become almost universal, stems from a superficial interpretation of Buddhist psychology in general and the Buddhist idea of renunciation in particular.

To begin with, it may be emphasized that neither *taṇhakkhaya* or "the waning of craving" nor *virāga* or "absence of lust," two terms often used as synonyms for *nibbāna* or freedom,[115] in any way imply the elimination of *vedanā* or sensation/emotion. It is the mistaken *identification* of pleasant sensation (*sukhāvedanā*) with craving (*taṇhā*) and lust (*rāga*) that seems to be the cause of this confusion and misunderstanding. While it is true, and this is actually the position held by the Buddha, that pleasant sensations *could* give rise to craving and lust, and unpleasant sensations (*dukkhā vedanā*) can be the cause of aversion or hatred (*dosa*), the causal relation is not a one-to-one relation.

The abandoning of pleasant sensations, of joy (*pīti*) and happiness (*sukha*) are encouraged during the initial stages of meditation.[116] The purpose, however, is not to abandon them forever. The temporary cessation of all joyous and pleasant sensation, leading up to the cessation of all forms of perception and the felt (*nirodha-samāpatti*) has the salutary effect of bringing about the realization of their non-substantiality. However, when one realizes their non-substantiality and dependent nature, by "melting" the solidified conceptualizations, one's thought (*citta*) is said to become less rigid (*mudu*) and flexible or malleable (*kammañña*). Having achieved such a flexibility, one can proceed to have an understanding of the experiential process, and whenever a pleasant sensation occurs, one would have the necessary understanding as well as conviction to prevent the emergence of lust or hatred, attachment or aversion. It is this form of restraint (*saṃvara*) on occasions of sense experience that is emphasized in the Buddhist texts. It is not a platonic attempt to develop a non-sensuous intuition or experience; rather an elimination of the harmful effects of sensation.

The above misunderstanding emerges as a result of an inappropriate interpretation of a recurrent passage in the early discourses that explains the process of restraining the senses (*indriya-saṃvara*). The passage reads thus:

> He, possessed of the noble body of moral habits, subjectively experiences unsullied happiness. Having seen a material object (*rūpa*) with the eye (*cakkhu*), he does not grasp on to the *nimitta* nor to the *anuvyañjana*. If he dwells with the organ of sight uncontrolled, covetiousness and dejection, evil unhealthy states of mind, might predominate. So he fares along controlling it; he guards the organ of sight, he comes to control over the organ of sight. (This is repeated with regard to the other senses as well, including mind, *mano*).[117]

The terms *nimitta* and *anuvyañjana*, occurring in the above passage, contributed to all the confusion. The term *nimitta* is the more cumbersome. Once its meaning is clarified, the term *anuvyañjana* can be more clearly defined. *Nimitta* is sometimes rendered as "appearance,"[118] and sometimes as "sign."[119] As may be seen, both translations are unsatisfactory. An examination of the context in which the negative term *animitta* occurs will help to clarify the use of the term. *Animitta* often occurs along with *suñña* (Sk. *śūnya*) and *appaṇihita* (Sk. *apranihita*, a semantic equivalent of *appatiṭṭhita/apratiṣṭhita*).[120] The translation of this term as "signless" gives the impression that the Buddha was looking for a non-conceptual reality abandoning any form of sense experience.[121] Indeed, when the Buddha describes the freed person as one who, *having seen the object*, does not grasp on to a *nimitta*, he cannot be saying that the freed one is not grasping after the "sign" or the "appearance." The freed one has already seen the object because the process of sense experience has taken place and this involves the perception of the appearance, any signs the object may have and even conception. What he is not grasping must be something completely different. And this is clearly explained by the occurence of the term *animitta* along with *suñña*, the latter being the denial of a substance. Thus, *nimitta* is strongly suggestive of a mysterious cause or substance, either in the eye or in the object that the eye perceives. If *nimitta* is the substance, then the *anuvyañjana* refers to its associate, namely, quality. Here is the famous metaphysical issue of substance and quality. As such, what seems to be recommended is the renunciation of the Lockean enterprise that recognizes qualities of the object which could not be explained without positing a mysterious substance where the qualities are established (*paṇihita, patiṭṭhita*).

It is true that the term *suñña, animitta* and *appaṇihita* are generally used to describe the "freedom of thought" (*ceto vimutti*) resulting from the attainment of the "state of cessation (*nirodha-samāpatti*).[122] However, emerging from the "state of cessation" one does not necessarily lose the "freedom of thought," if one had attained the knowledge of the "waning of influxes" (*āsavakkhaya*, see section on "Analytic Yoga"). Thus, when applied to sense experience, the terms *suñña, animitta* and *appaṇihita* refer to the non-substantialist approach to sensory experience, and not the complete cessation of such experience and conceptualization. Therefore, there is no need to deny intellectual and aesthetic feelings or emotions as being necessarily evil. They could be considered, along with the moral, as being part of the restrained or refined life of a human being or of society. The fact that this has been the case is amply demonstrated by the followers of the Buddha who produced some of the artistic wonders of the world, such as the paintings of Ajanta and the architectural pieces of Borobudur.

The paeons of joy expressed by the Buddha,[123] as well as by his disciples,[124] upon attaining enlightenment represent some of the most sublime intellectual emotions experienced by human beings. They are not qualitatively different from the intellectual emotions enjoyed by other beings in ordinary life, such as in the discovery of a previously unknown star in the sky, of a new chemical or even a new discovery in the sphere of linguistics, sociology or history. The discovery is immediately made part of that person's experience, and it even comes to be named after him with any attempt to misappropriate it being condemned as plagiarism. Yet the latter seems to be much shorter-lived compared to the former, which is more stable.

Finally, the aesthetic emotions are not blunted by the attainment of enlightenment and freedom. How a person who clings to brute pleasures cannot enjoy the serenity and beauty of a forest glade is emphasized by the Buddha.[125] It seems that he recognized the fact that most people cannot enjoy whatever is beautiful (*citrāni*) in the world unless they make it their own. The Buddha once remarked: "Whatever is beautiful in the world does not represent your desire. Such beautiful things remain. But a wise one restrains his longing in that context."[126]

This, indeed, is not an appeal to abandon experience of the beautiful, the experience of the aesthetic joy, but only to restrain one's craving or desire for them, for this latter converts even the most sublime aesthetic experience (i.e., *assāda*) into one of suffering, hence leading to unfortunate consequences (*ādīnava*).

Speaking of the so-called subtler emotions, James says:

> As far as *these ingredients* of the subtler emotions go, then the latter form no exception to our account, but rather an additional illustration thereof. In all cases of intellectual or moral rapture we find that, unless there be coupled a bodily reverberation of some kind with the mere thought of the object and cognition of its quality; unless we laugh at the neatness of the demonstration and witticism; unless we thrill at the case of justice, or tingle at the act of magnanimity; our state of mind can hardly be called emotional at all. It is in fact a mere intellectual perception of how certain things are to be called—neat, right, witty, generous, and the like. Such a judicial state of mind as this is to be classed among the awareness of truth; it is a *cognitive* act. As a matter of fact, however, the moral and intellectual cognitions hardly ever do exist thus unaccompanied. The bodily sounding-board is at work, as careful introspection will show, far more than we usually suppose.[127]

With such an understanding of both crude and subtle emotions, one can easily account for something that is generally considered to be miraculous, namely, the changes in the physical appearance of someone who is affected by the most refined emotions, such as the usual aura, the halo of light emanating from his body. Thus, a so-called miracle turns out to be a very natural phenomenon.

If the moral, intellectual and aesthetic emotions are an inalienable part of the human experience and if their refinement can produce tangible effect on that personality, there could be no reason why they could not have any effect on the society in which that personality is located, unless it is assumed that the so-called society consists of discrete individuals with no mutual relations. This latter assumption makes a mockery of moral emotions or sentiments, even if it were to leave the intellectual and aesthetic emotions unaffected.

This brings us face to face with the most significant aspect of the moral life of human beings. If the moral feeling, sentiment or emotion is an inalienable part of human experience, what could be the criterion by which its refinement or degradation is to be determined?

If an action were to lead to one's own harm or suffering, it could not be a moral action. Self-destruction could hardly be called a joyful action. A moth is attracted by the glow of the light, but if it has any awareness that it is harmful to itself, it would not be attracted by it. Human beings can be blinded like moths leading themselves to disaster. Even though self-destruction is often praised as a noble and altruistic ideal, there is no denial that even those who have sacrificed their lives would have, given the opportunity, made all attempts to preserve them.

Similarly, harming others could not be a moral action. Such action ignores everything that was said about human emotions. "Tooth for a tooth, an eye for an eye," cannot be a decent moral principle, if human emotions as well as ignorance are taken into consideration. On the contrary, the recognition of emotion as an inalienable part of the human personality makes it important that one take oneself as an example and neither strike nor kill another.[128]

Absolute inviolable laws have no place whatsoever in the metaphysic of experience discussed above. One is compelled to go beyond this metaphysic of experience in order to admit such absolute moral laws. This non-substantialism in the moral sphere is clearly expressed by the Buddha when he maintained that even the good things should be abandoned, let alone the bad.[129] This certainly is not a call for renouncing both good and bad for the sake of something transcendental and absolute. On the contrary, it is a warning that even good, when it is considered to be absolute and inviolable, can turn out to be bad. As James remarked: ". . . there is always a *pinch* between the ideal and the actual which can be gotten rid of by leaving part of the ideal behind."[130] As such, the criterion by which something is determined as good or bad is *pragmatic*.

It is not a mere accident that the Buddha formulated this pragmatic criterion in an obviously negative way. Instead of saying that a good action is one that leads to one's own happiness as well as the happiness of others, he maintained that it contributes neither to one's own suffering nor to the suffering of others.[131] Even when he spoke of the criterion of morality in more positive terms as one's own welfare (*atta-d-attha*) and the welfare of others (*parattha*), he was careful in insisting that having considered both, one should follow what appears to be the true welfare (*sad-attha*).[132] Such caution reflects the Buddha's fear that the criterion of morality could turn out to be an absolute and inviolable law instead of being a middle position.

The non-absolutism (*anatta*) that he perceived both in the subject and in the object is here extended to the moral life as well. Non-substantialism in moral philosophy does not imply the relinquishing of all morality as empty and vain behavior. Just as much sense experience is dependently arisen (*paṭiccasamuppanna*), so is moral, intellectual or aesthetic experience, for as pointed out earlier, the latter is dependent upon the former. Similarly, if experience, whether it be of sense or moral or intellectual or aesthetic, is non-substantial and dependently arisen, there could be no reason why the conceptualizations which are substitutes for such experience also could not be non-substantial and dependently arisen.

Chapter Nine Conception

The dominating spirit of Platonism in Western philosophy is clearly reflected in Kant's rejection of psychology as the "scandal to philosophy." Analytical philosophy has come to inherit this attitude when it confines itself primarily to an analysis of propositions, concepts and meaning. Conceptual analysis has progressed, as in mathematics and logic, to examining concepts as "they are," paying little attention to the manner in which they have "come to be." The purity of philosophical thinking is said to be preserved when concepts and propositions are considered in themselves and their meanings laid bare. Any attempt to examine concepts in terms of how "they have come to be" is looked upon as the psychologizing that pollutes philosophical thinking, as re-enacting the "scandal to philosophy."

The Buddha did not encounter such a sophisticated mathematical or logical tradition. Nyāya or Navya-Nyāya philosophers were unknown in India before the Buddha, even though the Buddha made constant references to logicians (*takkī*) and metaphysicians (*vīmaṃsī*). Thus, the field of philosophy was not so restricted for the Buddha, as it was for William James. While the Buddha was innocently introducing a detailed psychological analysis into his philosophical speculations, James' background made him constantly feel that he was "psychologizing, not philosophizing."[133] Yet, with their psychological speculations, both the Buddha and James were undermining the very foundations of pure philosophy. Two such instances have already been noted. First, the psychological investigations in Buddhism and in James revealed how the rationalist philosophers were committing a "psychologist's fallacy" in formulating the notion of a transcendental pure Ego as the foundation of human experience. Secondly, their analysis of human emotions deprives the so-called emotivist philosophers of the subject-matter for their particular thesis that ethics is a mere matter of emotion. Similarly, the treatment of conception by the Buddha as well as James provides no consolation to the analytical philosopher whose primary task is to examine the meaning of concepts without getting involved in the psychology of conception.

Let us consider James' ideas first. Before proceeding to explain his famous theory of "the stream of thought," James recognized two kinds of knowledge of things: knowledge of acquaintance and knowledge about.[134] When explaining conception James immediately returns to the consideration of these two kinds of knowledge, indicating that these are possible primarily because of a fundamental psychical peculiarity which he calls "*the principle of constancy in the mind's meanings*."[135] This principle is further elaborated as follows: "The same matters can be thought of in successive portions of the mental stream, and some of these portions can know that they mean the same matters which the other portions meant."[136] Having located conception within the context of the stream of thought, without introducing the psychologist's fallacy, James insists that this "sense of sameness" is the very keel and backbone of our thinking. The consciousness of personal identity, which gave rise to the so-called transcendental apperception, resposed on this *sense of sameness*, the present thought finding in its memories a warmth and intimacy which it recognizes as the same warmth and intimacy it now feels."

James, thereupon, proceeds to explain how this notion of personal identity based upon a sense of sameness was considered by some philosophers as the only vehicle by which the world hangs together. He also feels that the sense of identity of the known object could perform exactly the same unifying function, even if the sense of subjective identity were lost. In presenting subjective as well as objective identity in this way, James is preparing the ground for an exposition of conception that would not only account for its genesis in the stream of experience, but also expose the futility of admitting substantial entities either in the subject or in the object. In other words, the so-called unifying function belongs to conception and a clarification of its source as well as nature could eliminate many a philosophical controversy to which we shall return later.

Early Buddhism is generally considered a crusade against the belief in a permanent and eternal self (*ātman*) in the explanation of personal identity. Those philosophers who assumed that a permanent and eternal self is a necessary condition for explaining personal identity have characterized Buddhism as a nihilistic doctrine. As explained earlier, the Buddha's conception of a person steers clear of the two extremes of eternalism and annihilationism.

However, some interpreters of the Buddha's teachings assumed that the Buddha's emphasis on the non-substantiality of the self (*pudgala-nairātmya*) left him without any means of accounting for the unity and continuity of experience. Therefore, they attributed a theory of substantial elements (*dharma*) to the Buddha himself.[137] Thus, they were able to single out one of the Buddha's disciples, Nāgārjuna, and credit him with a "Copernican revolution" in Buddhism. Our more recent work on Nāgārjuna is an attempt in the direction of exposing this myth. The easiest way to expose the untenability of this age-old interpretation of the history of Buddhist thought is to demonstrate that according to the Buddha neither a permanent subject nor an eternal object is needed to explain the unity and continuity in experience. As shown above, the unity and continuity in subjective experience is adequately explained in terms of the "stream of consciousness" (*viññāṇsota*) or the "stream of becoming" (*bhavasota*), this in turn being based upon the conception of "dependent arising" (*paṭiccasamuppāda*). If it could be shown that the unity and continuity of objective experience is based upon "conception" founded on the stream of thought or becoming, and that this process of "conception" is also dependently arisen (*paṭiccasamuppanna*), the attribution of a substantialist theory of elements to the Buddha and early Buddhism or what may be described as the "scandal of Buddhist historical interpretation" can easily be avoided.

Instead of considering the Buddha's view as the contrary of the Upaniṣadic view of self, it is possible to look upon it as a middle position between the two extremes of subjective and objective identity conceived in metaphysical terms. The Upaniṣadic thinkers were not satisfied with the sense of identity in the knowing subject to explain how the world hangs together. They proceeded to perceive a similar identity in the object, which is then identified with the identity of the knowing subject. Apart from this, the Materialists attempted to conceive of identity in terms of the material object. As such, it could be rather surprizing if the Buddha, who was able to understand the problem relating to personal identity, failed to observe the equally substantialist conception of objective identity. Statements relating to the Buddha's refusal to recognize the substantiality of both subject and object and, therefore, of all phenomena (*sabbe dhammā anattā*) are found not only in the Pali Nikāyas but also in the Chinese Āgamas, thus indicating that it was not an innovation of the so-called Mahāyānists or of Nāgārjuna.[138] What remains to be explained is the epistemological justification of this conception of non-substantiality.

For the Buddha, the substantial identities are *overstatements* (*adhivuttipadāni*) about the content of human knowledge, whether such knowledge be sensory or extra-sensory.[139] He recognised two kinds of knowledge. The first is called *dhamme-ñāṇa* or knowledge of phenomena.[140] This is similar to what James calls knowledge of acquaintance. The second is *anvaye-ñāṇa.*[141] On a previous occasion we rendered this phrase as "inferential knowledge,"[142] since it pertains to the obvious past and the yet unexperienced future. Yet, by implication or when explained in relation to the metaphysic of experience, it also means what James calls "knowledge about." This is because experience as well as inference is founded on the fundamental psychical peculiarity described by James as "the principle of constancy in the mind's meanings."

Both the Buddha and James recognize the *sense of sameness* as the foundation of our thinking. Both present rather bold fronts in upholding this view. James would insist: ". . . that is, we do not care whether there be any *real* sameness in *things* or not, or whether the mind would be true or false in its assumption of it. Our principle only lays it down that the mind makes continual use of the *notion* of sameness, and if deprived of it, would have a different structure from what it has."[143] Questioned about the veracity of each one of the conflicting theories about the nature of the self, of the world, etc., the Buddha refused to go beyond "contact" (*phassa*), that is the sense organ, the object of sense and consciousness functioning harmoniously to produce experience.[144] No theories, no conceptions and no experience can go beyond contact and still remain meaningful. This same reluctance is expressed by James when he said: "The principle that the mind can mean the Same is true of its *meaning*, but not necessarily of ought besides."[145]

In order to avoid the belief in *something* "ought besides," the Buddha as well as James adopted a functional view of concepts, as they did with regard to consciouness. According to James, "*the function by which we thus identify a numerically distinct and permanent subject of discourse is called* CONCEPTION; and the thoughts which are its vehicles are called *concepts*."[146] The Buddha utilized the term *saṅkhā* to refer to concepts, and the functional use is often expressed by the verbal expression: *saṅkhaṃ gacchati* or "conceives."[147] The following passage is typical:

> Citta, just as from a cow comes milk, and from milk curds, and from curds butter, and from butter ghee, and from ghee junket; yet, when there is milk, there is no conceiving as 'curd' or 'butter' or 'ghee' or 'junket'; instead on that occasion there is conceiving as 'milk'.[148]

Such conceiving (*saṅkhā*) is based not only upon sense experience (*saññā-nidānā*),[149] but also the "sense of sameness" which, according to James, is the foundation of our thinking. Sense experience and thought are thus held together at the empirical level by a concept. Neither the Buddha nor James were willing to accommodate any conceptual knowledge that originates independent of perceptual particulars and raise it to the level of the noble and the divine. James is critical of the rationalist view that holds concepts such as "God, perfection, eternity, infinity, immutability, identity, absolute beauty, truth, justice, necessity, freedom, duty, worth, etc., and the part they play in our minds as being impossible to explain as a result of practical experience."[150] Both favor the empiricist view that these do result from practical experience. Not only do they reject the view that conceptual knowledge is self-sufficing and a revelation all by itself; they also have no sympathy for the opposite view that true experience is beyond all conceptual thinking. The latter view is not strictly philosophical, for philosophy is essentially talkative and explicit.

Could there be a middle standpoint between the two views mentioned above? For James, this consists of the pragmatic rule which is that "the meaning of a concept may always be found, if not in some sensible particular which it directly designates, then in some particular difference in the course of human experience which its being true will make."[151] This rule is applied as follows: If, questioning whether a certain concept be true or false, you can think of absolutely nothing that would practically differ in the two cases, you may assume that the alternative is meaningless and that your concept is no distinct idea. If two concepts lead you to infer the same particular consequence, then you may assume that they embody the same meaning under different names.[152] He rightly believes that this rule applies to concepts of every order of complexity, from simple terms to propositions uniting many terms. He is also aware that many disputes in philosophy hinge upon ill-defined words and ideas, each side claiming its own word or idea to be true.

This latter unfortunate consequence of the manner in which we understand the meaning of concepts has been the subject-matter of a discourse by the Buddha. Here he speaks of the "warring path" (*saraṇa-paṭipadā*) and a "peaceful path" (*araṇa-paṭipadā*), the former being the result of dogmatic and extremist attitude toward concepts and, therefore, of language, and the latter representing a more pragmatic attitude described above. The passage reads as follows:

> When it is said: "one should not strictly adhere to the dialect of a country nor should one transgress ordinary parlance," in reference to what is it said? What, monks, is strict adherence to the dialect of a country and what is transgression of ordinary parlance? Herein, monks, the same thing (*tad eva*) is recognized in different countries as *pāti*, as *patta*, as *vittha*, as *sarāva*, as *dhāropa*, as *poṇa*, as *pisīla* [these being dialectical variants for the word 'bowl']. When they recognize it as such and such in different countries, a person utilizes this conven-

> tion obstinately clinging to it and adhering to it [saying]: "This alone is true; all else is falsehood." Thus, monks, is strict adherence to the dialect of a country and transgression of ordinary parlance. And what, monks, is the strict non-adherence to the dialect of a country and the non-transgression of ordinary parlance? In this case, monks, the same thing is recognized in different countries as *pāti*, as *patta*, as *vittha*, as *sarāva*, as *dhāropa*, as *poṇa*, as *pisīla*. Thus they recognize it as such and such in different countries. "These venerable ones utilize it for this purpose," and thus saying he utilizes it without grasping. And thus, monks, is strict non-adherence to the dialect of a country and the non-transgression of recognized parlance.[153]

The treatment of concepts as ordinary modes of convention (*vohāra*, *vyavahāra*), neither ultimately true nor absolutely false, but as having pragmatic value, is highlighted in the above passage. While the above passage refers to one concept, i.e., the concept of a bowl described in different terms, another discourse, the *Mūlapariyāya-sutta*,[154] examines a variety of simple and complex concepts, explaining the attitude different people adopt with regard to them. The concepts listed are as follows:

1. earth, water, fire, air;
2. beings, gods, Prajāpati, Brahmā, the radiant ones, the lustrous ones, the Vehapphala (brahmās), the overlord;
3. the sphere of the extremity of space, the sphere of the extremity of consciousness, the sphere of the extremity of nothingness, the sphere of neither perception nor non-perception;
4. the seen, the heard, the reflected, the cognized;
5. unity, diversity;
6. everything, and
7. freedom.

There is no attempt made to distinguish between these different concepts. For the sake of clarity, we have put them under different categories. The first set includes gross material elements; the second, all beings, human and divine; the third refers to the four stages of higher contemplation; the fourth embraces the major forms of sense experience; fifth and sixth are abstract concepts, and the seventh refers to ultimate freedom. All of them are concepts or ideas (*dhammā*). What is important is the attitude different people adopt in regard to these concepts. The *first* is the ordinary unenlightened individualist (*assutavā puthujjano*). Having recognized each one of the ideas (earth as earth, . . . freedom as freedom), the individualist immediately develops the notion of a self, a transcendental unity of apperception (*maññati*) in relation to that particular perception. He considers himself to be made by it, of it; considers it his own and takes delight in it (*paṭhaviyā maññati, paṭhavito maññati, paṭhaviṃ meti maññati, paṭhaviṃ abhinandati*).

The *second* is a trainee who makes an attempt to comprehend the conception and, therefore, does not allow the notion of self or a transcendental apperception to interfere with his understanding. As such, he refrains from identifying himself with any of the ideas or concepts, and is not unduly enamored with them.

Finally, the *third* and the *fourth*, namely, the enlightened disciples and the Buddha himself, understand the nature of conception. They do not allow the notion of self to appear. They do not identify themselves with the conception. They remain unsmeared by them.

Here, there is no denial of sense experience or conception based upon such experience. All that is avoided is the conception of a metaphysical self and, as a result, neither the perception nor the conception culminates in obsession (*papañca*). The Buddha, as pointed out earlier, was a vehement critic of the Upaniṣadic notion of self. He could not have been unaware of the manner in which Upaniṣadic thinkers attempted to utilize this notion of self in explaining sense experience and conception. The following passage occurs in a pre-Buddhist *Upaniṣad*:

> He who inhabits the earth, yet is within the earth, whom the earth does not know, whose body the earth is, and who controls the earth from within—he is your self, the inner controller, the immortal. [The statement is repeated in relation to the concepts such as water, fire, sky, air, heaven, sun, quarters, moon and stars, space, darkness, light, beings, breath, speech, eye, ear, mind, skin, intellect and organ of generation.][155]

The close similarity between the two lists is clear. The more or less parallel formulation in the *Mūlapariyāya-sutta* of somewhat similar subject-matter along with a denial of the very foundation of the Upaniṣadic explanation of perception and conception, without abandoning either perception or conception, was probably baffling to the five hundred monks, as it has been for many more later on, that we for the one and only time come across the statement at the end of the discourse expressing the inability of the monks to appreciate what the Buddha said, ("And thus spoke the Buddha, and those monks *did not* rejoice at his words," *idam avoca bhagavā, na te bhikkhū bhagavato bhāsitaṃ abhinandun ti*).[156] The conclusion is irresistible that it is this same difficulty on the part of the ordinary people in comprehending this selfsame problem that made the Buddha reluctant to preach what he discovered at the time of enlightenment. The *ālaya* referred to by the Buddha on that occasion is the psychological mooring or anchoring that prevents a person from abandoning the notion of a self or a transcendental unity of apperception as the primordial ground for all sensory experience and conception.

A similar evaluation of conception by William James has met with equally dogmatic resistence in the modern world. Having stated the view that "*The intellectual life of man consists almost wholly in his substituting a conceptual order for the perceptual order in which his experience originally comes*," James proceeded to explain that conceptual order in the following passage:

> Trains of concepts unmixed with percepts grow frequently in the adult mind; and parts of these conceptual trains arrest our attention just as parts of the perceptual flow did, giving rise to concepts of a higher order of abstractness. So subtle is the discernment of man, and so great the power of some men to single out the most fugitive elements of what passes before them, that these new formations have no limit. Aspect within aspect, quality after quality, relation upon relation, absences and negations as well as present features, end by being noted and their names added to the store of nouns, verbs, adjectives, conjunctions, and prepositions by which the human mind interprets life. Every new book verbalizes some new concept, which becomes important in proportion to the use that can be made of it. Different universes of thought thus arise, with specific sorts of relation among their ingredients. The world of common-sense "things;" the world of material tasks to be done; the mathematical world of pure forms; the world of ethical propositions; the world of logic, of music, etc. — all abstracted and generalized from long-forgotten perceptual instances from which they have as it were flowered out — return and merge themselves again in the particulars of our present and future perception. By those *whats* we apperceive all *thises*. Percepts and concepts interpenetrate and melt together, impregnate and fertilize each other. Neither, taken alone, knows reality in its completeness. We need them both, as we need both our legs to walk with.[157]

Here James is not maintaining that there is a complete reality that is to be known or grasped through a non-sensuous and non-conceptual means. He is merely emphasizing the need to depend upon both sense experience and conception in order to understand what reality is. What is significant to note is that both the Buddha and James, while recognizing the need to depend upon sense experience and conception, also admit the problems and limitations associated with such perceptual and conceptual knowledge. For the Buddha, such a realization constitutes the path to enlightenment and freedom. And one who has attained such enlightenment and freedom is succinctly described in the following passage:

> For him who has renounced conceit, there are no bonds. All his bonds of deemings are exhausted. And the prudent one who has overcome the notion of self may say: "I speak," or "They speak to me." Yet the adept, having understood the worldly convention, speaks conforming to such mere convention (*vohāramattena*).[158]

The elimination of the belief in a metaphysical self, a pure Ego, is here described as the necessary condition for abandoning conceit (*māna*), which is sometimes defined as *ahaṃ-kāra* (literally, "I-making"). Such a (*nir-ahaṃ-kāra*) person can continue to use linguistic conventions like "I say," or "They say to me," without running into any conflicts or difficulties. For him, such statements are no more than "mere conventions" (*vohāra-matta, vyavahāra-mātra*). The fact that they are mere conventions do not deprive them of pragmatic value in the matter of communicating one's experiences; only they are neither ultimate realities nor absolutely false imaginations.

These "mere conventions" (*vohāra-matta*) are meaningful (*attasaṃhita*) only when they can "return and merge themselves again in the particulars of our present and future perception."[159] Thus, impermanence returns and merges with the impermanent, unsatisfactoriness with the unsatisfactory, non-substantiality with the non-substantial, emptiness with the empty, dependent arising with the dependently arisen. Such returning and such merging prevents us from soaring into the realm of substantialist metaphysics, into the so-called divine world of abstractions, into linguistic transcendence, into Absolutism.

Chapter Ten
Analytic Yoga

In the *Upaniṣads*, yoga or meditative absorption turned out to be the means by which the ultimately real self (*ātman*) is realized.[160] This required the complete transcendence of the sensory process, even though this self was considered to be part and parcel of the objects of sensory experience. The Upaniṣadic claim was first rejected by the Materialists without even making an attempt to analyse the process of meditation and demonstrating to what extent that claim was either true or false. We have already noted how the Buddha analysed the process of sense experience in order to show that there is no permanent and eternal self, thereby initiating one of the earliest psychological speculations known to man. In the same way, he turned out to be the first person in the Indian context to provide a detailed treatment of the psychology of yoga, and this once again was necessitated by his failure to verify the existence of a permanent and eternal self through the so-called transcendental intuition. Even though both Sāṅkhya and Yoga schools of Indian philosophy can be pre-Buddhist in the sense that their methodologies in the treatment of experience were available in the *Upaniṣads*, there is almost no evidence that their systematizations are pre-Buddhist. The system of yoga attributed to Patañjali may, therefore, be considered a re-working of Upaniṣadic epistemology in order to counter the Buddha's criticism.

The Buddha's perception that the metaphysical views of the Upaniṣadic thinkers as well as some of the Materialists like Ajita Kesakambali, who undoubtedly were practitioners of yoga, are the products of the so-called yogic insight is clearly expressed in the *Brahmajāla-suttanta*. Here we find sixty-two different views involving eternalism, annihilationism, creationism, etc. being attributed to the rationalists (*takkī, vīmaṃsī*) as well as to the contemplatives, the latter following the method of yoga (*atappaṃ anvāya padhānaṃ anvāya anuyogam anvāya*).[161] The Buddha's failure to verify such claims made him characterize these views or theories as "overstatements" (*adhivutti-padāni*).[162] His conception of non-substantiality (*anatta*), which is a denial of any mysterious and eternal self or substance, and his notion of dependent arising (*paṭiccasamuppāda*), which explains the manner in which the non-substantial phenomena come to be and cease to exist, are the results of a two-pronged investigation of yogic contemplation. This two-pronged investigation, which eventually contributed to the two forms of freedom—freedom of thought (*ceto-vimutti*) and freedom through wisdom (*paññā-vimutti*)—came to be known as the processes of "appeasement" (*samatha*) and "insight" (*vipassanā*), the latter being predominantly *analytic* as implied by the term.

The attainment of such higher stages of contemplation calls for a long and strenuous training in morality and self-restraint.[163] Four types of self-culture are required even before one can get to the preliminary stages of meditation. The *first* is the possession of a noble body of moral habits (*ariya sīlakkhandha*). These consist of avoidance of any behavior that leads to one's own suffering as well as the suffering of others, and the adoption of harmless professions. The *second* is called the noble restraint of the senses (*ariya indriya-saṃvara*). It may be noted that this is a prescription given by the Buddha who had followed the contemplative process to its very extreme and failed to discover an ultimate reality. Hence, in explaining the restraint of the senses, he is recommending that a pre-conceived search for substance (*nimitta*) and quality (*anuvyañjana*), which dominates ordinary unrestrained modes of sense experience, be abandoned at this early stage, so that it does not color the perceptions and conceptions (or even the non-perception and non-conception) that may follow. In other words, the non-grasping after substance and qualities allows a person to perceive and conceive of things as they fall within his limited epistemological range and capacities with which he has come to be endowed. This is preparing the ground for the knowledge of things as they have come to be (*yathābhūta*). The *third* requirement is noble mindfulness (*ariya-sati-sampajañña*) and this is necessitated by the sort of restraint of the senses recommended earlier. While not looking for mysterious substances, etc. one is expected to be conscious of what has so far happened. In fact, knowledge of things as they have come to be (*yathābhūta*) would not be possible unless one remains constantly mindful. Forgetfulness (*muṭṭhassati*) is inimical to any form of knowledge and understanding. The *fourth* and final condition also follows from the second, namely, the abandoning of a metaphysical search. Such abandoning may be looked upon as being harmful to investigation and discovery. The Buddha, therefore, recommends "contentment" (*ariya-santuṭṭhi*), not with the intention of stultifying or neutralizing the process of discovery and encouraging complacency, but with the hope of promoting true discoveries by abandoning over-enthusiastic expectations often dominated by pre-conceptions.

After such training, when one settles down to practice contemplation in an appropriate surrounding, the yogin is expected to overcome the five constraints (*nīvarana*). The five constraints are excessive greed (*abhijjhā*), malevolence (*vyāpāda*), sloth and torpor (*thīna-middha*), excitement and worry (*uddhacca-kukkucca*) and doubt (*vicikicchā*). The importance of overcoming these constraints cannot be overemphasized. Cleansing one's thought in this manner, one develops not only moral rectitude but also openness to whatever one experiences. Excessive greed is abandoned and absence of greed cultivated. Malevolence is replaced by a concern for the welfare of all living beings and compassion for them (*sabba-pāṇa-bhūta-hitānukampī*). Sloth and torpor are relinquished making room for brightness and sharpness of perception and reflection. Excitement and worry that often compel a person to arrive at hasty conclusions and views are abandoned in favor of appeasement of thought, thus providing a foundation for balanced and sober judgement. Finally, constant doubt or extreme skepticism that does not often allow room for cautiously formulated and pragmatically relevant ideas (*kusala-dhamma*) is renounced providing opportunities for constant verification. The actual process of meditation thus begins after a person has transformed himself morally and intellectually from a dogmatic, unreceptive and close-minded person to a tolerant, compassionate and open-minded one. It may be noted that intellectual pursuits are here not divorced from moral concerns, for whatever knowledge and understanding that emerges as a result of yogic contemplation will have rippling effects on the moral and spiritual concerns of humanity.

Perceiving oneself to be free from the five constraints, a yogin is said to generate a feeling of enjoyment (*pāmujja*), leading to joy (*pīti*). A person whose mind is permeated with joy experiences bodily relaxation (*kāyo passambhati*) and, thereby, enjoys happiness (*sukhaṃ vedeti*). This experience of happiness paves the way for the concentration of thought. Hence the first preliminary stage of meditation.

The Four Preliminary Stages of Contemplation

The first stage of meditation consists of being aloof from desire (*kāma*) and unwholesome or evil ideas (*akusala dhamma*) and the attainment of a sense of joy and happiness born of *such* aloofness, yet associated with reasoning (*vitakka*) and investigation (*vicāra*). His whole body comes to be permeated by such joy and happiness. During the *second* stage of meditation, reasoning and investigation are dropped, for if such reasoning and investigation were to be carried on without interruption, these could lead not only to the dissipation of one's energies, but also obsession and frustration. The joy and happiness one enjoys during this second stage is born of concentration (*samādhijaṃ*). During the *third* stage the yogin attempts to remain aloof from the feeling of joy and cultivates a sense of equanimity in relation to whatever he experiences and he becomes very mindful and alert (*sato sampa-*

jāno). This is described as the happiness of one who is equanimous and mindful, and is distinguished from the joyful feeling one experienced before. It is free from such joyful feeling (*nippītika*). As in the previous stages, this form of happiness pervades his entire body. Finally, in the fourth stage the yogin attempts to further purify that practice of equanimity and mindfulness by getting rid of both happiness and unhappiness. This is a neutral (*adukkham-asukhaṃ*) stage of feeling when he is able to direct his mind to the perception and understanding of phenomena.

The above explanation of the four preliminary stages of contemplation (*jhāna*) occurs in a stock passage prefixed to the description of the higher stages of contemplation, referred to as the "contemplation on immateriality" (*arūpajjhāna*) as well as the higher forms of knowlege (*abhiññā*). Unfortunately, the prevalent explanations of Buddhist epistemology, and especially the psychology of yoga in Buddhism, are based upon a completely inappropriate reading of this stock passage, especially the terms *vitakka* and *vicāra*, and this has caused innumerable problems for the exposition of the Buddha's empiricist teachings. In spite of Rhys Davids' rendering of the terms *vitakka* and *vicāra* as "reasoning" and "investigation" repectively,[164] which seems more appropriate, scholars have continued to explain them as "initial thought" and "discursive thought." Thus, when in the second stage, these are abandoned, these scholars were able to justify their search for a transcendental intuition and a perception of truth that is beyond linguistic expression. Unless one depends entirely upon the "rational psychology" of the scholastics (see below), there is no need or even justification for translating these two terms as "initial thought" and "discursive thought."

The four stages represent a concerted attempt to cleanse the thought process and prepare it for understanding truth or reality. For the Buddha, who emphasized knowledge of things "as they have come to be" (*yathābhūta*), instead of knowlege of things "as they are," reasoning based upon reflection and investigation are important epistemological means. The term *vitakka* occurs in the description of the process of sense experience discussed earlier, and does not represent a stage of "initial thought." Neither is *vitakka* considered to be necessarily bad or unhealthy. It is only the *vitakka* that is founded upon the conception of a "pure Ego" that is said to contribute to obsession (*papañca*). However, *vitakka* understood as "reasoning" (which is invariably associated with reflection) and *vicāra* as "investigation" can also turn out to be obsessions if their limitations are ignored.

It is possible for reasoning based on reflection to be an obsession if and when one assumes that it is the only means of arriving at an understanding of truth. Such assertion would mean that *everything* has to be understood in relation to the past *only*. Deterministic views are often generated as a result of such reflection. Any novelty or creativity would remain unexplained or problematic. Similarly, obsession with investigation can contribute to dissatisfaction with what is given or discovered, and this can re-introduce the search for a metaphysical or mysterious *something*. Therefore, when, in the second stage, the *appeasement* of reasoning and investigation (*vitakka-vicārānaṃ vūpasamā*) is called for, what is suggested is that a person, having made appropriate use of these, should concentrate on the given. There is no appeal here to abandon thought and conception. This latter occurs only during the final stage of the higher contemplation (i.e., *nirodha-samāpatti*).

Just as much as reasoning and investigation can turn out to be obsessions, even so joy and happiness may prove to be stumbling blocks. The passage emphasizes the difference between joy and happiness experienced on occasions of ordinary sense experience and the joy and happiness one experiences during the contemplations. The latter is said to be more exalted (*panītataraṃ*). The reason for this may be that the joy and happiness that one obtains in ordinary sense experience is the result of our experience fitting into our pre-conceived perspectives, while in the contemplations a perspective emerges out of our experience gained in the context in which that experience occurs. While the former tends to satisfy our ego, the latter allows us to experience novelty. However, in the end, what is required is the equanimity necessary for careful consideration or close scrutiny (*upekkhā*, derived from *upa* + $\sqrt{}$*īkṣ* "to see," "to perceive"). This does not mean abandoning sense experience and conception at all. The description of this stage of contemplation as "the purification of equanimity and mindfulness" (*upekkhā-sati-pārisuddhi*) does not mean that it is an experience without content. What is most prominent is the ability to scrutinize or examine a given object or a situation without being swayed by likes and dislikes (that is, with *upekkhā*), with full alertness or mindfulness (*sati*).

In fact, thought (*citta*) concentrated and purified in this manner leaving no trace of taint or defilement is said to be supple and ready to act, firm and imperturbable, not rigid and uncontrollable. There is no indication whatsoever that at this stage the total truth or reality appears revealed to the yogin. In fact, except in the case of the development of the higher contemplations which are intended to eliminate perception and conception, it is said that the yogin has to direct and bend his thought (*cittaṃ abhinīharati abhininnāmeti*) toward whatever he wants to understand.

The Higher Stages of Contemplation

The evidence available in the *Ariyapariyesana-sutta*[165] is that the process of contemplation in relation to which the Buddha received instruction from Ālara Kālama and Uddaka Rāmaputta before his enlightenment involves the "contemplations on immateriality" (*arūpajjhāna*), rather than higher knowledge (*abhiññā*). Furthermore, it is clear that he was dissatisfied with their attainments and, therefore, left them. However, when, after a long "search for something good" (*kiṃ-kusala-gavesī*), he decided to return to the process of contemplation he learned under them, he was not really attempting to justify their methods or views. Rather, he was proceeding to verify the claims made on the basis of such attainments. Interestingly, the process seems to have revealed the unreasonableness of their claims as well as the inappropriateness of their ideas.

The four higher stages are once again explained in a stock passage in the discourses. Unlike in the case of the development of higher knowledge, here there is no attempt to direct or bend the mind to examine some object or event, for this process of contemplation is intended to peel off every structure and penetrate deeper and deeper into the available experience to see whether it represents an ultimate reality. Thus, the material object or situation which was the focus of scrutiny in the fourth *jhāna* is gradually abandoned. This abandoning is facilitated by the contemplation on "space," where no perception of material form (*rūpa-saññā*) or perception of resistence (*paṭigha-saññā*) or the perception of difference (*nānatta-saññā*) are obtained. The conception of infinite space (*ananto ākāso*) enables one to move around one's thought unobstructed for a while until one realizes that in attempting to discover the "extremity of space" (*ākāsañcāyatana*), one was merely dealing with the consciousness of space. This allows him to slip into the next stage of contemplation about "consciousness" (*viññāṇa*). If the person were to remain in this stage, it would be possible for him to reach the conclusion that ultimate reality is "consciousness," and thus advocate some form of extreme idealism. However, consciousness has its limits, in the same way as material form and space are limited. Thus, the "extremity of consciousness' (*viññānañcāyatana*) can easily yield to the conception of "nothingness" (*akiñci*) as a sphere of experience. This was the stage recognized as the highest by Ālara Kālama. It seems that for him the search for reality in experience and conception ended in nothingness. The stage was thus prepared for the negation of empirical phenomena. Uddaka Rāmaputta's attainment described as "the state of neither perception nor non-perception" (*neva-saññānāsaññāyatana*) reflects the Absolutist's dilemma, namely, to discover an experience that accounts for unity while retaining plurality. The Buddha's skepticism regarding such an enterprise seems to have compelled him to relinquish Uddaka's tutorship. However, when he, before his enlightenment, returned to this method of contemplation, he made a determined attempt to break through this barrier and reached a stage where all perceptions and all that has been experienced ceased (*saññā-vedayita-nirodha*).

The last two stages, namely, the state of nothingness and the state of neither perception nor non-perception, seem to have left a different impression upon the Buddha than they did on both Ālāra and Uddaka. While Ālāra and Uddaka were attempting to go beyond sensory experience in their search for an ultimately real experience, the Buddha seems to have ended up with the complete cessation of sense experience and conception without discovering a "transcendental intuition." What happened in the process may have taken the Buddha by surprise. It seems to have weakened his hold on the belief in an ultimately real subject or an absolutely incorruptible object. If either the subject (*ātman*) or the object (*dharma*) were ultimately real, these could have survived the annihilation of the sensory process and conception. However, the cessation of these processes did not leave him with any other perception or cognition. The realization of the non-substantiality of all phenomena (*sabbe dhammā anattā*) dawned upon him as he emerged from the state of cessation (*nirodha-samāpatti*).[166] It was like the peeling off of the trunk of a plantain tree looking for the ultimate essence and discovering that no such essence or substance existed.

At this stage, it is possible to raise the question as to why contemplatives of the pre-Buddhist tradition like Ālāra and Uddaka failed to realize what the Buddha himself realized after practicing such contemplation. As the above description of the preparatory stages would indicate, the search for a mysterious substance in phenomena has to be abandoned even before one gets on with the higher contemplations, especially at the time of the restraining of the senses (*indriya-saṃvara*), and so Ālāra and Uddaka could have proceeded beyond their attainments and realized the state of cessation (*nirodha*) without having to remain satisfied with the two previous stages. It is most probable that the preparatory stages were actually recommended by the Buddha *after* he discovered the state of cessation by sheer accident, and this indeed was the turning point in Buddhist yoga. In fact, when the Buddha spoke about his training under Ālāra and Uddaka, he did not refer to any such preparation, especially the relinquishing of the search for an ultimate reality. The complete description is given only *after* his attainment of enlightenment.

Eight forms of release (*vimokkha*) are referred to in the *Saṅgīti-suttanta.*[167] The last four among them are the four higher stages of contemplation referred to above. The selfsame discourse explains these eight forms of release as bodily experiences (*kāyena sacchikaraṇīyā dhammā*).[168] This is a definite denial of any cognitive content in such attainments. All that is experienced is probably peace and tranquillity of body, not knowledge and insight. For this reason, the Buddha was willing to compare and contrast the state of cessation (*nirodha*) with the state of a dead person (*mato kālakato*).[169] In the case of a dead person, the bodily, verbal and mental dispositions (*saṅkhāra*) have ceased, life has waned, breath is appeased, and the faculties are destroyed. Even in the case of a person who has attained the state of cessation, the bodily, verbal and mental dispositions come to cease. Yet his life has not waned, breath has not been appeased and the faculties are extremely clear. Even though the faculties are clear and bright (*vippasannāni*), since no perception or cognition is taking place, the Buddha maintained that complete freedom from influxes can be achieved only as a result of perceiving through wisdom (*paññā*).[170] This represents a clear admission that the practice of the higher contemplations do not lead to any wisdom or insight. In fact, as mentioned earlier, the realization of the non-substantiality of all phenomena takes place when the yogin has emerged from that state, not when he is in it.

The Sixfold Higher Knowledge

Such being the nature of the highest stage of contemplation or absorption (*jhāna*), it is of utmost importance to note that the so-called higher knowledge (*abhiññā*) or wisdom (*paññā*) does not occur immediately following the attainment of the state of cessation. Indeed, all explanations of knowledge and vision (*ñāṇa-dassana*) are preceded by the first four preliminary stages of contemplation, i.e., before proceeding to the higher contemplations where perception and conception are gradually flushed out. In other words, after practicing the higher contemplations, the Buddha seems to have realized the *epistemological limitations* of yoga, rather than its unlimited capacity which is emphasized in the Brahmanical tradition.

The process that leads to knowledge and vision begins, as mentioned earlier, after the fourth preliminary stage of contemplation (*catutthajjhāna*).

The Buddha's discourse on the "Fruits of Recluseship" (*Sāmaññaphala*) represents a detailed description of this knowledge and vision. Interestingly, this description is appended to a text that is devoted to an analysis of the heretical views of the materialists and the skeptics, rather than to the views of the traditional soul-theorists. It seems to indicate that the higher contemplations described earlier demonstrated the futility of recognizing an eternal subjective reality called *ātman*. The knowledge and vision described in the present context may, therefore, be taken as a means of discrediting the materialist's view about an ultimately real object as well as his skepticism regarding psychological and moral phenomena.

Once again, it may be remembered that the fourth preliminary stage of contemplation did not involve the relinquishing of sense experience or conception. Only the search for an ultimate reality was abandoned. In a majority of the discourses, the six forms of higher knowledge (*abhiññā*) are enumerated immediately after the fourth *jhāna*, always with the statement that a yogin directs or bends his thought toward the object of such knowledge, thus indicating that selectivity and attention are once again required as in sense experience. However, the *Samaññaphala* differs slightly from other descriptions in that, before the development of the so-called higher knowledge, the yogin directs his attention to his own psychophysical personality:

> With his thought thus serene, made pure, translucent, cultured, devoid of evil, supple, ready to act, firm and imperturbable, he applies and bends down his thought to knowledge and vision. He comes to know: "This body of mine has material form, it is made up of the four great elements, it springs from mother and father, it is continually renewed by so much boiled rice and juicy foods, its very nature is impermanence, it is subject to erasion, abrasion, dissolution and disintegration, and there is in this consciousness of mine, too, bound up, on that does it depend."[171]

In the first place, it is an understanding that counters the materialist's view according to which the self is identical with the body (*taṃ jīvaṃ taṃ sarīraṃ*).[172] The Buddha's vision leaves the material body a product of the various conditions and liable to decay and destruction. Any underlying unity is thus rejected. Secondly, it is a perception that goes against another pre-supposition of materialism, that consciousness is a mere by-product of matter. The Buddha's description of consciousness as something associated or dependent upon rather than being a product of the body represents a different vision altogether.

The perception that follows is also not found in many other texts. It is described as follows:

> With his thought thus serene . . . and imperturbable, he applies and bends down his thought to the creation of a mind-made body (*mano-mayaṃ kāyaṃ*). From this body he creates another body, having material form, made of mind, possessed of all limbs and parts, not deprived of any organ.[173]

It is most plausible that, having rejected the materialistic conception of unity by explaining the material body as being dependently arisen, the Buddha is here explaining the "psychologist's fallacy," the so-called transcendental unity of apperception, explaining it as nothing more than the product of *manas* (*mano-maya*). The apparent permanence of this self is, then, due to the continuous creativity of *manas*.

While the four higher stages of contemplation proved the *absence* of any experience that would indicate the existence of a permanent and eternal entity, the last two perceptions provided *positive* information regarding the nature of the human personality as well as the functioning of the human mind.

The higher forms of knowledge are then listed in the *Sāmaññaphala-suttanta*. These are explained in the same way elsewhere. The purified and concentrated thought is now directed at psycho-kenesis (*iddhi-vidha*), which is more of a power or ability to perform the so-called miracles, rather than a knowledge. Clairaudience (*dibba-sota*) is an extension of the range of hearing. Telepathy (*cetopariya-ñāṇa*) represents the penetrating observation of another's thought process, whether it is lustful or free from lust, hateful or free from hate, confused or free from confusion, etc. The metaphor utilized to illustrate this is suggestive. It is compared to the perception of one's face as reflected in a clean mirror or a clear pan of water. Retrocognition (*pubbenivāsanussati-ñāṇa*) represents how this purified and concentrated thought can bring back the memories of the past lives. The next is the knowledge of the decease and survival of beings (*sattānaṃ cutūpapāta-ñāṇa*), which is also called clairvoyance (*dibba-cakkhu*). Most important of all is the knowledge of the waning of influxes (*āsavānaṃ khaya-ñāṇa*).

It seems that these powers and knowledge have often appeared rather mysterious and transcendent not only to those ordinary folk who have not developed their intellectual capacities, but even to those who have developed such capacities and who, unfortunately, have directed such capacities toward discovering still more mysterious causes and substances in the world. The Buddha's analysis of the higher knowledge seems to indicate that if the search for a mysterious self (*ātman*) or a substance (*dharma*, *svabhāva*) were to be abandoned, the knowledge referred to above could turn out to be commonplace.

Even though psycho-kinesis is a power that can be developed by someone who has control over his thought process, the Buddha often discouraged the use of such powers. It is true that he himself utilized such powers to convert the hard-headed during the early days of his mission, but realized their inadequacy to bring about lasting knowledge and understanding in persons so converted.

Among the other five forms of knowledge, the Buddha considered the fourth and fifth as being relevant, and the final one essential for enlightenment and freedom. Retrocognition and clairvoyance are relevant since they provide more information regarding human life than is normally available. The possibility of human survival after death, although not *absolutely* essential for inculcating the sort of moral life recommended by the Buddha, yet strengthens it. He utilized rebirth in the same way as Blaise Pascal employed the "wager" in order to inculcate the belief in God.[174] However, it should be kept in mind that it was not used *merely* as a means (*upāya*), as some of the modern interpreters have assumed. It was not an unverified hypothesis, but rather one that was personally verified by the Buddha and a whole host of his disciples. Yet, the Buddha's conception of "dependent arising" (*paṭiccasamuppāda*), unlike the Upaniṣadic conception of a permanent and eternal self, did not allow him to predict with absolute certainty that all human beings, whatever the circumstances are, will be reborn.

For the Buddha, the last form of knowledge is the most significant and essential. Wisdom (*paññā*) has the waning of influxes (*āsavakkhaya*) as its object.[175] As such, *paññā* is synonymous with *āsavakkhaya-ñāṇa*. Waning of influxes is what takes place within the individual. Whether one allows oneself to be overwhelmed by such influxes in the future, after they have been overcome, depends upon various factors such as the conviction that they are harmful and the determination not to be lured by them. The enlightened ones who have been convinced of the evil effects of the influxes and who have developed the strength of character to ward off the assault of such influxes, have claimed certainty about this form of knowledge more than any other. The paeons of joy expressed by them after realizing the waning of influxes represent such an exultant and jubilant attitude resulting from the triumph over suffering and frustration, that it is almost impossible for them to allow any room for the influxes in the future. Hence their claims: "(Future) births have waned, the higher life has been lived, done is what has to be done, there is no more of this in the future."[176]

As the previous discussions would indicate, human beings are subjectively affected by most forms of experience and their responses to such experience based upon "interest" can gradually solidify into "disposition" (*saṅkhāra*). These dispositions can move in two different directions, generating likes or dislikes, greed or hatred, in relation to whatever is experienced or conceived. The so-called influxes (*āsava*) are such subjective affectations and these are often referred to as four.

1. *Kāmāsava*, influx of desire or constant thirst for the pleasurable; hatred (*dosa*) representing an excessive desire to avoid the unpleasant.
2. *Bhavāsava*, the influx of becoming, which is a constant yearning for self-aggrandisement; its other extreme being self-destruction (*vibhava*).
3. *Diṭṭhāsava*, the influx of views. These could constitute metaphysical views relating to both ultimate existence (*atthitā*, *astitva*) and nihilistic non-existence (*n'atthitā*, *nāstitva*), being and non-being, somethingness and nothingness.
4. *Avijjāsava*, the influx of ignorance. The elimination of this influx would mean the emergence of absolute knowledge or omniscience. The waning of influxes (*āsavakkhaya*) should thus lead to "knowledge of everything" (*sabbaññutā*). Yet, nowhere is this equation made in the Buddhist texts. The waning of influxes always leads to knowledge of the four truths, and not any metaphysical knowledge. For this reason, the influx of ignorance (*avijjā*) is more appropriately understood as confusion (*moha*), with the other two defilements: desire and hatred being involved in the influxes referred to above. This confusion is sometimes referred to as perversion (*vipallāsa*, Sk. *viparyāsa*) by the Buddha.[177] Four such perversions pertaining to perception (*saññā*), thought (*citta*) and views (*diṭṭhi*) are enumerated. These occur with the identification of
   (a) the impermanent with the permanent (*anicce niccan ti*),
   (b) the not unsatisfactory with the unsatisfactory (*adukkhe dukkhan ti*),
   (c) the non-substantial with the substantial (*anattani attā ti*), and
   (d) the unpleasant with the pleasant (*asubhe subhan ti*).

It is clear that the elimination of these four perversions does not leave the individual without any sense experience, conception or even emotion. The four perversions involve intellectual as well as emotional confusion. The elimination of such confusions would leave the person with more refined intellectual and emotional attitudes which enable him to perceive the world as it has come to be (*yathābhūtaṃ*).

Nāgārjuna's inclusion of a complete chapter on the perversions (*viparyāsa*) just before proceeding to examine the concepts of truth (*satya*) and freedom (*nirvāṇa*) clearly demonstrates his understanding of the Buddha's position with regard to the nature of human knowledge and wisdom.

The fact that this form of knowledge is listed at the end of the so-called higher knowledge (*abhiññā*) which, as indicated above, appeared to the ordinary person as something mysterious, seems to have contributed to the view that wisdom (*paññā*) has nothing to do with sensory experience and conception and is, therefore, completely and absolutely transcendent. Yet, what happens when one has realized the waning of influxes is that he knows things as they have come to be (*yathābhūtaṃ pajānāti*). This provides him with the knowledge that such and such is suffering (*idaṃ dukkhaṃ*), that such and such is the arising of suffering (*idaṃ dukkha-samudayo*), that such and such is the cessation of suffering (*idaṃ dukkha-nirodho*) and that such and such is the path leading to the cessation of suffering (*idaṃ dukkha-nirodha-gāminī-paṭipadā*), etc. His perception of suffering of the human beings is so clear like the perception of shells, pebbles and fish in a stream of clear water.

Wisdom (*paññā*) or knowledge of the waning of influxes (*āsavakkhaya-ñāṇa*) is not only the unprejudiced understanding of the world as being dependently arisen (*paṭiccasamuppanna*) but also a genuine realization that there is suffering in it. The realization that there is suffering in the world provides the strongest incentive and commitment to a life of compassionate behavior toward oneself as well as others, avoiding the extremes of self-indulgence and self-mortification. It is the inexhaustible source of the moral life of man. What is *not* discovered by such knowledge is either a permanent and eternal self as the unity of subjective thought or an incorruptible and eternal substance as the unity of objective experience, these latter being unfounded (*abhūta*) conceptualizations.

Realizing that the pursuit of mystery is of little relevance to human happiness, the Buddha, for the first time in the Indian tradition, presented a system of meditation or reflection that could be cultivated by almost anyone interested in a solution to the problem of suffering in the world. This is popularly known as the "establishment of mindfulness" (*satipaṭṭhāna*). Unfortunately, the search for mystery seems to have once again overwhelmed this meditative or reflective method of investigation and understanding to such an extent that, in South and South-East Asian countries where this practice is prevalent, the practitioners often look for a "state of transcendence of ordinary sense experience" as the ultimate goal. Yet, the Buddha's own description of this method leaves no room for such transcendence. Instead, it simply emphasizes the importance of what may be called the "radical empiricist" approach to an understanding of human experience, thought and life.

Even though the term *satipaṭṭhāna* ("setting up of mindfulness") may give the impression that the intention here is to stabilize the mental faculty without allowing it to roam all over in an unrestrained manner thereby preparing the way for the perception of a static reality, the process of perception recommended is totally different. Mindfulness (*sati*) is to be established by a process of "re-flection" or "re-cognition" (*anu-passanā*) or looking back, that is, not concentrating upon the immediate moment or point-instant without any attention to what has occurred, but rather looking at the "historical present" in order to understand the nature of life. James' metaphor of "the saddle-back [instead of the knife-edge] with a certain breadth of its own on which we sit perched and from which we look into two directions in time"[178] is illustrative of this approach. Indeed, the Greek god Janus, with its two heads facing the opposite directions and serving as a symbol for the month of January, is equally illustrative.

The re-flection (*anu-passanā*) is to be applied to four kinds of objects or events, namely, (i) the human body or the physical personality (*kāya*), (ii) feeling or sensation (*vedanā*), (iii) thought (*citta*), and (iv) facts in general (*dhammā*).[179]

The first form of reflection pertains to the nature and functioning of the human bodily organism. It requires the understanding of the bodily organism in all possible ways: its constitution, the various elements that go into its constitution, its modes of functioning such as breathing and formation of habits (*kāya-saṅkhāra*) as well as its impermanent nature. Such reflection can enable a person to know its capacities as well as its limits, and thereby refrain from placing unnecessary strain upon it.

The second is feeling or sensation (*vedanā*) which, as mentioned earlier, is the foundation of experience involving emotive as well as cognitive functions. These represent a variety of feelings: pleasant, unpleasant, and neutral pertaining to sensuous experience (*sāmisa*) and the more refined aesthetic experiences (*nirāmisa*).

The third represents reflection relating to the vehicle of experience, namely, thought (*citta*), paying attention to distinctions such as good and bad, superior and inferior, fruitful and unfruitful, clear and confused, subjective and objective, etc. These thoughts or concepts are to be pursued only to the point where they produce knowledge (*ñāṇa-matta*), and not beyond, for, as emphasized earlier, conceptions carried beyond their limits can lead to substantialist metaphysics and hence to insoluble problems for human life.

Finally, a variety of ways in which reflection can be carried out in relation to phenomena (*dhammā*) is described. These pertain to subjective attitudes as well as objective facts, to bondage and freedom.

In brief, the establishment of mindfulness, considered to be the most important means to the attainment of freedom from suffering, is not a search for an essence, a substance or an Absolute, but an attempt to perceive things as they have come to be (*yathābhūta*). It is, indeed, the form of reflection and understanding that came to be embodied in the Buddha's doctrine of "dependent arising" (*paṭiccasamuppāda*).

Formulating his radical empiricism, James remarks:

> To be radical, an empiricist must neither admit into its constructions any element that is not directly experienced, nor exclude from them any element that is directly experienced. For such a philosophy, *the relations that connect experiences must themselves be experienced relations, and any kind of relation experienced must be accounted as 'real' as anything else in the system.*[180]

It may be observed that the "establishment of mindfulness" (*satipaṭṭhāna*) in the Buddhist context is intended to avoid any element that is not directly perceived and include all elements that are perceived when the question of truth or reality is discussed.

Such is the nature and function of yoga in Buddhism. It does not involve any mysticism or extreme form of spiritualism. Yoga is here completely demystified in order to provide an epistemological means to gain an analytic view of truth. However, the non-availability of information regarding this form of yoga in the Western world during James' lifetime probably made James rather unpopular among psychologists and philosophers who seem to have assumed that every form of yoga involved the mystical and the spiritual, and were therefore frightened away by his involvement. Yet James was more perceptive and was not taking a blind leap when he got involved in discussions of yoga.

Speaking about mysticism in *The Varieties of Religious Experience*, at first James assumed that cosmic or mystical consciousness sporadically appearing in the individual is methodically cultivated by the Hindus, Buddhists, Mohammedans, and Christians.[181] This is the practice of yoga. His sources of information are Vivekananda and Vihari Lal Mitra.[182] For him, yoga meant "the experimental union of the individual with the divine." He was unaware of the great differences between the Brahmanical and Buddhist understanding of the methods as well as the goal of yogic practice. He says:

> It is based on persevering exercise; and the diet, posture, breathing, intellectual concentration and moral discipline vary *slightly* in the different systems which teach it. The yogi,

or disciple, who has by these means overcome the obscurations of his lower nature sufficiently, enters into the condition termed *samadhi*, "and comes face to face with facts which no instinct or reason can ever know" (italics mine).[181]

After quoting a passage from Vivekananda to substantiate his explanation of the practice of yoga, James proceeds to comment on the Buddhist practice. In this case his source of information is C. F. Koeppen's *Die Religion des Buddha* (1857). He refers to the first four preliminary stages of contemplation discussed above. Koeppen's description of the fourth stage as one in which indifference, memory and self-consciousness are perfected [*upekkhā-sati-pārisuddhi*?] puzzles James. Just what "memory" and "self-consciousness" mean in this connection in unintelligible to him. Assuming that this is a stage that transcends ordinary human experience, he maintains that these cannot be faculties familiar to us in the lower life. Moving on to the highest stage of contemplation, namely, the state of cessation, James rightly assumes that it is not nirvana. However, he observes that it is "but as close an approach to it as this life affords." One cannot fault James on this latter observation when scholars more conversant with the Buddhist tradition go to the extent of equating the state of cessation (*nirodha-samāpatti*) with freedom (*nibbāna*).

In his essay on "The Energies of Men,"[184] James demonstrates a more detailed understanding of yoga, especially when he comments on the training involved in Hatha Yoga which he learnt from one of his European friends, a disciple of Vivekananda. James describes his friend as "an extraordinarily gifted man, both morally and intellectually, but has an instable nervous system, and for many years lived in a circular process of alternate lethargy and over-animation: something like three weeks of extreme activity and then a week of prostration in bed." Quoting from a sixty-page letter, James describes how his friend was able to gain physical stability by the practice of Hatha Yoga, how he excluded all emotions, involved himself in dry logical reading as intellectual diet, and finally wrote a Handbook of Logic.[185]

Interestingly James was not impressed by his friend's exulting experiences. He called it "dynamogenic" which "throws into gear energies of imagination, of will, of mental influence over physiological processes, that usually lie dormant, and that can only be thrown into gear at all in chosen subjects."[186] James responded to his friend saying that he could not possibly attribute any sacramental value to the particular Hatha Yoga processes. James would have been delighted to know that his was the Buddha's own response to the practice of "psycho-kinesis" (*iddhi*, *ṛddhi*) discussed earlier.

Commenting on the problem of "power" independent of the yogic practices, James says:

> And the power, small or great, comes in various shapes to the individual, power, as he will tell you, not to 'mind' things that used to vex him, power to concentrate his mind, good cheer, good temper; in short, to put it mildly, *a firmer, more elastic moral tone*. The most genuinely saintly person I have ever known is a friend of mine now suffering from cancer of the breast. I do not assume to judge of the wisdom or unwisdom of her disobedience to the doctors, and I cite here solely as an example of what ideas can do. Her ideas have kept her a practically well woman for months after she should have given up and gone to bed. They have annulled all pain and weakness and given her a cheerful active life, unusually beneficient to others to whom she has afforded help.[187]

James' conclusion is posed in the form of a question: "Can any one of us refine upon the conceptions of mental work and mental energy, so as later to be able to throw some definitely analytical light on what we mean by 'having a more elastic moral tone,' or 'by using higher levels of power and will'"?[188] This question was of momentous significance for James, the humanist, especially because the discipline of philosophy was gradually narrowing down its field of inquiry to an analysis of conceptual structures relating to objective experience without showing much interest in the psychology of human behavior, especially moral behavior. His friend Peirce was dissociating himself from the philosophical movement he founded because questions regarding "feelings" were being introduced into the discussion when pragmatism should be confined to an analysis of the conception of the "Outer World."[189] As is well known, lamenting the "kidnapping" of pragmatism, Peirce decided to re-designate his method as "pragmaticism."[190] However, James was pleased that his fellow-pragmatist from Italy, G. Papini, had adopted a new conception of philosophy called the *doctrine of action* from which point of view "philosophy is a *pragmatic*, comprehending, as tributary departments of itself, old disciplines of logic, metaphysic, physic, and ethic."[191] Yoga in Buddhism, as presented earlier, leading to the development of wisdom (*paññā*), and yielding information regarding the principle of dependence (*paṭiccasamuppāda*) applicable to both physical and psychological facts thereby generating serious discussions of the nature of moral and aesthetic experience and conceptualizations, can be seen as a way of throwing some definite analytic light on what we mean by "having a more elastic moral tone" (without implying any absolutistic moral conscience). It provided an epistemological foundation for a philosophy of action centered on compassion.

In the Buddhist context, genuine compassion (*karuṇā*) is neither an extension nor the result of passion or lust (*rāga*). Passion, lust (*rāga*), craving (*taṇhā*) or greed (*lobha*) are the primary cause of suffering in the world. The cultivation of dispassion (*virāga*) or the achievement of the waning of passion (*rāgakkhaya*) is considered to be freedom (*nibbāna*). It is a freedom from the egoistic tendencies. It has already been pointed out that elimination of egoism (*ahaṃ-kāra*) does not mean the annihilation of the empirical self (*ahaṃ*). Therefore, when the Buddha spoke of compassion (*karuṇā*) as the most beneficial and moral behavior, there was no need for him to exclude that empirical self from being the object of such compassion. For a non-absolutist like the Buddha, compassion for oneself and compassion for others are not mutually exclusive. For him, *freedom from* passion implies the capacity on the part of a person to have *freedom to* be compassionate.

Chapter Eleven Suffering

In the previous section it was mentioned that a genuine realization that there is suffering in the world dawns upon the enlightened one with the development of wisdom. What is genuine about this realization?

The Buddha's statement that there is suffering in the world, a statement reflecting the realization referred to earlier, has been the subject of much discussion among some of the leading philosophers in the modern world like Schopenhauer, Nietzsche and Jaspers. Unfortunately, most of these philosophers have attempted to understand the concept of suffering in Buddhism in terms of the conception of tragedy familiar to them in the Western philosophical and literary traditions reaching back to the early Greeks. As a result, we are left with the impression that Buddhism is a pessimistic religion. Whether such an interpretation of the Buddhist tradition is valid or not can be decided only after a careful study of the problem of suffering placed in the context of the non-substantialist and pragmatic teachings of the Buddha outlined above.

Pessimism and optimism are two contradicting attitudes adopted mostly by those who are prone to substantialist or absolutist ways of thinking. If the Buddha was a genuine non-substantialist or a non-absolutist, then there is no justification for applying such exclusive categories as pessimism or optimism to describe his teachings. Before proceeding to explain the psychology of suffering in Buddhism, it would be necessary to indicate how and when this unacceptable interpretation of Buddhism emerged.

In spite of the Buddha's emphasis on the idea that all experienced phenomena are non-substantial (*sabbe dhammā anattā*), substantialist thinking gradually infiltrated Buddhism, crystalizing itself in the doctrines of the Sarvāstivādins. The following discussion of happiness and suffering couched in extremely substantialist language is reported by Vasubandhu:

When [the Buddha] declared: "One should perceive happy feeling as suffering," both [happiness and suffering] are available therein. Happiness is *inherently* so, because there is pleasantness. However, eventually there is suffering, because

> of its changing and impermanent nature. When that [feeling] is perceived as happiness, it contributes to enlightenment, through its enjoyment. When it is perceived as suffering, it leads to release, by being non-attached to it.[192]

This discussion was generated as a result of the Sarvāstivāda attempt to recognize both happiness and suffering existing as substances (*svalakṣaṇataḥ sukhā vedanā*,[193] *svabhāvenaiva duḥkhā*[194]). Indeed, the Buddhist metaphysician seems to have been trapped by the substantialist Brahmanical opponents who continued to misquote the Buddha's statement regarding suffering. The Buddha's statement is sometimes couched in the language of universals. Thus we have the phrase: "All dispositions are suffering" (*sabbe saṅkhārā dukkhā*). He consistently, and it seems consciously, avoided considering all phenomena to be suffering. Nowhere in the discourses attributed to him do we come across the statement: "All phenomena are suffering" (*sabbe dhammā dukkhā*). However, the use of the term *sabbaṃ* ("all, everything") in the above context misled most interpreters, especially the Brahmanical thinkers and the later Buddhist metaphysicians, to assuming that the Buddha was making unqualified universal statements. They took the Buddha to be saying:

All is impermanent (*sabbaṃ aniccaṃ*).
All is suffering (*sabbaṃ dukkhaṃ*).
All is non-substantial (*sabbaṃ anattaṃ*).

They failed to realize the absolutist implication of the above statements in contrast to the universal statements that are identified, concretized or embodied in the following manner:

All *this* is impermanent (*sabbam idaṃ aniccaṃ*).
All *this* is suffering (*sabbam idaṃ dukkhaṃ*).
All *this* is non-substantial (*sabbam idaṃ anattaṃ*).

It is the failure to distinguish these two types of universal statements, the absolute and the limited, that led not only to the dilemma of the Sarvāstivādins (referred to in the passage quoted above) with their conceptions of happiness and suffering as two substantial entities that need reconciliation, but also to the interpretation of Buddhism as a doctrine of "universal suffering" by modern European scholars.

The Brahmanical and Buddhist ideological conflict continued until the disappearance of the latter from the Indian soil. Later Brahmanical philosophers like Udayana Acārya continued to attribute distorted statements like *sarvam duḥkham* ("all is suffering") to the Buddha, and revelled at their success in demolishing Buddhism, [195] hardly realizing that they were exposing the contradiction in their own substantialist thinking.

Nineteenth century Western philosophers like Schopenhauer, who pioneered the study of Asian thought in the West before careful editing and translating of Buddhist texts were carried out in Western languages, were most probably led by the Brahmanical interpreters of Buddhism. Schopenhauer was one of the first to characterize Buddhism as a pessimistic religion propounding a theory of "universal suffering," a characterization that seems to have appealed to his own inclinations and temperament. William James, quoting J. Misland (*Luther et le Serf-Arbitre,* 1884), notes that "Germanic races have tended rather to think of Sin in the singular, and with a capital S, as of something ineradicably ingrained in our natural subjectivity, and never to be removed by any superficial piecemeal operations," and that "undoubtedly the northern tone in religion has inclined to the more intimately pessimistic persuasion, . . ."[196]

Such being the manner in which Buddhism came to be looked upon as a pessimistic religion, it would now be possible to examine the implications of pessimism and optimism, and evaluate the Buddha's conception of suffering. In this connection James' two chapters in *The Varieties of Religious Experience* on "The Religion of the Healthy-mindedness," and "The Sick Soul" will be of great assistance. These two chapters are elaboration of two types of human beings referred to by Francis W. Newman as "the once-born and the twice-born."[197] James takes the "once-born" as an example of the "healthy-minded." A quotation from Newman illustrates the character of such a person:

> They see God, not as a Strict Judge, not as a Glorious Potentate; but as the animating Spirit of a beautiful harmonious world, Beneficient and Kind, Merciful as well as Pure. The same characters generally have no metaphysical tendencies: they do not look back into themselves. Hence they are not distressed by their own imperfections; yet it would be absurd to call them self-righteous; for they hardly think of themselves *at all.* This childlike quality of their nature makes the opening of religion very happy to them: for they no more shrink from God, than a child from an emperor, before whom the parent trembles: in fact, they have no vivid conception of any of the qualities in which the severer Majesty of God consists. He is to them the impersonation of Kindness and Beauty. They read his character not in the disordered world of man, but in romantic and harmonious nature.[198]

In the pre-Buddhist background, such an attitude seems to emerge in the substantialist tradition of the *Upaniṣads* where the individual empirical self is negated in favor of a more permanent and eternal self (*ātman*) which came to be looked upon as possessing the characteristics of "the real" (*sat*), "consciousness" (*cit*) and "bliss" (*ānanda*). The emphasis is on the blissful and harmonious self pervading the universe, including man, and suffering being confined to the individual empirical self which should not be the object of thought at all. This could not be considered the shallower version of the healthy-mindedness, sometimes depicted in the attitude of the materialists in India, but represents what James calls the more "profounder" level of healthy-mindedness. The contrary of this is the "sick soul" which "cannot so swiftly throw off the burden of the consciousness of evil, but are *congenitally fated to suffer from its presence*."[199]

The one school of thought in the Indian context that comes anywhere close to this way of thinking is Jainism. The Jaina view of life, in spite of its relationship to Buddhism in certain aspects, was criticized by the Buddha. Their view of karma is often referred to in the Buddhist texts as *pubbe-kata-hetu* which implies that all present experiences are the inevitable results of the inexhorable past actions. The Buddha initiates the criticism of this theory by raising questions regarding its epistemological foundations.

> From what you say, reverent Jains, you do not know whether you yourselves were in the past, or whether you were not; you do not know whether in the past you yourselves did this evil deed like this or like that; you do not know that so much suffering is worn away, or that so much suffering is to be worn away, or that when so much suffering is worn away, all suffering will become worn away; you do not know the getting rid of the bad states of mind here and now, or the arising of the good states.[200]

Having rejected the substantialist implications of the Jaina theory of karma,[201] the Buddha concludes:

> If, monks, the pleasure and pain which creatures undergo are due to what was previously done, certainly, monks, the Jainas were formerly doers of deeds that were badly done in that they now experience such painful, severe, sharp feelings. If, monks, the pleasure and pain which creatures undergo are due to creation by an overlord, certainly, monks, the Jainas were created by an evil overlord in that they now experience such painful, severe, sharp feelings. If, monks, the pleasure and pain which creatures undergo are due to destiny, certainly, monks, the Jainas are of evil destiny in that they now ex-

perience such painful, severe, sharp feelings. If, monks, the pleasure and pain which creatures undergo are due to their species, certainly, monks, the Jainas are of evil species in that they experience such painful, severe, sharp feelings. If, monks, the pleasure and pain creatures undergo are due to effort here and now, certainly, monks, the Jainas are of evil effort here and now in that they now experience such painful, severe and sharp feelings."[202]

The point made clear is that none of these causes, *taken in itself*, can be presented as *the* cause or condition of human experience to the neglect of everything else. Human experience is complex; so are the conditions that give rise to such experience. It is possible that James came to realize the difference between the Jaina and Buddhist theories of karma after he completed writing his Gifford Lectures, and in the postscript (referred to earlier) opted for the more non-substantialist Buddhist theory of karma.

In criticizing the Jaina thinkers for presenting a very deterministic theory of karma that leads to a pessimistic view of life, the Buddha raised questions regarding the epistemological means by which they reached their conclusions. To understand what these epistemological puzzles are it would be appropriate to return to James' examination of pessimism in the Western world. James quotes two interesting passages in order to explain the type of questions that eventually lead to a tragic or pessimistic view of life. The first is from the Greek classics.

Naked came I upon the earth, naked I go below the ground —why then do I vainly toil when I see the end naked before me? How did I come to be? Whence am I? Whereof did I come? To pass away. How can I learn ought when naught I know? Being nought I came to life: once more shall I be what I was. Nothing and nothingness is the whole race of mortals.[203]

Next is a quotation from Tolstoy, a pessimist from the modern world of science and technology.

This is no fable, but the literal incontestable truth which every one may understand. What will be the outcome of what I do today? Of what I shall do tomorrow? What will be the outcome of all my life? Why should I live? Why should I do anything? Is there in life any purpose which the inevitable death awaits me does not undo and destroy?
These questions are the simplest in the world. From the stupid child to the wisest old man, they are in the soul of every human being. Without an answer to them, it is impossible, as I experienced, for life to go on.[204]

The former quotation refers to the uncertainties regarding the past and the latter regarding the future. In both instances, the anxieties about the past and the future have become obstacles against dealing with the present. While the optimist's response to this anxiety may appear to be "childlike," the pessimist has lost all hope. The Buddha did realize, as did the Greeks and Tolstoy, that these are genuine questions raised by human beings. "Did I exist in the past or not? Will I exist in the future or not? Do I exist in the present or do I not exist in the present?"[205] are questions for which human beings have sought answers from the dawn of history. However, the Buddha also realized that human beings have often transgressed the limits of reflection and investigation in attempting to answer these questions (see section on "Epistemology and Psychology"). There is no need to list the variety of answers that one can find in the different traditions. Most of them fall under the broad categories of eternalism and annihilationism, and as far as the Buddha is concerned they are dispositional (*saṅkhāro so*) answers,[206] which can neither be confirmed nor denied. Abandoning such speculations and without carrying on the reflections and investigations to their extremes, the Buddha concentrated upon what is given in the historical past and the present in order to understand the nature of human life. As such, Tolstoy cannot quote the Buddha in support of his tragic or pessimistic view of life.[207]

The Buddha's explanation of suffering is presented in the following statement, regarding the first of the four truths he had realized through wisdom (*paññā*).

> Birth is suffering; old age is suffering; sickness is suffering; death is suffering. Sorrow, lamentation and dejection are suffering. Association with the unpleasant is suffering; separation from the pleasant is suffering; not getting what one wishes for is suffering. In brief, the five aggregates of grasping are suffering.[208]

Any attempt to understand the nature of this truth, and for that matter, any of the four truths, independent of the epistemological source, namely, wisdom (*paññā*) and the conditions that prevent the development of such wisdom, that is, the confusions or perversions (*vipallāsa, viparyāsa*) referred to in the previous section, would be utterly futile. It is, indeed, for this reason that an enlightened disciple like Nāgārjuna devoted an entire chapter to the examination of the four perversions (*Kārikā* XXIII) before undertaking an explanation of the four truths (*Kārikā* XXIV).

To repeat the four confusions or perversions listed earlier, they consist of the identification of

A. the impermanent with the permanent,
B. the not unsatisfactory with the unsatisfactory,
C. the non-substantial with the substantial, and
D. the unpleasant with the pleasant.

Here again, one needs to keep in mind the epistemological standpoint of the Buddha before proceeding to analyse the perversions. For example, perversions A and C are not on the same epistemological standing as perversions B and D. The Buddha recognized the impermanent and the non-substantial on the basis of experience. Yet he did not admit any experience that can provide us with knowledge of the permanent and the substantial. The rationalist method of assuming knowledge of the impermanent strictly on the basis of the knowledge of the permanent, and the knowledge of the non-substantial strictly on the basis of the knowledge of the substantial was not acceptable to the Buddha. Empirically, neither the permanent nor the substantial are *known*. However, this is not the case with the perversions B and D. Experience of pleasant and unpleasant sensations do occur even in the enlightened ones (see section of "The Psychology of Freedom"). Yet this does not indicate a sharp or absolute dichotomy between cognition and emotion. As pointed out earlier, it is indeed the excessive emotive element, namely, anxiety, that gives rise to the belief in the permanent and the substantial. Thus the difference between perversions A and C, on the one hand, and perversions B and D, on the other, is that in the former the cognition is stretched beyond its legitimate limit to assume the existence of permanent and substantial events, whereas in the latter what is given in experience is mixed up, that is wrongly identified.

Keeping these four perversions in mind, one can proceed to examine the Buddha's definition of suffering. For the annihilationist materialists (*ucchedavādī*) (as it is for some of the modern scientists), who seem to know almost with certainty that birth is the beginning of human existence and death is the ultimate end, the adoption of an optimistic view of life is easy. If birth is not a new phenomenon but the re-appearance of a permanent and eternal self, and death is not a real death but merely a temporary phase in the same permanent and eternal self that will eventually reach its source, as the eternalists (*sassatavādī*) of the Upaniṣadic tradition believed, optimism could again reign supreme. On the contrary, if one is extremly skeptical as to how birth has come to be, and what possibly could happen after death, the tragic sense can be heightened and there is reason for being pessimistic.

However, for the Buddha who was willing to recognize retrocognition as a valid source of knowledge, and for whom the beginning of the stream of consciousness need not be strictly confined to a definite point in the present life of a human being, birth (*jāti*) is the result of a process of dependent arising (*paṭiccasamuppāda*) involving physical as well as psychological factors. While excessive craving for survival (*bhava-taṇhā*) constitutes one of the psychological conditions for the birth of a human being, birth will not occur unless the necessary physical conditions provided by the parents are also available.[209] Furthermore, birth could be a source of suffering in the present life only if this craving for survival continues to dominate a person's life; not if he has, after being born, adopts an attitude of renunciation or dispassion (*virāga*) for such continuation. Birth is thus the result of excessive craving or passion for survival and the availabilty of other necessary physical conditions. Birth becomes a source of suffering only in this conditional, but not in an absolute sense. In other words, there is no intrinsic relationship between birth and suffering. If they were to be so related, there could not be any freedom from suffering for one who is born, at least in the present life.

The same holds true of decay or old age (*jarā*). It is the unwillingness to accept decay as a fact of life that causes frustration and unhappiness.

Death (*maraṇa*) turns out to be the most intolerable cause of suffering. Eternal life after death, or sometimes eternal life uninterrupted by death have been sought for as ways of overcoming this hazard of existence. For the Buddha, the only way to overcome suffering associated with death is through the realization of the impermanence of life and the renunciation of craving for its continuance beyond its possible limits. In this particular case, the nature of one's dispositions (*saṅkhāra*) plays a dominant role. While the dispositional tendencies involving excessive craving for life (*bhava-taṇhā*) can lead to re-birth (and a repetition of the process of suffering), the complete annihilation of such dispositional tendencies can result in premature death (i.e. suicide). Hence the Buddha's emphasis is on the appeasement of dispositions (*saṅkhāra-samatha, saṅkhāra upasama*, see section on "The Psychology of Freedom") as a means of avoiding suffering. The appeasement of dispositons enables a person to enjoy the satisfactions (*assāda*) of life[210] without being a slave to them and having to face either constant frustrations or fear and fret. In other words, it allows for the recognition of what is called the "life instinct" (*jīvitukāma*)[211] yet not making it an obsession.

Underscoring the condition that renders birth, old age, decay and death intolerable sources of suffering, thereby eliminating the joys of human life, the Buddha points out that "association with the unpleasant and not getting what one wishes for are suffering." In other words, it is one's excessive craving (*taṇhā*) or yearning (*chanda*) or obsession (*papañca*) that makes the unpleasant intolerable and the pleasant excessively satisfying. Pleasant and unpleasant experiences are, in a sense, not suffering. Only the greed for the pleasant and the aversion or hatred toward the unpleasant constitute suffering.

For this very reason, the Buddha summarizes his exposition of suffering by saying that the five aggregates of grasping are suffering (*pañc' upādānakkhandhā dukkhā*). This is sometimes taken to mean that the Buddha condemned the psychophysical personality as a putrid, despicable phenomenon to be gotten rid of or sacrificed without the least hesitation in favor of a more exalted and eternal personality after death. This is too hasty a conclusion. It is hard to find the statement in the discourses of the Buddha which reads: "The five aggregates are suffering" (*pañcakkhandhā dukkhā*). What the Buddha considered to be suffering is not the psychophysical personality consisting of the five aggregates, but grasping for it (*upādāna*).

The abandoning or relinquishing of grasping does not mean the immediate disintegration of the human personality. Grasping is not like a plaster that holds the pieces of the mosaic together. It is what causes suffering once the personality has come to be, even though its elimination can prevent the recurrence or the rebirth of a new personality after death (see section on "The Psychology of Freedom").

The Buddha's perception of life is therefore neither pessimistic nor optimistic. To use a term from James, it is rather melioristic.[212] Commenting upon Schopenhauer's attempt to see similarity between Buddhism and his own philosophical outlook, Walter Kaufmann has made the following remark:

> One might have expected Schopenhauer to realize all this, since he stressed the universality of suffering more than any previous philosopher. But at this point he felt a kinship to Buddhism—the universality of suffering is the first of the Buddha's "four noble truths"—and Buddhism and tragedy represent two utterly different responses to suffering.[213]

To this may be added in conclusion that the Buddha did not advocate a notion of "universal suffering" (see above) and, therefore, without looking upon human life as a *tragedy*, perceived it as an *opportunity*.

Chapter Twelve
The Dilemma of Freedom

The belief in strict determinism or in chaotic indeterminism, whether it be in ontology or in human behavior, was considered by the Buddha and James to be inimical to the conception of human freedom. The Buddha's awareness that the *ātman*-ontology of the *Upaniṣads* contributed to the strictly determined social clases which left no room for individual initiative, but eventually led to the reposing of faith in the grace of a Supreme Power, made him an unrelenting critic of both *ātman* and caste. Similarly, the theory of strict determinism in human behavior propounded by the Jainas, referred to as the *pubbekatahetu*, where all present and future experiences are attributed solely to past karma (see section on "Suffering"), was also rejected as it contributed to the denial of choice and free-will. The materialist denial of free-will, even though based on their conception of the indeterminism of human behavior, was backed up by a strongly deterministic theory of physical nature (*svabhāva*). Even though the Buddha made a persistent endeavor to avoid these extremes and follow the middle path of "dependent arising" (*paṭiccasamuppāda*) to explain the life-process (*saṃsāra*) as well as freedom (*nibbāna*), most critics of Buddhism as well as some of its followers have failed to understand the implications of his views. For them, any conception of causation or dependence, when universalized, becomes inimical to freedom of choice. Therefore, the Buddha's conception of karma is seen as conflicting with his view that all phenomena are dependently arisen. This has led to the unfortunate view that the Buddha admitted a total or absolute difference between the life-process (*saṃsāra*) and freedom (*nibbāna*). Thus, the transcendence of the life-process becomes a necessary condition for freedom. Freedom becomes the absolute, ineffable, ultimate reality.

In the context in which James lived, deterministic theories of existence were propounded with greater enthusiasm and sophistication. Proponents of determinism were influenced by the progress of scientific explanations and the belief that any event in the world, including human behavior, is necessarily determined solely by factors in its past. James directed a two-pronged attack on such theories of determinism. First, he insisted that human behavior cannot be *experimentally* proven. This was his criticism of behaviorism, which was gradually becoming the major theme in psychology. Secondly, he argued that scientific investigations arrive at deterministic theories by merely focussing attention on specific aspects of experience, leaving out its broader horizons. For James, the ability to focus attention on specific aspects of experience is itself indicative of human choice and the possibility of freedom. John K. Roth, in his excellent book, *Freedom and the Moral Life. The Ethics of William James*, states this view clearly:

> The selectivity of consciousness which focusses on certain parts of the world in terms of special interests, operates in the sciences. Assumptions concerning determinate relationships and even the discovery of causal regularities do not exhaust our world, and a nonreductive understanding of human experience will require us to place scientific investigations in a broader perspective that leaves freedom standing.[214]

The Buddha's conception of the life-process, as well as James' view of experience, properly understood, provides an explanation of the possibility of freedom. The resonances between the Buddha's conception of personhood, explained in terms of the life-process or the stream of consciousness (*viññāna-sota*) and James' description of the self on the basis of the stream of thought, have already been noted. Both the Buddha and James emphasized the centrality and importance of *selection*.

In the Buddha's explanation of perception (see above), this process of selection occurs at the initial non-reflective stage as well as the more self-conscious stage of perception. Selectivity based upon 'interest' occurs even in the pre-reflective stage beginning with the impinging of the sense object upon the sense organ culminating in feeling or sensation (*vedanā*). The need for selectivity even at this initial stage of sense experience is prompted by the inability of consciousness to deal with the "big blooming buzzing confusion." During the second stage, when sensations give rise to perception and reflection, the selectivity is conditioned by the stronger "dispositions," thereby leading to obsession and bondage during the final stage. This selectivity in consciousness accounts for the possibility and, therefore, the ability on the part of the human being to choose, think and act, and these represent the core of selfhood or personality in the Buddha's doctrine. Hence, his statement that the self is a "lump of dispositions" (*saṇkhāra-puñja*).[215]

Once the freedom of choice is recognized as a constituent part of human knowledge and, therefore, of life, the question arises as to how we go about deciding which alternative to choose. At this stage, both the Buddha and

James, introduce a moral component of human life as a criterion for deciding which alternative to choose. Referring to James' view, Roth says:

> However, it is one thing to argue that consciousness is efficacious and another to defend the view that the acts of consciousness are not parts of a rigidly determined sequence, James works to defend a theory of freedom against deterministic views and his arguments rest primarily on the moral importance of a belief in freedom.[216]

For this reason, James had no hesitation about branding determinism as an irrational view. Rationality, for him, had broader implications, and was not confined to the domain of scientific methods, assumptions and findings. It included ethical, aesthetic as well as religious components.

James was not unaware that some of the moral or religious determinists who ignored the determinism accepted by the scientific minds had sought refuge in equally deterministic moral imperatives and religious sanctions. Such moral determinism and religious dogmatism were as unacceptable to James as scientific determinism. The idea that even "part of the ideal has to be left behind"[217] was expresed by James in order to leave an open-ended universe and to preserve plurality as well as choice in the world of human experience.

The Buddha's way of introducing a moral element into the discussion of empirical facts is rather unique and basically pragmatic. Discoursing at a time when a sharp dichotomy between fact and value was not part of philosophical discussion, he utilized the term *dhamma* to refer to all empirical facts. Therefore, anyone would expect the Buddha to use the negative term *a-dhamma* to refer to non-empirical facts or anything that is denied existential status, like the metaphysical self or substance. Yet he never did so, even though some of the modern interpreters of Buddhism translated the phrase as "non-factor."[218] A careful reading of all the instances where the term *adhamma* occurs in the early discourses as well as in the texts like the *Prajñāpāramitā* and philosophical treatises like the *Mūlamadhyamakakārikā* reveals the undeniable fact that it is used in the sense of 'bad' or 'evil,' i.e., as a synonym for the "unwholesome" (*a-kusala*). The implication is clear. For him, even a fact is not a fact, an option is not an option, a choice is not a choice, so long as it is *devoid of* any moral or ethical significance. Thus, *dhamma* is not merely an empirical fact, but also a fact of some value, moral, aesthetic or religious, or of some significance for human life; and when a human person chooses a fact (*dhamma*), he is either choosing a fact that is either useful (*dhamma*) or harmful (*adhamma*), a neutral fact posing no difficulties in relation to choice. The criterion by which usefulness and harmfulness is to be determined is then examined.

In justifying an open-ended universe, James spoke of *possibilities*. However, when he comes to discuss morality and freedom, he is compelled to set limits. The following statement of James is specially relevant:

> A look at another peculiarity of the ethical universe, as we find it, will still further show us the philosopher's perplexities. As a purely theoretic problem, namely, the casuistic question would hardly ever come up at all. If the ethical philosopher were only asking after the best *imaginable* system of goods he would indeed have an easy task; for all demands as such are *prima facie* respectable, and the best simply imaginary world would be one in which *every* demand was gratified, as soon as made. Such a world would, however, have to have a physical constitution different from that of the one which we inhabit.[219]

Examples of the ideal world, the world of the best imaginable goods he is presenting is one in which we can spend our money, yet grow rich; take our holiday, yet get ahead with our work; shoot and fish, yet do no hurt to the beast; gain no end of experience, yet keep our youthful freshness of heart, etc.[220]

The ideal world presented in the pre-Buddhist *Upaniṣads* and continued to be justified in the later Hindu classic, the *Bhagavadgītā*, seems to embody such a system of imaginable goods, namely, eternal life unmarked by death; eternal enjoyment uninterrupted by pain; eternal light unobstructed by darkness, etc.

For the Buddha as well as for James, the world of ours is made on an entirely different pattern. The *actually possible* in this world is vastly narrower than all that is demanded. When the *world* comes into conflict with the *demand*, some may wish to abandon the world and satisfy his demand in another world totally different from this world. This would be some sort of moral solitude. Some others may want to abandon the demand and satisfy the world. Absolute self-denial could be one way of achieving this. The middle way between these two extremes would be to take the world as it has come to be and *appease one's demands*. It is this last choice that is advocated by the Buddha as well as James. James' position is clearly stated by Roth:

> In this life the individual cannot actualize all his possibilities. He must select the ones that are most important for him and drop out most others. This process of selection shapes the

> character of the individual, and the choices he makes with respect to himself also helps to determine the course of society as a whole.[221]

The Buddha's preference for a life that contributes to one's own welfare as well as the welfare of others as a morally good life is based upon similar considerations. While James may have arrived at such conclusions based upon reflection, the Buddha seems to have tested them out in his own life and achieved freedom (*nibbāna*), which would be the subject of discussion that follows.

Chapter Thirteen
The Psychology of Freedom

As is evident from the foregoing discussion of the various theories of human psychology, there is hardly any unanimity among the theorists as to the nature and constitution of the human mind. Most attempts at systematic formulation of human thought have culminated in theories that reduce the mind to mere material functions, as it is the case with behaviorism. On the other side of the scale is spiritualism that distinguishes the mental life from the so-called crude material world and, as such, from all forms of sensory experience. The Upaniṣadic thinkers were the forerunners in this latter enterprize. Its culmination is reached in the Vedānta. The Upaniṣadic and Vedāntic views on the transcendence of sense experience in the explanation of human freedom seems to have overwhelmed the interpretation of the Buddhist tradition in spite of the Buddha's clear and unequivocal rejection of such methodology. The Buddha's own "Discourse on Everything" (*Sabbasutta*)[222] rarely received proper treatment even from those who interpreted him as an "empiricist."[223] The Buddha's teachings got submerged in the Vedāntic flood to such an extent that even a very sincere and energetic disciple in the modern world like Ñāṇananda would insist: "Not only has the concept 'I' (*papañca par excellence*) undergone combustion, but it has also ignited the data of sensory experience in their entirety. Thus, in this *Jhāna* of the Arahant, the world of concepts melts away in the intuitional bonfire of universal impermanence."[224]

The concepts of universal impermanence, unsatisfactoriness, non-substantiality, emptiness, dependent arising, etc., instead of returning and merging with the impermanent, the unsatisfactory, the non-substantial, the empty, the dependently arisen, etc., and thus relating themselves with the concrete world of sense experience, soar upward into the absolute like kites or helium-filled baloons released into the sky. Freedom or nirvana seems to have no relationship whatsoever to the concrete world of sense experience and consciousness and, therefore, to the world of conceptual thinking. The Buddha's revolution in epistemology is thus abandoned.

In 1969 Rune Johansson attempted to explain the psychology of freedom without making much effort to deal with the psychology of the person in bondage.[225] This deficiency was to some extent corrected by Ñāṇananda when he devoted a greater part of his analysis to the problem of *papañca*, the cause of bondage. However, Ñāṇananda was preoccupied with a stage of meditation (*jhāna*) that is free from any objective support as representing the consciousness of the *Tathāgata*.[226] This, in fact, is an identification of the psychology of freedom with the so-called state of cessation (*nirodha-samāpatti*) or the state of cessation of perception and what is felt (*saññā-vedayita-nirodha*). It is the same mistake committed by Johansson.[227] Ñāṇananda seems to depend heavily on a passage which emphasizes the practice of *jhāna* that has no recourse either to sense experience or to the higher forms of consciousness.[228] However, he fails to realize that this is the same as the state of cessation. The *Ariyapariyesana-sutta* in which the Buddha refused to equate freedom with the state of cessation should have served as a corrective to this wrong identification. In fact, as pointed out earlier, the state of cessation is to be experienced by the body (*kāyena sacchikaraṇīyā dhammā*), rather than to be realized through wisdom (*paññā*).[229]

Thus, on the one hand, Ñāṇananda clearly sees that the enlightened one continues to have sense experience and resort to conception. On the other hand, he seems to recognize a totally different form of consciousness in the *Tathāgata*, and this is prompted by his emphasis on the state of cessation. The dilemma is resolved only by a dogmatic assertion that the *Tathāgata* has an intuition that transcends both sense experience and conception. This latter assertion becomes irrelevant, if we are to carefully examine the psychology of freedom as expressed by the Buddha in several passages quoted by Ñāṇananda himself.

The first is the Buddha's admonition to Bāhiya Dārucīriya, as found in the *Udāna*. The passage reads thus:

> Then, Bāhiya, thus must you train yourself: "In the seen there will just be the seen; in the heard, just the heard; in the reflected, just the reflected; in the cognized, just the cognized." That is how, Bāhiya, you must train yourself. Now, Bāhiya, when in the seen there will be to you just the seen; . . . just the heard; . . . just the reflected; . . . just the cognized, then, Bāhiya, you will not identify yourself with it. When you do not identify yourself with it, you will not locate yourself therein. When you do not locate yourself therein, it follows that you will have no "here" or "beyond" or "midway-between." and this would be the end of suffering.[230]

The passage is a clear denial of the identification of oneself with what is given in sense experience, whether that oneself be the material body or the spiritual self. The phrase *na tena* carries the same implication as the term *a-tammaya* occurring in another passage quoted by Ñāṇananda.[231] This latter passage implies a rejection of the transcendental unity of apperception discussed earlier. It is a rejection of the metaphysical search for *something* (*na kiñci maññati*), a search for some *location* (*na kuhiñci maññati*) and a search for some *agency* (*na kenaci maññati*).[232] It may be noted here that it is the same kind of search that Nāgārjuna was rejecting when he maintained: "The Buddha did not teach the appeasement of all objects, the appeasement of obsession and the auspicious as something to someone at some place."[233]

Explaining the process of perception, we have already pointed out that the Buddha recommended non-grasping for *nimitta* and *anuvyañjana* on occasions of sense experience. We have interpreted the former as "substance" or "mysterious cause" and the latter as "quality." When the Buddha admonished Bāhiya to train himself in such a way that "in the seen there will just be the seen" (*diṭṭhe diṭṭha-mattaṃ bhavissati*), etc., the Buddha was not advising him to abandon seeing, but only the search for a mysterious *something* (*kiñci*) in the object of perception that would provide for its unity. The constant human search for either a unity of the subject (a self or a transcendental apperception) or a unity of the object was the subject of previous discussions. The Buddha's teaching represents an unrelenting criticism of this almost universal search.

Abandoning the search for such metaphysical entities and causes, a search for things as they are, the Buddha was willing to recognize things as they have come to be (*yathābhūta*), that is to take—

1. the seen as the mere seen (*diṭṭha-matta, dṛṣṭa-mātra*),
2. the heard as the mere heard (*suta-matta, śruta-mātra),*
3. the reflected as the mere reflected (*muta-matta, smṛta-mātra*),
4. the cognized as the mere cognized (*viññāta-matta, vijñāta-mātra*), and this attitude, as noted previously, was to be extended to all conception and, therefore, conventions, i.e. to take—
5. the convention as the mere convention (*vohāra-matta, vyavahāra-mātra*).

The use of the term *matta* (Sk. *mātra*) in the above contexts is extremely significant. It does not mean the abandoning of any and every search for the conditions that give rise to events, occurrences, etc. Indeed, the knowledge of the conditions depending upon which events occur represents the most significant form of empirical knowledge. The principle of "dependent arising" (*paṭiccasamuppāda*) was formulated by the Buddha on the basis of the perception and knowledge of "dependently arisen phenomena (*paṭiccasamuppanna dhamma*). Such knowledge and understanding is relevant to the development of the human personality and the attainment of freedom. What is being rejected by the use of *matta* is the search for non-empirical, metaphysical causes and conditions. The theological arguments for the existence of God as the cause of everything that happens in the universe are illustrative of what the Buddha was rejecting. The arguments for "an unmoved Mover," "an uncaused First Cause" or "a necessary cause" are non-empirical arguments about which hardly any agreement or consensus could be reached, without first asserting the argument to be proved. The conceptions of self or substance are no more different. Such mysterious causes and conditons have eluded human grasp and understanding for centuries. For the pragmatic Buddha, the search for such ultimate causes and conditions is as futile as the search for the unseen beauty queen (*janapada-kalyāṇī*).[234]

It is the search for metaphysical causes that contributes to constant doubt and perplexity. A call for the recognition of "omniscience" (*sarvajñatva*) provides one way of overcoming such doubt and perplexity. Being a human being, the Buddha was not willing to lay claim to such omniscience. Nor was he prepared to repose faith on some other unseen being or power that could possess such knowledge.

The answer to skepticism, therefore, did not lay in omniscience. Instead, it depended upon the avoidance of the metaphysical search itself and the recognition of empirical causes and conditions, as reflected in the Buddha's statement regarding enlightenment: "When things appear before the brahman who is ardent and contemplative, his doubts disappear as he understands their causal nature."[235]

Excessive lust (*rāga*), not only for the pleasurable objects of sense, but also for stimulating ideas and concepts prevents man from understanding them as mere objects of perception (*diṭṭha-matta*) or mere ideas of cognition (*viññāta-matta*) or mere conventions (*vohāra-matta*). When that lust is exhausted, completely uprooted and not allowed to re-emerge, the manner in which the pleasurable objects affect him, the way in which ideas influence him, may be seen in a totally different light. This seems to be the transformation of the personality that the Buddha was advocating.

Lust (*rāga*), craving (*taṇhā*) or desire (*kāma*) are not invariable concomitants of sense experience. While there is a general tendence in human beings to be attracted to pleasurable objects of experience and repulsed by the unpleasurable (*sukha-kāmā hi sattā dukkha-paṭikkūlā*),[236] such tendencies may vary from person to person not only with regard to the quality of the pleasure or revulsion, but also to the degree to which one is attracted and repulsed. The realization of this fact enabled the Buddha to cultivate pleasures neither harmful to himself nor to others. The avoidance of pleasures that are harmful to oneself as well as to others requires a great deal of restraint (*saṃvara*). Such restraint is not easily cultivated so long as one is constrainted by an internal sickness (*ajjhattaṃ rogamūlaṃ*) and an external sickness (*bahiddhā rogamūlaṃ*). The belief in a permanent and eternal self constitutes the former, while the grasping for a real object represents the latter.[237] The obsession (*papañca*) relating to these two metaphysical conceptions constitutes the most potent form of constraint (*saṅga*). Freed from such constraint, a person is able to experience happiness without giving occasion to lust, craving or desire.

The Buddha insisted that desire (*kāma*) is not identical with the pleasurable or the verigated objects in the world (*na te kāmā yāni citrāni loke*).[238] It is merely the thought of lust (*saṃkappa-rāgo*), which is normally generated by wrong ideas or misconception (*miccha-saṃkappa*), primarily the metaphysical conceptions of self and object. As such it is possible to maintain that on occasions of sense experience, which are represented by the coming together (*saṃgati*) of the subject and object, the subject does come to be affected in a certain way and this is conditioned by the views it holds regarding its own nature as well as the nature of the object. It is only in this sense that one speaks of influxes (*āsava*) associated with sense experience.

In the "Discourse on the Noble Quest" (*Ariyapariyesana-sutta*), where the Buddha recounts his struggles before his enlightenment, his final attainment of enlightenment and freedom and his first preaching, it is stated that the phenomenon that beclouds the perception of dependent arising (*paṭiccasamuppāda*) and the attainment of freedom (*nibbāna*) is *ālaya*.

> These human progeny are delighting in *ālaya*, delighted by *ālaya*, excited by *ālaya*. By these progeny delighting in *ālaya*, delighted by *ālaya* and excited by *ālaya*, this situation is not easily perceived, namely, this conditionality, this dependent arising (*idappaccayatā paṭiccasamuppādo*). This situation is also not easily perceived, namely, the appeasement of all disposition, the relinquishing of all grasping, the waning of craving, cessation (of craving) and freedom.[239]

The term *ālaya*, an extremely important term in the Yogācāra tradition, is literally rendered as 'abode,' 'settling place,' 'house' and, therefore, by implication as 'attachment,' 'desire,' 'clinging,' 'lust,' etc. The foregoing discussion of the psychology of a human person clearly identifies the two primary ideas in which human beings take refuge, namely, the notion of a permanent and eternal self within and an external object without. Indeed, all other forms of attachment, desire and clinging are secondary, compared with this obsession with the metaphysical inquiry and search for subjective and objective realities. One who continues the search for such metaphysical entities is called a *kiñcana*, and one who has abandoned such a search is referred to as *akiñcana*, a synonym for the freed one. Similarly, the state in which one anchors oneself to such ideas is called *ālaya*, and the state where no such anchoring is found is called *anālaya* or release (*vimutti*).[240]

The history of Buddhist thought since the Buddha represents a constant struggle on the part of his disciples to prevent the re-introduction of this search for metaphysical entities.

However, when the metaphysical beliefs in self and ultimately real objects are relinquished the influxes (*āsava*) such as desire (*kāma*), becoming (*bhava*), views (*diṭṭhi*) and ignorance (*avijjā*) cease. The constant thirsting for this and that causing worry and frustration ceases along with it. With the waning of influxes (*āsavakkhaya*), the constraints relating to perception (*sañña*) and conception (*saṅkhā*) are removed. Yet the removal of constraints does not mean that the perceptions and conceptions are themselves eliminated. Only that one is not strictly confined or constrained by any of the perceptions and conceptions. A flexibility is achieved whereby perceptions and conceptions can be usefully utilized for the sake of human happiness, both of oneself and of others.

Elimination of constraints (*nīvaraṇa*) represents freedom (*nibbāna*). This elimination of constraints would definitely bring about a transformation of the human personality. The transformation would be both physical and psychological. Physically the freed one (*nibbuta*) enjoys great relaxation and appeasement (*kāya-passaddhi*), free from any form of hypertension or internal disorders. He could be immune to many a disease that others may pick up at the slightest contact. Yet he cannot remain completely unconstrained by the physical body or its environment. He cannot overcome ageing, decay and final death in this life. Reading the early discourses, one cannot avoid the impression that even the Buddha was not able to completely overcome the physical constraints. At the age of eighty he compared his body to an old cart, worn and decrepit (*jara-sakaṭa*).[241] Only the devotion on the part of his uninitiated disciples was responsible for depicting him as one who did not have a wrinkle on his face at the time of death.

However, with the attainment of enlightenment and freedom, he is able to overcome most other constraints—economic, political, social or ideological.

His way of treating perception and conception enables him to respond to the outside world without conflict and strife. His reluctance to admit absolute certainty with regard to empirical knowledge and his pragmatic interpretation of sense experience coupled with his non-absolutistic approach to conception and convention, as clearly illustrated in the "Discourse on the Analysis of Non-strife" (*Araṇavibhaṅga-sutta*, see section on "Conception"), provided the means for avoiding most of these constraints.

Economic, social and political constraints follow more frequently from cosy conceptual super-structures laid down with absolute precision by economists as well as social and political scientists. Prediction of economic growth, social evolution and political changes is carried out with great precision and insignificant margins of error. These provide the foundations for absolute laws relating to the economic, social and political life of man. Predictability, instead of serving as a *guide*, can turn out to be the fountain-head of monstrous and inhuman laws. Suffering for oneself as well as others is inevitable. The Buddha comments:

> Beings, dominated by prediction (*akkheyya*), established upon prediction, not understanding prediction, come under the yoke of death. However, having understood prediction, one does not assume oneself to be a fore-teller. When such a thought does not occur to him, that by which he could be spoken of, that does not exist for him.[242]

Thus, non-substantiality (*anatta*) applied in the realms of experience as well as conception deals a staggering blow to absolute laws formulated on the basis of prediction (*akkheyya*). For one who has realized the non-substantiality of all phenomena, including the conceptually formulated laws, human happiness becomes a criterion of economic, social as well as political ordering and organization. Motivated by such a noble ideal (*paramattha*), unconstrained by economic, social and political laws, the freed one leads a life contributing to his own happiness as well as the happiness of others. He has no remorse, no frustration, no mental depression, not because he has served the fiat of an almighty and supreme power or the dictates of an ultimate reality, but because he has served man. The Buddha's conception of duty is clearly and succinctly expressed in his admonition to his own son. Rāhula:

> But if you, Rāhula, while reflecting thus should find, "That deed which I am desirous of doing with the body is a deed of my body that would conduce neither to the harm of myself nor to the harm of others nor to the harm of both; this deed of my body is skilled, its yield is happy, its result is

happy"—a deed of body like this, Rāhula, may be done by you.[243]

The early discourses do not seem to permit any other reading of the psychology of freedom (*nibbāna*). The question as to what happens to the freed one who is not reborn after death is raised only by the metaphysician who is enamored with the notion of substantial and permanent self.

James was more of a critic of religion, a psychologist and philosopher who made a consistent attempt to evaluate and understand the different expressions of religious experience, not one who tried his hand at experimenting with all these religious exercises, except maybe those with which he was familiar from his childhood. He states this clearly at the end of his exhaustive analysis of the most extreme types of religious experience known to him. "We who have pursued such radical expressions of it (i.e. religions experience] may now be sure that we know its secrets as authentically as anyone can know them *who learns them from another*."[244]

James' ideas about freedom are embodied in his lengthy chapters on "Saintliness" and "The Value of Saintliness." Having been brought up in the Western religious tradition and intellectually nurtured by a father whom he described as "a religious prophet and genius,"[245] James could not help devoting more space in these two chapters to the examination of "saintliness" as expressed in the Western religious traditions, even though he occasionally makes references to other non-Western religions. Therefore, in speaking about the "fruits of the religious life" [*sāmañña-phala*?],[246] James picks up self-mortification as a prominent feature and refers to three minor branches of it as indispensable pathways to perfection.[247] These are chastity, obedience, and poverty. His remarks are confined to obedience and poverty. With regard to the former, James has appreciation as well as criticism.[248] The latter, he says, is "felt at all times and under all creeds as one adornment of a saintly life."[249] He refers to the Hindu fakirs, Buddhist monks, Mohammedan dervishes, Jesuits and Franciscans who have idealized poverty as the loftiest individual state, and proceeds to examine the spiritual grounds for what he calls "a seemingly unnatural opinion."

Unlike his ambivalence about obediance, James seems to be most impressed by this aspect of saintliness. He considers the opposition between men who *have* and the men who *are* to be immemorial. He has a quotation from an anarchist poet, Edward Carpenter, who loathed "capital" [and, along with it, probably, the philosophy of "possessive individualism," which is generally recognized as the foundation of the capitalist system[250]]. Carpenter's poem rings the *Dhammapada*-bell and, therefore, deserves to be quoted here.

Not by accumulating riches, but by giving away what you have,
Shall you become beautiful;
You must undo the wrappings, not case yourself in fresh ones;
Not by multiplying cloths shall you make your body sound and healthy, but rather by discarding them . . .
For a soldier who is going on a campaign does not seek what fresh furniture he can carry on his back, but rather what can leave behind;
Knowing well that every additional thing which he cannot freely use and handle is an impediment.[251]

James is impressed by this aspect of the religious life. He understands this to be freedom. "In short, lives based on having are less *free* than lives based either on doing or on being, and in the interest of action people subject to spiritual excitement throw away possessions as so many clogs. Only those who have no private interests can follow an ideal straight away. Sloth and cowardice creep in with every dollar and guinea we have to guard."[252]

However, James' religious background immediately surfaces when he says:

But beyond this more worthily athletic attitude involved in doing and being, there is, in the desire of not having, something profounder still, something related to that fundamental mystery of religions experience, the satisfaction found in absolute surrender to the larger power.[253]

In this last assertion, however, the Buddha and James would part company. There is nothing in the Buddha's explanation of freedom that would make room for ***absolute surrender to the larger power***, unless this larger power be interpreted as the "happiness of oneself as well as of others," as emphasized in the Buddha's admonition to his son, Rahula, quoted above. Thus, instead of *having*, there is here *doing*, that is, working for one's own happiness and for the happiness of others. There is also *being*, in the sense of being happy together.

James was aware that there are excesses involved in some of the reported religious experiences he had examined. Hence his remark: ". . . and we have next to answer, each of us for himself, the practical question: what are the dangers in this element of life? and in what proportion may it need to be restrained by other elements, *to give the proper balance*?"[254]

One thing that James wanted to avoid at all costs is one of the great pastimes of more recent students of comparative religion, namely, to look for the unity of the various religious experiences or traditions. After raising the question regarding the way in which we can restrain the extremist elements in religions experience in order to give a proper balance, James says:

> First, though, let me answer one question, and get it out of the way, for it has more than once vexed us. Ought it to be assumed that in all men the mixture of religion with other elements should be identical? Ought it, indeed, to be assumed that the lives of all men should show identical religious elements? In other words, is the existence of so many religious types and sects and creeds regrettable?
> To these questions I answer "No" emphatically. And my reason is that I do not see how it is possible that creatures in such different positions and such different powers as human individuals are, should have exactly the same functions and the same duties.[255]

This is James' pluralism, which was in a way opposed to his father's monistic view.[256] In assessing the value of saintliness, or rather providing what he calls a "Critique of pure Saintliness," James utilizes the pragmatic method he adopts from Charles Sanders Peirce.[257] He says:

> *We* cannot divide man sharply into an animal and a rational part. *We* cannot distinguish natural from supernatural effects; nor among the latter know which are favors of God, and which are counterfeit operations of the demon. We have merely to collect things together without any special *a priori* theological system, and out of an aggregate of piecemeal judgments as to the value of this and that experience—judgments in which our general philosophic prejudices, our instincts, and our commonsense are our only guides—decide that *on the whole* one type of religion is approved by the fruits, and other type condemned.[258]

Whether James was familiar with the Buddha's discourse to the Kalamas will remain an open question.

Part Two: Revisions and Resurrections

Chapter Fourteen
Psychology in the Abhidharma

The Buddha realized that the substantialist notions of self and object led to inevitable conflict, for there could be no easy agreement between those who uphold different metaphysical standpoints (*diṭṭhi*, *dṛṣṭi*). Metaphysical positions did not lend themselves to flexibility and agreement. A simple call for rejecting metaphysics by appealing to experience was not a very effective way of dealing with the problem. If such a recourse was going to be successful at all, the conflicts among philosophers in the Western world could have disappeared after David Hume's compilation of the *Treatise of Human Nature*. The Buddha, however, proposed an effective way of avoiding such metaphysics. This was by appeasing one's dispositions (*saṅkhāra-samatha*). Yet it was not an easy way. Hence his final admonition: "All dispositions are subject to change. Strive with diligence."[259]

Even though he believed that his teachings were appropriate for all occasions and were not confined to any particular time (*a-kālika*), the difficult path that he was recommending prepared the stage for an ongoing conflict between the "tender-minded" and the "tough-minded."

Evidence for the existence, even during the Buddha's day, of tender-minded disciples who could not abandon the belief in the substantiality of self and object and, therefore, were unable to appreciate the Buddha's analysis of the nature of concepts, has already been referred to. The non-discursive treatment of the doctrine as embodied in some of the discourses like the *Vedalla-suttas* and the *Vibhanga-suttas* of the *Majjhima-nikaya*[260] were intended for such monks. The treatises included in the *Abhidhamma Piṭaka* could easily be described as the work of those tough-minded disciples who were keen on preserving the non-substantialist teachings of the Buddha. The treatment of subject-matter in the Abhidharma texts, whether these belong to the Southern tradition or the Northern schools, does not lend itself to a substantialist interpretation at all. What is achieved in the Abhidharma analysis is clarification and definition of terminology, without sacrificing the non-substantialist tenor of the teachings of the Buddha.

One of the earliest summaries of the contents of the Pali *Abhidhamma Piṭaka* was prepared in English by the late Nyanatiloka Mahathera. Reading through this carefully compiled summary entitled: *Guide Through the Abhidhamma Piṭaka* (1938), one can hardly come across any idea that can be considered incompatible with the teachings embodied in the discourses. Explaining the contents of the first book of the Abhidhamma, namely, the *Dhammasaṅganī* which, along with the *Paṭṭhāna*, is said to constitute the quintessence of the entire Abhidhamma, Nyanatiloka says:

> According to the Abhidhamma, all phenomena of existence may be classified under three ultimate terms or Realities (*paramaṭṭha*): 1. states of consciousness (*citta*), 2. mental concomitants (*cetasika*), 3. corporeality (*rūpa*); to them, as the fourth Reality, Nibbāna is added. Now in the *Dhammasaṅganī*, the first three Realities are treated from the ethical, or more exactly, the karmical standpoint, and divide accordingly to A. karmically wholesome phenomena (*kusala-dhamma*), B. karmically unwholesome phenomena (*akusala-dhamma*), C. karmically neutral phenomena (*avyākata-dhamma*), which make up the first Triad of the Abhidhamma Matrix. Consciousness and mental concomitants may be either karmically wholesome, unwholesome or neutral, whilst corporeality is always karmically neutral; and so is the fourth Reality, Nibbāna.[261]

Ignoring the terminology utilized by Nyanatiloka, such as Reality, etc., it could be said that this is an elaboration or specific formulation of the definition of *dhamma* available in the early discourses of the Buddha (discussed previously). However, in his appraisal of the nature of the Abhidhamma treatment of its subject-matter, Nyanatiloka, while remaining faithful to the nature of the treatment, seems to move away from the both the discourses and Abhidhamma in the way in which he explains the nature of the subject-matter itself. The following quotation is illustrative of this unconscious transition from the discourses and Abhidhamma texts to the interpretation found in the commentarial tradition that represents an entirely different metaphysical perspective.

> Regarding the difference between the Sutta and Abhidhamma, the 'Higher Doctrine', it does not really concern the subject, but rather its arrangement and treatment. Subject in both is practically the same. Its main difference in treatment, briefly stated, may be said to consist in the fact that in the Suttas the doctrines are more or less explained in the words of the philosophically incorrect 'conventional' every-day language (*vohāra-vacana*) understood by anyone, whilst the Abhidham-

> ma, on the other hand, makes use of purely philosophical terms true in the absolute sense (*paramattha-vacana*). Thus, in the Sutta it often is spoken of "individuals', 'persons', of 'I', 'you', 'self', even the rebirth of 'self', etc. as if such so-called individualities really existed. The Abhidhamma, however, treats of realities (*paramattha-dhamma*), i.e., of psychical and physical phenomena, which alone may be rightly called realities, though only of momentary duration, arising and passing away every moment. For in reality, or in the 'absolute sense' (*paramattha*), as the expression runs, there does not exist any real, self-dependent, permanent '*entity*', no such thing as the so-called '*Ego*', but only this ever-changing process of momentarily arising and passing phenomena. Hence, the whole Abhidhamma has to do only with the description, analysis and elucidation of such phenomena.[262]

While most of the above description of the method of treatment in the Abhidhamma may be correct, Nyanatiloka is unaware that he is introducing two concepts not traceable in either the discourses or the Abhidharma texts and which produced most of the unacceptable metaphysical theories. These are the conceptions of "momentariness" (*kṣaṇika-vāda*) and "ultimate reality" (*paramārtha-vāda*), both being the result of adoption of the principle of "reduction." It is this reductionism that led to the sharp distinction between conventional reality (*sammuti*) and ultimate reality (*paramattha*). Just as much as these two terms do not occur in the early discourses in the sense in which Nyanatiloka is using them, they do not occur at all in the canonical Abhidhamma that Nyanatiloka was summarizing. The only occurrence of the term *paramaṭṭha* is in the *Kathāvatthu* where the 'person' (*pudgala*) is said to be unavailable in the sense of ultimate truth and reality (*saccikaṭṭha-paramaṭṭhena*). In fact, a sharply distinguished doctrine of two realities is found only in the commentarial tradition.

Almost every controversy in Buddhist psychology has been generated by the theory of momentariness. Stcherbatsky's *The Central Conception of Buddhism and the Meaning of the Word 'Dharma'*, based upon Vasubandhu's *Abhidharmakośa*, not merely expounds that doctrine of momentariness and reductionism, but also attributes them to the Buddha himself. For some very strange reasons, this work has remained popular and authoritative among modern scholars in spite of all the evidence presented against its fundamental thesis.

The fact that the problems in Buddhist psychology generated by the acceptance of these doctrines did not infect the teachings in the canonical Abhidhamma can be easily demonstrated simply by pointing out to the source material utilized for discussions of these problems. One of the early and comprehensive treatments of the controversies relating to Buddhist psychology appears in E. R. Saratchandra's *Buddhist Psychology of Perception* (1958). Part I of this work includes two chapters, one on "Perception in the Abhidhamma" and another on "The Physiology of Perception."[263] Even a cursory glance at the source material utilized for these two chapters as well as all that follows will reveal one single and undeniable fact, namely, that they all come from the commentaries on the Abhidhamma, especially those of Buddhaghosa, and not a single reference is made to any canonical text of the Abdhidhamma. The conclusion is certain, if anything can be certain, that the canonical Abhidhamma remains untouched by the metaphysical speculations producing controversies that plagued later Buddhist psychology.

It is obvious to critical scholarship that the canonical texts of the Abhidhamma are not the Buddha's own words, in the same way as the discourses are. However, they gained canonical status, and rightly so, because they are merely the systematizations and not improvements or modifications of the Buddha-word. For this very reason, a text like *Kathāvatthu*, said to have been composed during the third century B.C. by Moggaliputta-tissa, needed special justification for inclusion within the canon.[264] Such special justification was not called for in the case of other texts of the Abhidhamma, even though the entire *Abhidhamma Piṭaka* was looked upon as possessing an "exalted status," hence the story of the Buddha's preaching it to the 'gods' in heaven.[265] However, the fact that the *Kathāvatthu* gained canonical status is significant.

Of the 219 controversies discussed in the *Kathāvatthu*, which are not grouped in any systematic way and most of which pertain to minor disciplinary issues, three major philosophical issues stand out. These are (i) the nature of the self (controverted topic 1), (ii) the nature of the objective world (controverted topic 6) and (iii) the nature of freedom (topics 11–53, 176–184, etc.). There can be very little doubt that the controversial views regarding these three issues were gradually emerging in the Buddhist tradition after the Buddha's death and continued to do so during the centuries that followed. These controversial views were not abandoned in spite of Moggalīputta-tissa's criticsm, and they finally blossomed forth as the basic pre-suppositions of the Sautrāntikas (*pudgalavāda*), the Sarvāstivādins (*svabhāva-vāda*) and some of the Mahāyāna schools (*lokuttaravāda*).

Rather sophisticated rationalizations that solidified these three views may not have been available before the third century B.C., even though a movement toward such rationalizations had already begun. Even if these existed, they were not accommodated within the canonical literature. They were, in fact, preserved in the commentarial literature and kept separate from the so-called canonical books. In the Theravada tradition, a whole mass of commentaries grew up side by side with the canonical texts and utmost care was taken not to mix them up. The commentaries that grew up in this manner and come to be preserved in Sri Lanka received final form in the hands of Buddhaghosa, Dhammapāla and others. A similar commentarial tradition is represented by the *Vibhāṣā*, believed to have been compiled a century or so after the Asokan council. Only digests of these commentaries, especially the points of controversy, are available to us in the *Abhidharmakośa*, *Abhidharmadīpa*, etc.

Thus, it would be necessary to observe these differences between the discourses and the Abhidharma, on the one hand, and the commentarial tradition, on the other. It seems that all the evidence is *against* recognizing any set of ideas as being uniquely Abhidharmic or as representing "Abhidharma psychology" that is different from the early Buddhist psychology discussed in the previous sections. In fact, Nyanaponika Thera, who has devoted most of his *pabbajjā* to the study and practice of the so-called "Abhidhamma psychology," has the following to say:

> It is on this very doctrine of Non-self (*anatta*) that all Abhidhamma thought converges and this is where it culminates. The elaborate and thorough treatment of Anatta is also the most important *practical* contribution of the Abhidhamma to the progress of the Buddha's disciple towards liberation. The Abhidhamma provides him with ample material for his meditations in the field of insight (*vipassanā*), concerning Impermanence and Impersonality, and this material has been analysed down to the subtlest point and is couched in strictly philosophical language.[266]

It is indeed the tough-minded approach in psychology represented by non-substantialism that refused to be lulled into a complacent acceptance of any ultimate realities, whether that pertained to something (*kiñci*) that unites the subjective world or the world of objectivity and which remains forever eluding human experience. This can be contrasted with the tender-minded approach in the explanation of human psychology that sought refuge in ultimately irreducible elements (*dharma*), sometimes "flashing forth into existence from nowhere" (as in the atomistic Sautrāntika school), or remaining permanent and eternal in the form of some substance (*svabhāva*), the "unknown support of all those qualities we find existing, which we imagine cannot subsist, *sine re substante*, without something to support them,"[267] (as in the Sarvāstivāda school), or even as "originally pure mind" lying in the hidden recesses of subjective life and which can be brought to the surface when once the doors are slammed on the polluting senses (as in the case of some later Theravāda and Mahāyāna traditions). This tender-minded approach is to be found in the commentaries and manuals containing the psychological speculations of the scholastics who attempted to *interpret* the ideas embodied in the discourses and the Abhidharma, and may properly be called "rational psychology."

Chapter Fifteen
Rational Psychology

The problems raised by the rationalists in Buddhist psychology are many and varied. Most of them are discussed in detail in Saratchandra's *Buddhist Psychology of Perception.*[268] Only those ideas that contributed to unacceptable metaphysical theories will be examined here.

Whereas early Buddhism was satisfied with the explanations of consciousness (*viññāṇa*) as being dependent upon the sense organ and the sense object, the resulting contact being subject to the selectivity of consciousness, the scholastics were involved in further rationalizations as to the nature of this consciousness and the manner in which contact can be explained. This led them to almost insoluable problems relating to consciousness as well as contact.

First, they were compelled to recognize a form of consciousness undiscriminated by selective activity. It is identified as the mere awareness of the presence of the object and is said to produce no knowledge.[269] Knowledge is thus confined to reflective understanding of the object, whereas consciousness itself represents a pre-reflective stage. Several metaphysical presuppositions can be justified by this analysis, and these are the presuppositions that the Buddha endeavored to avoid at all cost.

The notion of pre-reflective consciousness provides a basis for the speculations that the external object can be known as it is without the intervention of any human interest, capacity or dispositions. It could be taken as the stage in which the object can be *experienced* as "it is," even though it cannot be *known* as "it is." This is an extremely substantialist or reductionist approach that highlights the immediate impression as the incorruptible datum on the basis of which knowledge is *constructed.* This is the manner in which the distinction between conceptual (*savikalpa*) and non-conceptual (*nirvikalpa*) forms of knowledge came to be made by the metaphysicians. *Nirvikalpa*, in that context, describes not merely the absence of metaphysical discriminations, as was understood by philosophers like Nāgārjuna and Vasubandhu (see below), but also the non-existence of any form of conception. We have pointed out how, in the early Buddhist context, one can speak of perception as well as conception, without involving oneself in absolute distinctions and discriminations.

A second possible view that emerges as a result of the recognition of a pre-reflective experience is that *knowledge* necessarily involves a "transcendental unity of apperception," an idea that was rejected by the Buddha. In fact, such an implication cannot be ruled out when reading a passage from the *Abhidharmadīpa*, a genuinely Sarvāstivāda text, such as the following:

> The substance called the eye is of the nature of that which sees [i.e., a seer]. In it is produced an action of seeing, when its power is awakened on account of the emergence of the totality of its causes and conditions. The eye does not apprehend independently of consciousness (*vijñāna*), nor does the eye-consciousness know the object unsupported by the active eye. The eye as well as eye-consciousness, with the help of such accessories as light, cooperate simultaneously toward bringing the preception of a given object. The object, the eye, the eye-consciousness, and the light, all manifest their power, i.e., become active and flash forth simultaneously. The object appears, the eye sees, and the eye-consciousness knows it. This is called the direct knowledge of the object.[270]

The substance or the power referred to in the above passage, in relation to both consciousness and the object, represents another way of expressing the metaphysical unity.

The third metaphysical pre-supposition that emerges as a result of the rationalist analysis of consciousness is the existence of an unconscious process constantly interrupted by conscious activity, an idea that gave rise to the extremely metaphysical notion of *bhavaṅga* (comparable to the *ālaya-vijñāna* of the *Laṅkāvatāra*, but wrongly identified with the *ālaya-vijñāna* of Vasubandhu). The most difficult issue that the *bhavaṅga*-theorists had to deal with is how the unconscious process gets disturbed and begins to function as a conscious process. Saratchandra explains it thus:

> In attempting to anwer some of these questions, the scholastics assert that selective consciousness subjectively directed begins after initial sentience. In this stage of *viññāṇa* there is no attention or voluntary direction of the mind towards the objects. This voluntary aspect of attention is variously termed *āvajjanā* (sometimes *āvaṭṭanā*), *ābhoga*, *samannāhāra* and *manasikāra*. But the involuntary act of focussing the senses on an object is also an act of attention, and involves the operation of the mind. It is performed by a variety of 'mind element' (*kiriyamano dhātu*). This act of attention begins to operate after a stimulus has made the unconscious

mind conscious. When unconscious is no more, and attention
is objectively directed, conscious processes start.[271]

Here the emphasis is upon the impinging of the external object on the unconscious in order to produce conscious awareness. A truly unconscious mind would not only be unaware of the external objects but also its own inner composition, namely, its dispositional tendencies. As such, the recognition of a pure and luminous mind is not too far away in the horizon. The stage is made ready for the introduction of the *tabula rasa*, as it happened in the *Laṅkāvatāra*.

Just as much as a reductionist analysis of consciousness gave rise to a series of metaphysical assumptions, even so a similarly reductionist treatment of the physiology of perception brought forth ideas that may seem to go against the earlier doctrine of "dependent arising" (*paṭiccasamuppāda*). Once again we refer to Saratchandra's outlining of the problems faced by the scholastics in attempting to explain how the object of sense comes to impinge upon the sense organ. The question is whether the senses apprehend their objects by coming into contact with them in some manner or other, or whether they apprehend them at a distance. Against the non-Buddhist theories that posited mysterious substances like *vṛtti* that produce the contact, the Buddhist scholastics assumed that the sense organs were composed of matter and that there was nothing psychic about them. However, the Buddhist scholastics, both of the Theravāda and Sarvāstivāda schools, who recognized two distinct types of contact, the eye and the ear functioning without direct contact (*asampattagocara*, *aprāpyakārī*), still had to explain the difference. In fact, Buddhaghosa, who introduced this theory into the Theravāda tradition, had to argue against the prevailing commentarial view that all the five physical senses come into direct contact with their respective objects.[272]

Yet, speculating in this manner, the scholastics were compelled to recognize two aspects of the sense organ, the non-sensitive portion (*sasambhāra*) made of gross matter (*mahābhūta*) and a sensitive portion (*pasāda*) made of subtle matter: the sensitivity of touch being diffused all over the skin. The final solution to such inquiries ends up with recognizing some form of pre-established harmony among different kinds of material objects and the sense organs in producing such sensitivities. In fact, Buddhaghosa had to make a special effort to deny such pre-established harmony[273] which eventually left his explanation rather weak.

Even though the conception of an unconscious mind (*bhavaṅga-citta*), discussed earlier, enabled the scholastics to explain the notions of karma and rebirth with great facility,[274] this same conception contributed to views regarding freedom that are not in conformity with the teachings of early Buddhism.

Buddhaghosa, who was probably thinking of the conception of *ālaya-vijñāna* as explained in the *Laṅkāvatāra* and which he looked upon as a soul-theory in disguise, sets forth the theory of *bhavaṅga* as a better alternative. In contrast to the active thought process, which he calls *vīthi-citta* (*vīthi* meaning 'pathway' or process, and therefore equivalent to the *pravṛtti-vijñāna*), he considered *bhavaṅga* as *vīthimutta*, i.e., mind free of thought-process. In addition to positing a mind free of thought, which in itself may be inconsistent with the conception of mind discussed above in relation to early Buddhism, Buddhaghosa referred to this as the *natural* condition of the mind. Surprisingly, he did not realize that he was presenting a strongly metaphysical view comparable to that of the *Laṅkāvatāra*. In fact, he was utilizing the terminology of the *Laṅkāvatāra* when he described the thought-free (*vīthimutta*) mind as *pakati-mano* (= *prakṛti-prabhāsvara-citta*).[275]

The *bhavaṅga-citta* is thus taken to be the natural state of mind, not only free from all impurities but also of all sense impressions that cause such impurities; hence shining forth in its own radiance. It loses its lustre as a result of external influence. The *ālaya-vijñāna* of the *Laṅkāvatāra* is explained in identical terms (see below), with the further notation that it is also the consciousness of the *Tathāgata* or the womb of the *Tathāgata* (*Tathāgata-garbha*) preserved in its pristine purity.

The above explanation of *bhavaṅga-citta* introduced a totally different interpretation of the notion of freedom (*nibbāna*) from what was recognized in the early Buddhist tradition. *Bhavaṅga-citta* or the *vīthimutta*, distinguished from the sensory activities and thought processes (*vīthi-citta*, or *pravṛtti-vijñāna*), is an echo of the state of cessation (*nirodha-samāpatti*) which, as mentioned earlier, was often mistakenly identified with the conciousness of the freed one (*nibbuta*). The tendency to look upon the consciousness of the freed one as being different from consciousness involved in sensory experience seems to have been strengthened in the Theravāda tradition as a result of Buddhaghosa's theorizing. Ñāṇananda's view, that in the state of freedom both sense experience and conception are totally eliminated and replaced by a new kind of awareness (see section of the "Psychology of Freedom"), represents a continuation of this transcendentalist view advocated by Buddhaghosa, and before him the *Laṅkāvatāra*. Furthermore, the popular Mahāyāna idea of the *bodhi-citta*, which, *sans* metaphysics, may be explained as the possibility of everyone attaining enlightenment provided one makes an effort, now receives a more metaphysical interpretation at the hands of the rational psychology, that it is nothing more nor less than the "original mind" (*pakati-mano*) or the "originally pure thought" (*prakṛti-prabhāsvara-citta*). Freedom, in such a context, becomes the ineffable, non-conceptual, ultimate reality.

It is interesting to note that while Buddhaghosa was inadvertantly or advertantly introducing this substantialist view of consciousness into the Theravāda tradition, Vasubandhu was making a determined attempt to clean up the mess created by the equally substantialist psychology in the *Laṅkāvatāra*.

The psychological speculations explained above are based primarily upon Buddhaghosa's commentaries. Buddhaghosa is said to have arrived in Sri Lanka during the sixth century A.D. and translated the Sinhala commentaries into Pali. To what extent Buddhaghosa remained faithful to the orignal commentaries, no one will ever know, since the original Sinhala commentaries disappeared immediately after Buddhaghosa rendered them into Pali. What happened is still a mystery.

Some of Buddhaghosa's statements provide reasonable grounds for the hypothesis that Buddhaghosa was at least partly responsible for introducing certain metaphysical ideas into the Sinhala Buddhist tradition. Foremost among them is the theory of moments (*kṣaṇa-vāda*) which produced most of the philosophical controversies in the Buddhist tradition. This theory, according to Buddhaghosa's own testimony, was not part of the original Theravāda tradition.[276] Buddhaghosa's commentaries as well as the subsequent manuals make profuse use of this theory. The theory of moments as well as its corollaries, like the conception of *bhavaṅga* and *svabhāva*, were topics hotly debated by the Buddhists in India long before Buddhaghosa arrived in Sri Lanka. Indeed, most of the controversies were appearing in rather sophisticated form even before Nāgārjuna. Nāgārjuna's philosophical enterprise makes sense in the context of such metaphysics only.

Chapter Sixteen
Nāgārjuna and the Mādhyamika School

It may be true that Nāgārjuna was not conversant with the Buddhist literary tradition that came to be introduced into Sri Lanka during the reign of the Emperor Aśoka and which is now referred to as the Southern Tradition. Yet it is almost impossible for a Buddhist scholar like Nāgārjuna to be unfamiliar with a similar Buddhist tradition that was prevalent in India. The Prakrit version of the Āgamas, although different from its Pali counterpart in terms of arrangement of the *sūtras*, was not different at all with regard to the contents. The same holds true of the canonical Abhidharma versions.

The Buddhist scholastic tradition in India came to be incorporated in the *Vibhāṣā*, generally recognized as the compilations of scholars like Vaśumitra during the reign of King Kālāśoka. Whether this scholastic tradition reached the far south before Buddhaghosa cannot be verified as a result of the disappearance of the original Sinhala commentaries. However, Nāgārjuna's familiarity with the entire Buddhist literary tradition—the Āgamas, the canonical Abhidharma, the early Mahāyāna *sūtras* as well as the metaphysical views of the scholastics (Sthaviravāda as well as Mahāyāna)—is clearly demonstrated by his *Mūlamadhyamakakārikā*. As pointed out in our recent work on Nāgārjuna, there is no evidence that he was adopting or attempting to justify any sectarianism in Buddhism. On the contrary, there is a very strong evidence that he was making a determined effort to resurrect the teachings of the Buddha, for which he had to depend mostly on the early discourses. It is therefore unavoidable that Nāgārjuna had to be involved with the philosophical as well as psychological issues dealt with in the early discourses.

Unfortunately, some modern interpreters of Nāgārjuna, following certain philosophical schools in the Western world which still uphold the view that psychology is the "scandal to philosophy," endeavor to present him as a strictly critical and analytical philosopher, thereby neglecting even the limited involvement in psychology which he inherited from the Buddha's discourses. Not only does Nāgārjuna criticize the metaphysical conception of substance (*svabhāva*), but he also takes up the so-called "psychologist's fallacy" that gave rise to the notion of self. Nāgārjuna would primarily be a "critic," as is generally believed, if he were to confine himself to the refutation of such metaphysical views only. However, having critically examined these views, Nāgārjuna occasionally elaborates upon the Buddha's own statements relating to the psychology of perception, of karma and rebirth, or moral responsibility and even the psychology of freedom.

After criticizing the metaphysical theories of causation (Chapter I) and change (Chapter II), Nāgārjuna immediately takes up the problem of perception (Chapter III). Although the general assumption about this chapter is that it is a rejection of sense experience, a careful examination of its contents indicates that it represents a refutation of the "psychologist's fallacy."

Seeing does not perceive itself, its own form. How can
that which does not perceive itself, see others.[277]

There could not be much difficulty in understanding what Nāgārjuna is referring to in this context. The "seeing" referred to here is "seeing one's own self" (*svam ātmānaṃ darśanaṃ*) and is no more than the *cogito* that made "thinking" a mental substance. It is one way of arriving at the notion of an eternal self on the basis of sensory experience. Nāgārjuna begins his analysis with a simple rejection of this fallacy, and then proceeds to explain the philosophical inconsistencies that are generated as a result of such an assertion. This chapter is then followed by another (Chapter IX) in which Nāgārjuna takes up the more sophisticated argument of the rationalists, namely, the transcendental apperception, which is looked upon as a necessary condition for the unity in experience without which the "tender-minded" are generally left with a sense of insecurity. Nāgārjuna was not only conversant with the Buddha's response to such speculations,[278] but also utilized the Buddha's own argument that all perceptions, apperceptions and conceptions are dependently arisen.

Examining the early Buddhist notion of self, it was pointed out that just as much as the belief in a permanent and eternal self constitutes an extreme, the complete annihilation of the notion of self is also an extreme. The two extremes are the results of solidified dispositional tendencies (*saṅkhārā*). The selfless self was, therefore, presented as the middle position. Nāgārjuna's correct understanding of the Buddha's middle standpoint enables him to emphasize the "appeasement of the modes of self and selfhood" (*samād ātmamanī-nayoḥ*),[279] instead of their absolute negation. Thus, Chapter XVIII provides an excellent interpretation not only of the conception of self, but also the extent to which language and thought are intertwined[280] leaving no room for an unnameable and ineffable ultimate reality.

Chapter XVII of the treatise is a good illustration of how Nāgārjuna was able to deal with the Buddha's conception of karma, rebirth and moral responsibilty without having to utilize the idea of a permanent and eternal self or substance, a problem that caused much uneasiness for many Buddhists, including some of the Buddha's immediate disciples, and in modern times, for many a student of Buddhist thought. Some modern interpreters of Nāgārjuna, who looked upon him as a critical philosopher with no thesis to propound, have often glossed over the contents of this chapter, insisting that he had nothing to do with such concepts.

However, Nāgārjuna begins the chapter by praising the Supreme Sage (the Buddha) who explained the psychology of human behavior in terms of volition (*cetanā*). His first attempt is to get rid of the metaphysical explanations of karma and its fruits, according to which the latter is inherent in the former. For him, the view that a person's action remains even when it has not matured (*apākakālāt*), i.e., when it has not produced results, is a physicalistic and substantialist way of looking at the problem of moral responsibility. What is meant by the imperishability of karma is only the survival of responsibility, and this is illustrated by examples like signing a promissory note or falling into debt. Even if the promissory note were to be destroyed, the responsibility for signing it remains until one's obligations are fulfilled. Unless a person does not recognize the importance of volitional action (*cetanā*), he can ignore such promises, thereby rendering all promises meaningless. Here the critical and analytical Nāgārjuna gets involved in the psychological foundations of human behavior and, through that, in moral and social praxis.

The problems of karma and moral responsibility leads Nāgārjuna to the more cumbersome issue of rebirth or human survival. Yet, he was not willing to abandon the teachings of the Buddha in favor of what someone would consider to be a critical standpoint. Looking at the human personality as a psychologist would, Nāgārjuna recognizes the possibility of a person possessing a variety of similar or dissimilar traits of character. Avoiding a substantialist's assumption that if there were to be survival the total personality should survive, Nāgārjuna follows the Buddha's doctrine of "dependence" when he recognizes that survival or rebirth is meaningful even if one of such several traits of character were to be continued.[281]

It is often assumed that a substantialist interpretation of the Buddha's conception of freedom or *nirvāna* can be avoided if it were to be explained as something beyond conceptual thinking and, therefore, transcending description. More often this has led to some form of Absolutism. Nāgārjuna's chapter on the "perversions" (*viparyāsa*), preceding his explanation of both "truth" (*satya*) and "freedom" (*nirvāṇa*), introduces a totally different element into the discussion of these two popular topics. The perversions involve ontological, psychological, moral as well as aesthetic confusions and, as such, play an important part in the determination of truth and freedom, as they did in the early Buddhist tradition.

The four perversions are not the innovations of Nāgārjuna, nor do they receive a purely intellectualist treatment in his hands. The Buddha's own treatment of the subject in the *Aṅguttara-nikāya*[282] is repeated by Nāgārjuna (see section on "Suffering"), with the warning that these perversions and the resulting defilements cannot be explained satisfactorily by adopting a substantialist mode. The perversions are both cognitive and emotive and these are dependent upon one another. However, Nāgārjuna begins his analysis with the emotional, and proceeds to deal with the more cognitive or intellectual confusions that arise as a result. Thus, a proper understanding of the pleasant and the unpleasant (*śubha-aśubha*) distinction can lead to the appeasement (*upaśama*) of grasping for all the categories through which subjective and objective experience is interpreted,[283] thereby paving the way for the understanding of truth (*satya*) and the attainment of freedom (*nirvāṇa*).

With the intellectual and emotional transformation of the human personality resulting from the appeasement of dispositions (*saṃskāropaśama*), the possibilty of adopting substantialist metaphysics in the explanation of truth and freedom is also eliminated. Nāgārjuna's two chapters on truth and freedom reflect this awareness as he continues to battle with his opponents to preserve the pragmatic definition of truth and to resurrect the Buddha's teachings relating to human suffering, its cause, its elimination, and the path leading to its elimination. After that battle, Nāgārjuna settles down to outline in *twelve* verses the *twelvefold* factors (*dvādasāṅga*) utilized by the Buddha to explain the human personality both in the state of bondage and in final *parinirvāṇa*.

We have already presented a detailed study of Nāgārjuna's *Mūlamadhyamakakārikā* in relation to the discourses included in the Pali Nikāyas and Chinese Āgamas. In that study, we have provided sufficient evidence to show that Nāgārjuna was merely re-stating the philosophical "middle path" propounded by the Buddha as stated in his "Discourse to Kaccāyana," (*Kaccāyanagotta-sutta*). It was also pointed out that Nāgārjuna's energies were spent primarily in exposing the futility of metaphysics, especially those of the Sarvāstivādins and the Sautrāntikas. The former, while advocating the non-substantiality of the individual, presented a theory of substantial elements (*dharma*). This substantialist view came to be popularly designated as *svabhāva-vāda*. The Sautrāntikas, who opposed a theory of substantial elements, advocated a form of nominalism (*prajñapti-vāda*), even though they surreptitiously re-introduced the notion of a metaphysical self (*pudgala*).

Utilizing the Buddha's theory of "dependent arising" (*pratītya-samutpāda*), Nāgārjuna demonstrated the futility of these metaphysical speculations. His method of dealing with such metaphysics is referred to as a "middle way" (*madhyamā pratipad*). It is the middle way that avoided the substantialism of the Sarvāstivādins as well as the nominalism of the Sautrāntikas. On the basis of the Buddha's view that all experienced phenomena (*dharmāḥ*) are "dependently arisen" (*pratītya-samutpanna*), Nāgārjuna insisted that all such phenomena are empty (*śūnya*). This did not mean that they are not experienced and, therefore, non-existent; only that they are devoid of a permanent and eternal substance (*svabhāva*).[284] Since they are experienced elements of existence, they are not mere names (*prajñapti*).[285]

Following the method adopted by the Buddha in arriving at a conception of "dependent arising" (*pratītya-samutpāda*) on the basis of the experience of "dependently arisen phenomena" (*pratītya-samutpanna*), Nāgārjuna recognized "emptiness" (*śūnyatā*) as the principle derived from the experience of "empty" (*śūnya*). The attempt on the part of the metaphysicians to convert "emptiness" (*śūnyatā*) into an ultimate reality was foiled by Nāgārjuna when he qualified it as a "dependent concept" (*upādāya prajñapti*).[286] Thus, emptiness is a concept (*prajñapti*), but it is based upon the empirical phenomena that are empty.

The emphasis upon "concept" (*prajñapti*) and the denial of an ultimate reality in the world of experience, which is the implication of the conception of "emptiness" (*śūnyatā*), did not make Nāgārjuna a nominalist. The reason for this is that the concepts, grounded in experience, possessed pragmatic value. Thus, a *prajñapti* or *vyavahāra* or *saṃvṛti* would not be meaningless fabrications of mind. They produce fruits (*artha*) which, in the sphere of morals, turn out to be ultimate fruits (*paramārtha*).

Apart from Chapter XXVI, which contains a positive explanation of the human personality, Nāgārjuna's whole treatise is an unrelenting negation of metaphysical views. Almost 26 out of the 27 chapters are negative in this sense. This created the wrong impression that he was a thinker with no positive thesis to propound. This impression seems to have gained ground during the next two centuries. Popular dissatisfaction with this apparently negative tenor in Nāgārjuna's thought is clearly brought out in the *Laṅkāvatāra*.

Chapter Seventeen
Transcendental Psychology in the *Laṅkāvatāra*

One of the earliest available sources presenting distinctly idealistic thought is the *Laṅkāvatāra-sūtra*. D. T. Suzuki, who has published the most detailed study of this work, describes it thus:

> All that we can say is this that the *Laṅkā* is not a discourse directly given by the founder of Buddhism, that it is a later composition than the Nikāyas or Āgamas which also developed some time after the Buddha, that when Mahāyāna thought began to crystallise in the Northern as well as in the Southern part of India probably about the Christian era or even earlier, the compiler or compilers began to collect passages as he or they came across in their study of the Mahāyāna, which finally resulted in the Buddhist text now known under the title of *Laṅkāvatāra-sūtra*.[287]

The *Laṅkāvatāra* is not far removed from its predecessor, the *Saddharma-puṇḍarīka-sūtra*, in attempting to bring about a unity among the different sectarian views that emerged in Buddhism, except for the fact that the former concerns itself more with philosophical ideas, while the latter concentrated on the means to salvation. The text is definitely Mahāyānistic.[288] Following upon Suzuki's observation regarding the compilation of the text, it may be observed that the collection and presentation of passages dealing with Mahāyāna philosophy is very unsystematic. Indeed, it appears to be one of the earliest attempts to provide a philosophical justification for the Absolutism that emerged in Mahāyāna in relation to the concept of Buddha. The philosophy of Nāgārjuna, especially as it is presented in his *Mūlamadhyamaka-kārikā*, did not provide such justification. On the contrary, it was critical of some of the ideas like "inherent thought of enlightenment" (*bodhi-citta*) inculcated in the popular Mahāyāna.[289] A life of extreme self-sacrifice or self-immolation recommended for the *bodhisattva* was not acceptable for Nāgārjuna and, therefore, he advocated a life of self-restraint rather than self-sacrifice.[290]

If Nāgārjuna's attempt during the second century A. D. was to return to early Buddhism, rejecting the metaphysics of some of the Sthaviravādins as well as the Mahāyānists, it is reasonable to assume that the Mahāyānists needed a more philosophical treatise in order to substantiate their Absolutism. Even if the nucleus of the *Laṅkāvatāra* were to be pre-Nāgārjuna, yet the manner in which the available text has been put together is indicative of the urgency with which ideas were assembled in order to have an authoritative text with which the influence of such negativism could be countered.

One way of arriving at a transcendental conception of reality was already available in the Brahmanical tradition. This is by a complete and unequivocal denial of the subject-object duality and an adoption of a non-dual spiritual reality. Without any hestiation, the *Laṅkāvatāra* takes this route. As explained above, early Buddhism did emphasize the importance of psychology in any epistemological investigation. However, it did not consider consciousness an ultimate reality to the neglect of all other aspects of experience. Yet statements like "The world is led by thought"(*cittena nīyati loko*),[291] "Ideas have mind as a pre-condition" (*manopubbaṅgamā dhammā*),[292] etc. were frequently found in the early discourses. These were sufficient for the Mahayanists to justify their attempt to formulate an idealism as a foundation for their absolutism.

In explaining Nāgārjuna's chapter on "The Examination of *Tathāgata*" (*Tathāgata-parīkṣā*, XXII) we have shown how, among all the epithets used to refer to the enlightened one (*buddha*), the concept of *tathāgata* was most amenable to metaphysical interpretations.[293] Nāgārjuna's treatment of the concept was no consolation to any metaphysician. Yet, the transcendentalist speculation regarding the enlightened one (*buddha*) or enlightenment (*bodhi*) continued among the Mahāyānists in association with the concept of *tathāgata*. The *tathāgata-garbha* in the *Laṅkāvatāra* represents that speculation. The *tathāgata-garbha* could not be anything ordinary for it is the seat of the Absolute. [In this connection, it is interesting to note that in the later Theravāda tradition the sacredness of the *tathāgata-garbha* receives a more physicalistic interpretation when it is stated that Māyā's death had to occur seven days after the birth of Siddhārtha because her womb was so sacrosanct that it could hold no other being.[294]] There was no question of identifying it with the ordinary mind that is polluted but which can be cleansed as a result of training or culture (*bhāvanā*). The conception of mind in the early Buddhist tradition allowed for such possibilities. Thus the non-luminous mind (*na pabhassaraṃ cittaṃ*), which is compared to gold-ore (*jātarūpa*, lit. "the form in which it is born"), could be cleansed and purified through culture, just as gold-ore could be purified in order to produce gold (*suvaṇṇa*) through a process of smelting and washing.[295] Such change could not be part of the Absolute. Therefore, for the first time the "luminous mind" (*pabhassaraṃ cittaṃ*) of early Buddhism, becomes an "*originally* luminous or pure mind" (*prakṛti-prabhāsvara-citta*).[296] With this concept of the pure mind, there comes to be a shift in the meaning of the simile of gold-ore (*jātarūpa*) as well. It is not the gold-ore that gets converted to gold, but the brightness (*kānti*) of gold as well as the pebbles of gold-ore that become visible through purification,[297] the implication being that the brightness is already there and is not the result of purification. This idea, that what is already present is being manifested, an idea that carries all the metaphysical implication of substance (*svabhāva*), could not be acceptable either to the Buddha or to Nāgārjuna.

This originally pure mind needs to be located or identified in some way. Neither the sixth sense organ (*manas*), nor the six types of consciousness that are conditioned by the six senses and the six objects could be associated with this "originally pure mind." *Ālaya*, with its sense of source or location (*sthāna*),[298] rather than its earlier meaning of "attachment," turns out to be the only thing with which such an absolute mind can be identified. This is readily accepted by the *Laṅkāvatāra*. Thus, in addition to the sixth sense (*manas*) and the six types of consciousness (*ṣaḍ-vijñāna*), *ālaya* comes be recognized, which makes a total of eight (*aṣṭa*)[299] forms of consciousness. Since *ālaya*, whatever it represents, is associated with the pure mind and the womb of *tathāgata*, it becomes the original source with *manas* as the troublemaker in producing the notion of self and the six types of consciousness as providing the notion of other (*para*) or the external object (*bāhya*). Eliminating the last two, the *ālaya* regains its original purity or aboriginal status.

"This 'mind' (*citta*) is everything (*sarvaṃ*) in every place (*sarvatra*) and every body (*sarva deha*). Multiplicity is grasped by the evil-minded. This is the 'mind-only' without any characteristics (*citta-mātram alakṣaṇam*)."[300]

We have already indicated how, in spite of many positive statements made by Nāgārjuna, his overwhelming and constant negations of metaphysics created an uneasiness in the minds of those who came after him. While Nāgārjuna's negations were strictly confined to metaphysics of identity and difference, substance and quality, self-nature and other-nature, etc., the universalization of that negation resulted in a wrong understanding of his philosophy by the author(s) of the *Laṅkāvatāra* which is perpetuated to some extent by modern scholarship. *Laṅkāvatāra* lays down its criticism of [Nāgārjuna's] "middle standpoint" (*madhyamaṃ*) with the following statement: "An existent exists in terms of non-cause; it is devoid of permanence and annihilation. Having avoided the two extremes of existence and non-existence, they conceive of a middle."[301]

There could be no mistake about the identity of these philosophers. They were the ones who upheld a middle standpoint (*madhyamaṃ*), not only avoiding existence (*sat*), and non-existence (*asat*), but also permanence (*śāsvata*) and annihilation (*uccheda*) *by* resorting to a theory of uncaused (*akaraṇataḥ* = *anirodhaṃ anutpādaṃ*) existence. If Nāgārjuna's negations of arising (*utpāda*) and ceasing (*nirodha*) are universal, and not confined to metaphysical entities, the idealists of the *Laṅkāvatāra* are right in their criticism. On the contrary, if his negations have only a limited application (and this has been shown to be the case in our detailed study of Nāgārjuna), then the author(s) of *Laṅkāvatāra* (as well as their modern counterparts) are guilty of propounding a metaphysical theory of "mind-only" for wrong reasons.

Chapter Eighteen
Psychology in the Yogācāra

For several obvious reasons, Maitreya and Vasubandhu are here selected as representatives of Yogācāra. Maitreya, who was looked upon as a mythical figure by modern scholars for a long time, has now been recognized as the actual founder of the school. In the Buddhist tradition, Vasubandhu always enjoyed a pre-eminent position as the systematizer of Yogācāra. The publication of *Madhyāntavibhāga-bhāsya* by Gadjin M. Nagao (1964) has confirmed the relationship between Maitreya and Vasubandhu, the latter being definitely attributed the authorship of the *bhāsya*, instead of Asaṅga. Even though our major interest is in providing an account of Yogācāra on the basis of the more systematic treatment of it by Vasubandhu in the *Vijñaptimātratāsiddhi*, we have thought of presenting at least the first chapter of Maitreya's treatise, with comments taken from Vasubandhu's exegesis. This, in fact, would facilitate understanding of Vasubandhu's actual contribution.

The use of the term *yogācāra* to refer to this system has left the Brahmanical interpreters and some of their modern followers with a basic pre-supposition about the nature of its doctrines. For them, yoga could not mean anything other than the method by which sense experience comes to be eliminated and a "transcendental intuition" developed. Thus, as soon as the term *vijñānavāda* is utilized to characterize the epistemological or philosophical standpoint of this school, the Brahmanical interpreters and their Western counterparts had no hesitation in branding this system as a metaphysical "idealism," contrasting it with the "realism" of early Buddhism and "criticism" of Nāgārjuna and the Mādhyamika school. For many a modern Buddhist scholar, especially from the Tibetan Buddhist tradition, for whom Vasubandhu represents a great luminary, and sometimes even a divinity, this distinction between the Buddha and Vasubandhu has caused great discomfort. With the existing interpretations it is not possible for them to look upon either Maitreya or Vasubandhu as true disciples of the Buddha, for they are more aligned with the Hindu tantricism.

Even if Maitreya and Vasubandhu were to be called *vijñānavādins*, there seems to be no justifiable reason for considering them to be idealists advocating some form of an Absolute like the Hindu Brahman. Such an interpretation could emerge only if the yogic method they were advocating as *yogācārins* were to be equated with that of the Brahmanical schools. It is this wrong equation, along with the hidden premise that a philosophy interpreting the way of yoga should necessarily involve a denial of the objective world of experience, that has solidified the view that *vijñānavāda* is "idealism."

In our analysis of the method of yoga in the early Buddhist tradition, we have indicated the manner in which the Buddha brought about a revolution in the contemplative tradition in India by avoiding any form of transcendence of sense experience and conception. If Maitreya and Vasubandhu were true disciples of the Buddha, there is no reason why they could not have adopted the methodology of their master. Both of them could be good "psychologists" without being Absolutists or Transcendentalists. If they could, then *vijñānavāda* need not necessarily mean "idealism" in a metaphysical sense. It could be "psychology" (*vijñāna* = *psyche, vāda* = *logos*) as well. Maitreya's *Madhyāntavibhāga* is intended to provide just such an exposition of psychology. Vasubandhu, who wrote the *bhāṣya* on Maitreya's treatise, presents the same ideas in a more systematic form in his own *Vijñaptimātratāsiddhi*. It is evident from Vasubandhu's commentary on the *Madhyāntavibhāga* that he does not disagree with Maitreya. As such, there seems to be no significant difference between their views. However, their psychological speculation can be clearly distinguished from the more metaphysical ideas presented in the *Laṅkāvatāra*. What, then, is the character of the so-called Mahāyāna to which these two philosopher-psychologists belong? This is similar to the question we raised regarding the Mahāyāna of Nāgārjuna.

With the evidence we presented in relation to Nāgārjuna's *Mūlamadhyamakakārikā* and the information provided here with regard to Maitreya's *Madhyāntavibhāga* and Vasubandhu's *Vijñaptimātratāsiddhi*, it would be possible to discover two forms of Theravāda and two forms of Mahāyāna. Reminding ourselves of these different varieties of Theravāda and Mahāyāna may be helpful in placing the psychological speculations of Maitreya and Vasubandhu in proper perspective.

It has been pointed out that the Theravāda of Moggalīputta-tissa is different from that of Buddhaghosa. The substantialist metaphysics (*pudgala, svabhāva*, as well as *lokuttara-vāda*) is not found either in the early discourses or in the Abhidharma, if this corpus of literature were to be recognized as that of the Theravāda. The moral life inculcated in some of the *Jātakas*, where self-destruction is praised as a noble ideal, is contrary to the ideas expressed in the discourses as well as the *Dhammapada* that emphasizes the avoidance of suffering for oneself as well as others. It seems that we are left with two forms of Theravāda: the non-substantialist and the substantialist. Similarly, the Mahāyāna of Nāgārjuna not only avoids the metaphysics of the substantialist version of Theravāda but also of the substantialist Mahāyāna advocating ideas like the "inherent thought of enlightenment" (*bodhi-citta*), etc. Neither the transcendentalism of *Laṅkāvatāra* nor the absolutism of the *Saddharmapuṇarīka* would be compatible with his teachings, whereas the philosophy of the *Kāśyapaparivarta* and the *Vajracchedikā* would be consistent with his "middle way." Furthermore, the Mahāyāna ideal of self-destruction appearing in the *Avadānas* and the *Saddharmapuṇarīka* cannot be considered a middle path in the moral life recognize by Nāgārjuna.[302] Here again we are confronted with a non-substantialist Mahāyāna and a very substantialist one.

Thus, in relation to metaphysics as well as the moral life, there are two different versions of Theravāda and similarly different versions of Mahāyāna. As two philosophers who emphasized psychology, where do Maitreya and Vasubandhu stand? It is very clear that they were rejecting the transcendentalist psychology of the *Laṅkāvatāra*, and along with it the rational psychology of the scholastics of the Theravāda. The following analysis of the Yogācāra tradition is undertaken with these distinctive traditions in both the Theravāda and Mahāyāna in mind. Just as much as Moggalīputta-tissa and Nāgārjuna were attempting to restore the non-absolutistic and empiricist *philosophy* of the Buddha, Maitreya and Vasubandhu were striving to resurrect the non-absolutist and empiricist *psychology* of the Buddha. Both superficiality and sectarianism need to be overcome in order to appreciate the distinctive genius of these extraordinary thinkers.

Maitreya

Maitreya's treatment of Yogācāra seems to be an attempt to eliminate the *apparent* negative impression caused by Nāgārjuna's explanation of the "middle way" (*madhyamā pratipat*). This negative impression is probably the result of the failure on the part of popular Mahāyāna, as reflected in the *Laṅkāvatāra* (see above), to understand the implication of the eight negations with which Nāgārjuna began his treatise, namely, *anirodhaṃ, anut-*

pādaṃ, anucchedaṃ, aśāsvataṃ, anekārthaṃ, anānārthaṃ, anāgamaṃ and *anirgamaṃ*. Nāgārjuna laid bare the metaphysical implications of the two extremes of substantial existence and nihilistic non-existence and rejected them by utilizing the eight negations. Having done so, he proceeded to explain "dependent arising" as the middle way following which one could achieve ultimate freedom represented by the "appeasement of dispositions" (*prapañcopaśama*) and auspiciousness (*śiva*). He did not make any attempt to relate these three processes in any explicit manner, thus giving the false impression that he was not much concerned with the inappropriate views, but was interested only in the right view developed by the enlightened one. Even though, as shown earlier, Nāgārjuna explained the reasons for rejecting metaphysical views, such views were treated separately, not in relation to the right view.

Nāgārjuna's treatise is intended for the professional metaphysician, not the ordinary person. An ordinary person reading the text would not only be baffled, but also completely put off by it. Thus, if there is any apparent deficiency in Nāgārjuna's philosophy, it is his non-involvement in a clear-cut presentation of the psychology behind his epistemological standpoint. While he utilized a sophisticated analytical method in order to get rid of metaphysics, and constantly used the pragmatic criterion in order to distinguish substantialist from non-substantialist truths, he did not spend much time explicating the psychological foundations of that pragmatism. An epistemological inquiry into the foundations of pragmatism naturally leads one to the psychology of perception, if not human psychology in general. This position is exemplified by the two forms of pragmatism in the Western world, namely, the pragmaticism of Charles Sanders Peirce and the more psychologically oriented pragmatism of William James.

Maitreya's most important contribution toward eliminating this apparently negativistic impression created in the mind of ordinary people is embodied in his treatment of the "three natures" (*tri-svabhāva*), a doctrine that was destined to be extremely popular among the Yogācārins. The three natures are:

i. the unfounded conception (*abhūtaparikalpa*), which is also called the "purely conceptual nature" (*parikalpita-svabhāva*).
ii. the dependent nature (*paratantra-svabhāva*), and
iii. the accomplished nature (*parinispanna-svabhāva*).

The use of the term *svabhāva* in the present context seems to have caused much confusion among the interpreters of Yogācāra. It was a concept criticized and rejected in almost every other verse in Nāgārjuna's treatise. However, even on very rare occasions, Nāgārjuna was compelled to use terms like *-bhāva* (in compound expressions) to denote the idea of "nature".[303] This latter carried no metaphysical implication of an "inherent nature," signifying an ontological reality apart from the phenomena that are being described. It is, in fact, similar to the conception of *dhammatā* or *-dhamma* (in the compound expressions (*jarāmaraṇa-dhamma, vipariṇāma-dhamma*, etc.) in the early Buddhist texts. In other words, the "three natures" (*tri-svabhāva*) did not represent three different ontological commitments, but an explanation of the three psychological processes, namely false conception, right conception and ideal conception.

There is, indeed, an enormous difference between the metaphysical Yogācāra of the *Laṅkāvatāra* and the more empirical Yogācāra of Maitreya and Vasubandhu. When the former speaks of "consciousness only" (*citta-mātra, vijñāna-mātra*, etc.) and proceeds to distinguish three natures (*svabhāva*), it is compelled to distinguish three different forms of consciousness, the first having no authentic existence, the second possessing relative existence and the third representing pure or absolute existence. It is this dilemma that seems to have led Chatterjee to make the following remark concerning what he calls Yogācāra Idealism:

> All forms of absolutism are necessarily committed to the doctrine of plurality of truths. An absolutistic metaphysics cannot stop with empirical experience; it must make a distinction between what *is* and what *appears*. What exists is real; what appears to exist has only a semblance of reality. In itself it is naught. This distinction between phenomena and noumenon, between the relative and the Unconditioned, is the very essence of absolutism. The acceptance of a plurality of Truths—the real (*paramārtha*) on the one hand and the apparent (*saṃvṛti*) on the other—is common to all systems other than rank realism. The realist identifies these two; for him the apparent is the real.[304]

As indicated in our earlier discussions, neither the Buddha nor Moggalī-putta-tissa nor Nāgārjuna recognized "an absolutistic metaphysics." They were quite prepared "to stop with the empirical experience." For that very reason, they did not feel that they "*must* make a distinction between what *is* and what *appears*." Maitreya was probably conversant with what the founder of his system, the Buddha, meant, even if he had second thoughts about what some others in the tradition maintained. Therefore, he "stopped with empirical experience." Because "empirical experince" was the limit, he recognized the importance of consciousness (*vijñāna*). However, in explaining the three natures (*svabhāva*), he wanted to avoid any ontological commitments, and utilized conception (*vijñapti*) to refer to the manner in which what is given in empirical consciousness is conceived of by the different individuals.

The foundation of experience is empirical consciousness characterized by dependence (*paratantra*). There is no denial of duality or even plurality here. Empirical consciousness is dependently arisen (*pratītyasamutpanna*), as the Buddha himself maintained. The rejection of a metaphysical theory of momentary destruction (*kṣaṇa-bhaṅga*) as well as its corollary, the assumption of causal efficiency, do not necessarily mean the abandoning of empirical causation or dependence. Similarly, this empirical consciousness does not allow for the existence of either an independent subject, an *ātman*, or an independent substantial object, a *svabhāva*, both of which are unfounded conceptions (*abhūta-parikalpa*) on the part of the "tender-minded."

A radical empiricist, who is also a pragmatist, now needs to formulate an ideal conception (*parinispanna*) based upon the empirical and dependent consciousness. Without such an ideal conception he would be like a "sessile sea-anenome" waiting for the waves to bring his nourishment. The empiricist moves forward, all the time forming ideal conceptions and modifying the old. As such the ideal conception is not a static reality. However, for the "tender-minded" this ideal conception could turn out to be the ultimate reality in the face of which everything else continues to recede into nothingness like a mirage. For the "tough-minded," this is no more than an abstract founded on a concrete experience. Emptiness (*śūnyatā*) is evident not only in the unfounded conception (*abhūta-parikalpa*) but also in itself, in emptiness (*śūnyatā*), not because emptiness transcends all experience, but because it comes to be grounded in empirical consciousness. The "dependent" (*paratantra*) thus becomes the middle ground on which our dispositions create either a *substructure* in the form of eternal and permanent subject and objects, or a *superstructure* in the form of an ideal. It is this middle ground and the two extremes that constitute the subject-matter of Maitreya's treatise, the *Madhyāntavibhāga*, "The Analysis of the Middle and the Extremes."

Vasubandhu

With such an understanding of Maitreya, it is not difficult to see how Vasubandhu would abandon his Sautrāntika leanings and embrace the discipleship of Maitreya, compiling a commentary upon the *Madhyāntavibhāga*. His older brother, Asaṅga, may have been instrumental in this conversion. Yet it is to be noted that Vasubandhu has not indicated any disagreement whatsoever with Maitreya. The only improvement

Vasubandhu made to the psychological speculations of Maitreya is providing a refutation of the substantialist views as Nāgārjuna did. Vasubandhu's philosophical arguments against the substantialists are embodied in his *Viṃśatikā*. The *Triṃśikā* deals with the same psychological material presented by Maitreya in his *Madhyāntavibhāga*. The selection of the two terms: *Viṃśatikā* (Twenty Verses," even though the text contains twenty-two verses—*Dvāviṃśatikā*?) and *Triṃsikā* ("Thirty Verses") to refer to the two treatises is not unintentional because the former is intended to refute the *two* metaphysical extremes of existence and non-existence, and the latter aimed at expounding the *three* transformations.

*Vasubandhu's Philosophical Speculations (*Viṃśatikā*).* One of the first priorities for Vasubandhu would be to analyse the theories that seem metaphysical. As a Sautrāntika he had been involved in a long-drawn controversy with the Sarvāstivādins. Their theory of self-nature or substance (*svabhāva*) in phenomena was not acceptable to him. Could the Sautrāntika atomism, on the basis of which the Sarvāstivāda theory of substance was criticized, be a satisfactory alternative? It seems that when he abandoned the Sautrāntika perspective and accepted a Yogācarā position, he was primarily interested, not in justifying the metaphysics of popular Mahāyāna, but in finding a way out of the unacceptable epistemological implications of atomism. The acceptance of a metaphysical object, whether it is permanent substance (as in the case of Sarvāstivāda) or one made of atomic particles and, therefore, emitting a series of discrete momentary impressions, raises questions regarding objectivity itself. Any attempt to question such objectivity for the sake of clarity may appear to be unduly harsh on the universally accepted view that objects of experience exist independently.

Vasubandhu's *Viṃśatikā* is devoted entirely to an examination of this routinely accepted view of commonsense. Even though the theories he is criticizing are the metaphysical ones, his questions pertain to a fundamental assumption in commonsense that an object exists independent of experience. In this regard, it is useful to compare the reflections of James relating to "The Stream of Thought," with those of Vasubandhu. James says:

> The reason why we believe that objects of our thoughts have a duplicate existence outside, is that there are *many* human thoughts, each with the same objects, as we cannot help supposing. The judgment that *my* thought has the same object as *his* thought is what makes the psychologist call my thought cognitive of an outer reality.[305]

A challenge to this epistemologist's claim is posed by James in a footnote. "If but one person sees an apparition we consider it his private hallucination. If more than one, we begin to think it may be a real external presence.[306] This, indeed, is a more crude way of saying that revolutions in human knowledge are not always readily accepted. One does not have to quote instances from the so called "scientific tradition" in the modern world to justify this epistemological phenomenon.

A critical philosopher will be compelled to raise questions, in spite of their unpalatability, not because he is interested in demolishing the validity of all human knowledge, but because he is keen on getting rid of the dogmatism with which certain views are adhered to even by very sophisticated philosophers. Vasubandhu's *Viṃśatikā* is intended as an antidote to such dogmatism with regard to the object of experience, and not as a denial of objectivity itself. Just as James referred to the possibility of a hallucination becoming a reality, Vasubandhu is raising questions about reality becoming a hallucination. This is the reason for his examination of dream experience and experiences of "hell." In no way does this imply the abandoning of sense experience as a source of knowlege. What is sought for is a *criterion* by which the more illusory can be distinguished from the less illusory. And this involves an examination of all the conditions that are relevant to any perceptual situation, as well as an analysis of concepts that are relevant to an understanding of every perceptual act.

Having first equated dream experience with sense experience, Vasubandhu proceeds to show how they can be distinguished. In the case of dream experience, the mind is said to be *completely* overwhelmed (*upahataṃ*) by torpor or sluggishness (*middha*),[307] the implication being that in ordinary sense experience such torpor is not completely absent. This is a metaphorical way of indicating how human beings are lulled into a state of acquiescence, without having to think twice before they respond to sense experiences. For Vasubandhu, extreme skepticism regarding the real existence of the object independent of experience is a *means* to awaken a person from his "dogmatic slumber," and not the *goal* of epistemological inquiry. He was keen on demonstrating that conceptual thinking is equally strong in perceptual experience as it is in reflections about the unexperienced or the not-yet-experienced. In that sense, my immediate perception of a copy of Vasubandhu's *Vijñaptimātratāsiddhi* in front of me is not very different from my assumption that the sun will rise tomorrow. Both involve a variety of concepts which, in the immedate context, have become part of the perceptual process. James refers to a widely-held view (e.g., by thinkers like Schopenhauer, Spencer, Hartman, Wundt, Helmholtz and Binet) that considered perception to a be a sort of reasoning operation, more or less unconsciously and automatically performed. James, who was generally unwilling to accept any notion of an unconscious, was not favorably disposed to considering perception to be a mediate inference with a middle term that is unconscious. Instead, he attributes it to "habit-worn path in the brain,"[308] an idea that is more in conformity with that of the Buddha for whom dispositions (*saṅkhāra*) are threefold: bodily, verbal and mental. Thus, when Vasubandhu commenced his treatise with the statement: *Vijñaptimātram evedaṃ* ("This is a mere concept"), he was underscoring the conceptual element in all forms of knowledge claims, whether that be experience or reason.

The study of the *Triṃśikā*, without any reference to the *Viṃśatikā*, has become very popular, since Hsüan Tsang translated the former into Chinese with his own annotation based upon Dharmāpāla's commentary. Hsüan Tsang's motivation for doing so is not clear. However, the availability of several early commentaries on the *Triṃśikā* by Sthiramati, Dharmāpāla and Paramārtha and the absence of such commentaries upon the *Viṃśatikā*, except the one by Vasubandhu himself, should indicate something.

After compiling a treatise in two parts, it would make no sense if Vasubandhu were to compile a commentary on only one of them. The skepticism he raised in the first part of the treatise, namely, the *Viṃśatikā*, was resolved in the second part, the *Triṃśikā*. As such, Vasubandhu could not have left the second part of the treatise without elaborating upon his ideas. Vasubandhu's commentary on the *Triṃśikā* probably got lost at an early date. Since his own interpretation of the *Viṃśatikā* was available, there was no need for his later disciples to spend their energies trying to explain it. However, as no such explanation was available for the second, it was natural for them to write commentaries upon it, thus contributing to divergencies in interpretation.

Yet, there is no justification whatsoever for depending upon the *Triṃśikā* for a complete account of Vasubandhu's views. In fact, it is the absolute dependence upon the *Triṃśikā*, to the complete neglect of the *Viṃśatikā*, that contributed to an utter distortion of Vasubandhu's ideas as well as the position he deserves in the history of Buddhist thought. Indeed, it resulted in the obliteration of the very contribution of Vasubandhu in cleaning up the metaphysical entanglements in Buddhist psychology as presented in the *Laṅkāvatāra*.

Interpreting the *Triṃśikā* without the aid of the *Viṃśatikā*, it is possible to explain *vijñaptimātra* rather superficially as "mere-ideation." However, considering the metaphysical theories rejected by Vasubandhu as well as the extremely critical methods adopted by him in order to expose the untenability of such theories, it is difficult to assume that he would be so dogmatic as to assume the ultimate reality of "mere ideation" or "consciousness only" (*vijñāna-mātra, citta-mātra*).

One of Vasubandhu's major contributions to the psychological investigations in Yogācāra is in highlighting the notion of *vijñapti-mātra* that replaced the more metaphysical *citta-mātra* of the *Laṅkāvatāra*. The relatiship between *vijñapti* and *vijñāna* corresponds to the relationship between *saṇkhā* and *saññā* in early Buddhism and *prajñapti* and *prajñā* (or *prajñāna*) in Nāgārjuna. *Vijñapti* is the means by which *vijñāna* or consciousness is expressed or communicated. Hence it represents a "concept." In the statement *vijñapti-mātram evedaṃ*, the demonstrative pronoun *idaṃ* stands for the experience referred to, whether it be of the subject or of the object, and *vijñapti* defines the object so identified. However, any attempt on the part of a metaphysician to perceive correspondence between such experience and a concept is eliminated with the phrase *mātra*.

In other words, Vasubandhu's statement *vijñapti-mātram evedaṃ* carries the same implication as Nāgārjuna's famous dictum: *śūnyam idaṃ*. The only difference between them is that the former constitutes a more positive description of the experience than the latter. The former explains what is involved in an experience, namely, conceptualization, while the latter describes what is absent in it, namely, substance.

If we are to accept Vasubandhu's own statement, the establishment of *vijñapti-mātratā* was completed by him with the compilation of the *Viṃśatikā*[309]. In other words, the epistemological arguments supporting the centrality of concepts in human thinking are presented here. What follows in the *Triṃśikā* is merely the analysis of human psychology showing how conceptual thinking becomes an inevitable part of human experience. This represents a transition from the problems of philosophy to those of psychology.

Vasubandhu's Psychological Speculations (Triṃśikā). When Vasubandhu moved from an examination of philosophical issues, which he undertook in the *Viṃśatikā*, to an analysis of the psychology of perception in the *Triṃśikā*, he did not abandon either the philosophical method or the ideas he expressed in the former. The philosophical method he adopted was "non-substantialism" (*anātmavāda*). Neither a substantial subject (*ātman*) nor a substantial object (*dharma*) would be acceptable in explaining experience. The reason for this is that the ideas relating to both subject and object are the results of a combination of perceptual and conceptual activity. Neither the self nor the elements would be purely perceptual or purely conceptual. The purely perceptual would not be expressible, just as much as the purely conceptual would have no empirical basis. The empiricist-rationalist controversy or the realist-idealist controversy, comparable to the one that came to be staged in the Western world centuries later, were already known to Vasubandhu because of the speculations of certain Buddhist as well as Brahmanical schools.

Therefore, having abandoned the realist metaphysics, he could not proceed to adopt those of the idealists. The Buddha's own discourses probably prevented him from doing so. Even though the Buddha had emphasized the importance of psychology in any epistemological investigation, he carefully avoided any substantialist or metaphysical involvement. As such, there was no reason for Vasubandhu to adopt the ideas in the *Laṅkāvatāra*, especially after being a critical Sautrāntika. Most interpreters of Vasubandhu have noted that his "idealism" is different from that embodied in the *Laṅkāvatāra*. Yet, very few have gone to the extent of carefully examining what these these differences are. They perceive the differences to be primarily terminological. In the analysis of Vasubandhu's work (see Appendix II), we propose to show that the differences are not terminological only, but are much more radical. Indeed, the radical departures from the current idealistic speculations is reflected in the difference in terminology itself.

The introduction of the term *vijñapti* (concept), in place of *vijñāna* (consciousness), and its philosophical significance has already been referred to. Having established the view that the so-called "real or substantial object" (*sad-artha*) is a "mere concept" (*vijñapti-mātra*), in the *Triṃśikā* Vasubandhu immediately settles down to explain the transformation of consciousness (*vijñāna-pariṇāma*) in order to show how conceptualization takes place. This transformation is threefold: *vipāka*, *manana* and *viṣaya-vijñapti*.

The concept of *ālaya* is borrowed from *Laṅkāvatāra*; but it does not have the same characteristics nor does it function in the same way. It is neither "the originally pure mind" (*prakṛti-prabhāsvara-citta*) nor "the location of the womb (of enlightenment)" (*garbha-saṃsthāna*). As a philosopher, Vasubandhu was involved in a lengthy discussion of the Sarvāstivāda conception of substance (*svabhāva*) and its philosophical implications. To characterize *ālaya* as an "original" (*prakṛti*) is to bring back the Sāṅkhya notion of the "primordial" and along with it the conception of substance (*svabhāva*) with which *prakṛti* was identified. Like Nāgārjuna, he seems to have realized the significance of the Buddha's reluctance to get involved in speculations regarding absolute beginnings. Thus, in order to avoid the metaphysical implications, Vasubandhu first speaks of "resultant" (*vipāka*) and then proceeds to identify it with the *ālaya*[310]. In doing so, he clearly gives the impression that *ālaya* is an ongoing process of consciousness which is the result of various factors (not identified as yet). Such an explanation would bring out the earlier meaning of the term *ālaya* as "attachment," instead of any implication such as "a primordial source."

Indeed, a fresh understanding of the three transformations of consciousness could emerge from a consideration of the three types of correspondences suggested by Vasubandhu. They are:

(i) *vipāka* = *ālaya-vijñāna,*
(ii) *manana* = *mano nāma vijñāna,*
(iii) *viṣaya-vijñapti* = *ṣaḍvidhasya viṣayasya upalabdhi.*

Taking *vipāka*, *manana* and *vijñapti* as three different kinds of functions, rather than characteristics, and understanding *vijñāna* itself as a function (*vijānātīti vijñānaṃ*), Vasubandhu seems to be avoiding any form of substantialist thinking in relation to consciousness.

Furthermore, the dissipation (*vyāvṛtti*) of *ālaya* occurs at the time of the attainment of freedom (*arhatva*). This does not mean that the freed one is without consciousness or the function of being conscious. It only means that his consciousness is not polluted by another function, namely, the function of being attached. As such, *ālaya* in Vasubandhu turns out to be the same as *ālaya* in early Buddhism and *adhilaya* in Nāgārjuna.[311] In other words, it is synonymous with obsession (*prapañca*) which is the result of the process of perception on the part of an unenlightened human being.

With such attachment or obsession functioning in the *ālaya* consciousness it would not be a passive receipient of sensory impressions, a sort of *tabula rasa*. This is how Vasubandhu avoided the metaphysical assumption of the *Laṅkāvatāra*. However, since the other two transformations have not yet been explained, it would be tempting to describe the *ālaya* as an unconscious process or even "a collective unconscious," as has sometimes been done.[312] Vasubandhu's descripton of *ālaya-vijñāna* shows how nicely he avoids, not only the notion of a *tabula rasa*, but also a similarly metaphysical "unconscious" or the still more complicated notion of a "collective unconscious." This latter idea may be elicited from the statement in the *Laṅkāvatāra* (quoted earlier) that "this mind is everything, in every place and in every body." However, no such statement is found anywhere in Vasubandhu's writings.

A mistranslation of *Triṃśikā* 3–4 could possibly give the impression that Vasubandhu recognizes an "unconscious process." A careful examination of these two verses may provide an altogether different view. The two verses can be read as follows:

> It is unidentified in terms of concepts of object and location, and is always possessed of [activities such as] contact, attention, feeling, perception and volition. In that context, neutral feeling is uninterrupted and not defined. So are contact, etc. And it proceeds like the current of a stream.

Unless the term *asaṃviditaka* (not identified, not conceptualized) is taken as applying, not merely to the two concepts (*vijñapti*) of object and location, but to all activities such as contact, attention, feeling, perception and volition (which would make them meaningless), one cannot assume the recognition of an "unconscious process," let alone a "collective unconscious." The continued and uninterrupted flow of experience, together with fringes, with no excessive lust or hatred to break up the neutral feeling, with "flights and perchings" depending upon interest, makes this stream of consciousness the classical as well as the classic version of James' "stream of thought" for the exposition of which he spent almost sixty-six pages.

Finally, *ālaya* is not the mysterious unconscious process, because it is consciousness (*vijñāna*) conditioned by contact, attention, feeling, perception and volition. What leaves the wrong impression that this is an unconscious process is, indeed, the "psychologist's fallacy" generating the view that to be conscious, one must first be conscious of one's own self. This, according to Vasubandhu, is the second transformation.

As mentioned earlier, *ālaya-vijñāna* functions in terms of contact, attention, feeling, perception and volition. These latter can operate as long as there is an element of "interest," without any "self-view, self-confusion, self-esteem and self-love" (= *manana*). The distinction between interest and self-love is crucial. The former is always operative in *ālaya* and the latter comes to be functional in *ālaya* with the second transformation *only*, that is *manana*. Thus, the *vāsanā* that are always operative in *ālaya* could be interpreted as "interest", and the "self-love" (*ātma-sneha*) that is due to *manana* can be considered the "pure Ego." This difference can be seen as one of degrees and James' explanation would be helpful in understanding it.

> Each mind, to begin with, must have a minimum of selfishness in the shape of instincts of bodily self-seeking in order to exist. This minimum must be there as a basis for all further conscious acts, whether of self-negation or of a selfishness more subtle still. All minds must have come, by the way of the survival of the fittest, if by no direct path, to take an in-

terest in the bodies to which they are yoked, altogether apart from any interest in the pure Ego which they also possess.[313]

The fact that conscious experience can take place without the reflective consciousness of self (*manana*) is clearly asserted in the definition of *ālaya*. Vasubandhu's definition of *ālaya* is, therefore, a re-statement of the Buddha's own words: "Depending upon eye and visible form arises visual consciousness," (*cakkhuñ ca paṭicca rūpe ca uppajjati cakkhuviññāṇaṃ*). In this sense, *ālaya* is a resultant. Yet, *ālaya* also functions in terms of interest or instinct which can, in turn, give rise to a full-fledged notion of Self or pure Ego. As such, it contains the "seeds of everything" (*sarvabījakaṃ*). It may be noted that the term "everything" refers to the two other transformations of consciousness, namely, *manana* and *viṣaya-vijñapti*. *Alaya*, so defined, has the seeds of bondage as well as freedom. This is another way of saying that *ālaya-vijñāna* or the "stream of consciousness" can be defiled by allowing *manana* to overwhelm it, that is, allowing the "psychologist's fallacy" to generate the four defiling tendencies (*kleśa*). On the contrary, it can be purified by adopting a non-substantialist (*anātma*) perspective and thereby allowing the *ālaya*-part (i.e., attachment) to dissipate, leaving consciousness or the function of being conscious (*vijñāna*) intact.

The above explanation of *ālaya-vijñāna* makes it very different from that found in the *Laṅkāvatāra*. The latter assumes *ālaya* to be the eighth consciousness, giving the impression that it represents a totally distinct category. Vasubandhu does not refer to it as the eighth, even though his later disciples like Sthiramati and Hsüan Tsang constantly refer to it as such. Instead of being a completely distinct category, *ālaya-vijñana* merely represents the normal flow of the stream of consciousness uninterrupted by the appearance of reflective self-awareness. It is no more than the unbroken stream of consciousness called the life-process referred to by the Buddha. It is the cognitive process, containing both emotive and conative aspects of human experience, but without the enlarged egoistic emotions and dogmatic graspings characteristic of the next two transformations.

The emergence of consciousness of self and the transformation of interest into egoistic pursuits were expressed by the Buddha when he, in his description of the sensory process, changed the language of dependence to one of agency. Vasubandhu, taking over the notion of *manas* from the *Laṅkāvatāra*, defines it in such a way that it becomes more compatible with the Buddha's own explanation than with *Laṅkāvatāra's*. As in the case of *ālaya*, Vasubandhu begins with the description of the function—*manana*—and proceeds to identify it with the consciousness called *manas* (*mano nāma vijñāna*).

This, according to the *Laṅkāvatāra* as well as the later interpreters, is the seventh consciousness, distinct from the six forms of consciousness recognized by the Buddha. Here, again, Vasubandhu is completely silent. Instead, he defines it as another function that emerges depending upon the stream of consciousness (*ālaya-vijñāna*).

The use of the term *manana* is significant. It is "thinking" about the various perceptions occurring in the stream of consciousness. There seems to be little doubt that this is the situation where a human being commits the "psychologist's fallacy," comparable to what is expressed by the verb *maññati* in the early Buddhist tradition (see section on "Conception").

This is an unequivocal rejection of the very foundation of a conception of *sākṣin* ("the agent of perception") so dear to the Brahmanical tradition. It seems that every yogin who came out of his meditation and propounded a theory of *ātman* was committing the psychologist's fallacy. The result of this epistemological confusion is that, instead of being able to locate or identify the self, which many philosophers like the Buddha, Nāgārjuna, Maitreya, Hume[314] and James[315] found to be the most elusive entity, a person falls into a quicksand that engulfs him in no time. His interests and emotions, which enabled him to deal with the world of experience in a fruitful and harmless way, now turn out to be extremely defiled or disturbing tendencies. Vasubandhu refers to four such defilements or taints (*kleśa*), namely, self-view (*ātma-dṛṣṭi*), self-confusion (*ātma-moha*), self-esteem (*ātma-māna*) and self-love (*ātma-sneha*).[316] *Manas* is thus not a special kind of consciousness recognized in Yogācāra and not found in the early Buddhist tradition. As the Buddha aptly remarked, it is the sort of reflection that throws man into the lap of an unseen "beauty queen" (*janapada-kalyāṇī*).[317] Vasubandhu is simply elaborating upon the Buddha's view that the notion of a "pure Thinker playing the 'title-role'"[318] is the cause of all the desires and confusions that prevent man from enjoying the satisfactions in ordinary human life, let along the happiness of freedom.

If Vasubandhu were to be a true idealist, he should have considered *manana* as the most important function in experience, for an idealist would consider the sense of identity of the knowing subject, the pure Ego, to be the only vehicle by which the world hangs together. However, he has completely rejected the efficacy of such identity. Instead he has shown how such a notion of identity leads to attachment and confusion, rather than freedom.

His question then is: Would the sense of identity of the known object perform exactly the same unifying function, even if the subjective identity were abandoned? In other words, would the denial of the pure Ego and the assertion of the reality of the objective world settle the epistemological issue that causes confusion and prevents the attainment of enlightenment and freedom? The *Viṃsatikā* presented an emphatic denial of such a possibility.

What is most significant in Vasubandhu's explanation of the so-called object of perception is that he replaces *viṣaya-vijñāna* ("consciousness of the object") with *viṣaya-vijñapti* ("concept of the object"). If he were an absolute idealist, he could have simply denied the reality of the external object and maintained that it is "mere-consciousness" (*vijñāna-mātra, citta-mātra*). In that case, the responsibility of proving the non-existence of the object would have fallen upon him. This, certainly, is not going to be an easy task for any philosopher unless he is willing to plunge himself into metaphysical speculations more troublesome than the recognition of the external object. Thus, the metaphysical idealist's task is no more different from that of the metaphysical realist. As reiterated before, Vasubandhu who was extremely hostile to the views of the metaphysical realists, whether such views pertained to permanent and eternal substances (*svabhāva*) or discrete atoms (*paramāṇu*), could not be blind to the implications of the metaphysical idealism.

If the consciousness of the object is not grounded in the experience of an object, or if the object is a mere fabrication of consciousness, how did that consciousness come to fabricate it? Did consciousness carry within itself the ideas of objects as "innate ideas" from the first appearance of consciousness, whenever that may have been? Vasubandhu did not need any instruction regarding the problem of "innate ideas," especially after writing a treatise like the *Abhidharmakośa* dealing at length with "inherent nature" or "substance" (*svabhava*). If such ideas were not found inherently in consciousness, they could not have appeared there unless they were implanted by a Supreme Power. This was a view that even the metaphysically inclined Buddhists would not advocate. As such, Vasubandhu could not involve himself in any discussion of the *consciousness of the object* (*viṣaya-vijñāna*) as a metaphysical idealist would be willing to do.

However, there was nothing to prevent him from discussing the concept of object (*viṣaya-vijñapti*) and this he unhesitatingly does. In his explanation of *ālaya-vijñāna*, he has already accounted for the experience of the object (= cognitive) as well as the emotive and conative elements associated with that experience. With reflective thinking (*manana*) or the "psychologist's fallacy," he has explained the manner in which "owned" experiences turn out to be extremely personalized or private experiences. With the concept of the object, Vasubandhu describes how human beings are susceptible to grasping after the object (*viṣayasya upalabdhi*).

Vasubandhu is critical of the third transformation, not because it relates to the conception of an object, but because it generates grasping after a "real object" (*sad artha*), even when it is no more than a conception (*vijñapti*) that combines experience and reflection. Just as the stream of experience that continues to swell with cognitive, emotive as well as conative elements is often interrupted by reflection (*manana*), thereby producing a *feeling* of oneself, of individuality, so does the dissection of that stream of experience into segments leaving no fringes produce the notions of distinct objects that are *felt*. Just as the *feeling* of oneself, of individuality can strengthen the dispositions and transform the individual interests and emotions into "self-view, self-confusion, self-esteem and self-love," producing the notion of a permanent and eternal self or soul (*ātman*), so does the experience of distinct objects give rise to the belief in their independence and produce grasping (*upalabdhi*) that leads to a mass of defiling tendencies, both primary and secondary, of which Vasubandhu gives a long list.[319]

It would be tempting for someone to assume that the stream of experience or consciousness (*ālaya-vijñāna*), uninterrupted by reflection (*manana*) as well as by the conception of object (*viṣaya-vijñāpti*), is a "pure experience," comparable to the conception of pure experience developed by James in his essay on "Does consciousness exist?"[320] However, when doing so, one needs to qualify what is meant by the term "pure" in both contexts. The stream of experience recognized by both Vasubandhu and James is filled with cognitive, emotive as well as conative elements. As such, it contains the conditions or the seeds (*bīja*) that could produce wrong views about self as well as the objective world. But "pure experience" as developed in the European philosophical tradition could possible not recognize such conditions.

Something like the "psychologist's fallacy" seems to have been operative in the *Laṅkāvatāra* when it recognized *eight* different types of consciousness—the *ālaya, manas* and six *vijñānas*. Vasubandhu's reluctance to admit *ālaya* and *manas* as distinct forms of consciousness has already been mentioned. This fact is clearly brought out where Vasubandhu relates the fundamental consciousness (*mūla-vijñāna* = *ālaya-vijñāna*) to the five forms of consciousnes associated with the five physical sense organs: "The arising of the five forms of consciousness, together or separately, within the foundational consciousness, is like the waves in the water."[321]

The foundational consciousness is the uninterrupted flux of experience represented by the *ālaya-vijñāna*. It is within this foundational consciousness that all other forms of consciousness occur. The early Buddhist tradition did not recognize a consciousness (*viññāṇa*) distinct from the six types of consciousness that are conditioned by the six sense and their corresponding objects. The stream of consciousness (*viññāṇasota*) admitted by the Buddha represents all the six forms of consciousness, not a mysterious "unconscious process" that lies beneath conscious activity. The empiricist psychology discussed above does not provide any evidence that supports the theory of a hidden wilderness in the human mind. The dispositions (*saṅkhārā*) are sometimes interpreted as constituting this wilderness. But the statement of the Buddha quoted in support of this view simply says that dispositions can be formed through deliberate activity (*sampajāno*) or without such deliberation (*asampajāno*).[322] And this does not seem to imply the existence of an unconscious process. All that is admitted which may seem to require a theory of a hidden recess in the mind is memory. As pointed out earlier, a metaphysical unconscious process is not a necessary condition for explaining the phenomenon of memory. According to James, the brain process was sufficient to explain memory and it also places a limitation on what can be remembered. Without the assistance of such modern techniques as neurosurgery, the Buddha realized the limitations of the memory process because of his involvement in yoga.

Yoga, as understood by the Buddha, did not reveal a hidden wilderness. He did not discover a source of psychic energy or the various instincts that produce the energies of the so-called *id* to be restrained by those of the *ego* and the *superego*. These would be very substantialist concepts for him. The yoga of appeasement (*samatha*) enabled the Buddha to gradually get rid of sense experience and conception, and realize their emptiness and non-substantiality. This emptiness and non-substantiality are not the results of comparing the so-called artificial behavior of the conscious person with the natural instincts of the unconscious. He did not discover a hell beneath with murderers, perverts, robbers, lunatics, and others. All such human behavior is, for him, dependently arisen and represents the working of conscious experience and conception dominated, in varying degrees, by the *mano* in "search of a soul" (*bhava-diṭṭhi*) or seeking to annihilate it (*vibhava-diṭṭhi*). Avoiding such extremes, the appeased *mano* is said to bring about the blissful experience of freedom (*nibbāna*).

Chapter Nineteen
Conclusion: Philosophical Implications

If the interpretation of the mainline Buddhist psychological tradition is valid and its comparison with the analytical psychology of William James is appropriate, it is also possible that the philosophical reflections of Buddhism and James could also be compatible. Such a comparison will require a separate volume. Yet, on the basis of the psychological material presented above, it will be possible to indicate briefly how and why Buddhist and Jamesean pragmatism came to emphasize the relevance of ethics for the determination of both logic and aesthetics, when the more substantialist thinkers were subordinating ethics to logic or aesthetics.

The above presentation of the psychological material in Buddhism may appear rather haphazard to those who are used to treating psychological topics in a rather systematic way, dealing first with bare sensation or feeling, then with perception and conception. In fact, the present treatise contains no chapter entitled "Sensation." Instead, the material is examined in the chapter on "Emotions and the Foundation of Moral Life," which follows, instead of preceding, the chapter on "Perception." This was prompted by the need to clarify the Buddha's notion of self, especially in the context of enormous misunderstanding or misinterpretations of his notion of no-self (*anatta*). In fact, Buddhist psychology may aptly be called an adventure in non-substantialism. For this reason, the analysis of feeling or sensation is undertaken after the chapter on the "Selfless Self." When a philosopher with a speculative bent of mind proceeds on the *a priori* assumption that the first impression of sense appear on the luminous and blank screen called the mind, a genuine empiricist, even according to Peirce, cannot afford to ignore that "our percepts are the results of cognitive elaboration." According to Peirce, " . . . in truth, there is but one state of mind from which you can 'set out,' namely, the very state of mind in which you actually find yourself at the time you do 'set out'—a state in which you are laden with an immense mass of cognition already formed, of which you cannot divest yourself if you would; and who knows whether, if you could, you would not have made all knowledge impossible to yourself?"[323] This indeed, is what compelled both the Buddha and James to take a good look at the total personality before proceeding to analyse the nature of feeling or sensation.

However, in spite of Peirce's above statement, this analysis of feeling tends to be more rationalistic, as is evident from his explanation of the principles of phenomenology. Outlining his theory of Firstness, Peirce says:

> Among phanerons there are certain qualities of feeling, such as the colour of the magenta, the odor of attar, the sound of a railway whistle, the taste of quinine, the quality of the emotion upon contemplating a fine mathematical demonstration, the quality of feeling of love, etc. *I do not mean the sense of actually experiencing these feelings, whether primarily or in any memory or imagination.* That is something that involves these qualities as an element of it. But I mean the qualities themselves which, in themselves, are mere may-bes, not necessarily realized.[324]

Where Locke recognized the experienced qualities and believed that there *ought* to be a substance in which these qualities "inhere," Peirce explicitly denies such inherence[325] and places the qualities themselves in the same position as Locke's substances. Thus, Firstness is attributed to outward objects which have capacities in themselves and which may or may not to be already actualized. "In the idea of being, Firstness is predominant, not necessarily on account of the idea of *abstractness* of that idea, but on account of its *self-containedness*. It is not in being separated from qualities that Firstness is most predominant, but in being something peculiar and idiosyncratic. The first is predominant in *feeling*, as distinct from objective perception, will and thought."[326]

This conception of the Firstness or the positive qualitative possibility which may be defined as a "pure feeling" enables Perice to admit the primacy of aesthetics. He says "Aesthetics is the science of ideals, or of that which is objectively admirable without any ulterior reason. I am not well acquainted with this science; but it ought to repose on phenomenology. Ethics, or the science of right and wrong must appeal to Aesthetics for aid in determining the *summum bonum*. It is the theory of self-controlled, or deliberate conduct. Logic is the theory of self-controlled, or deliberate, thought; and as such, must appeal to ethics for its principles."[327]

Peirce considers "honesty" as an important pre-requisite for all forms of probable inference.[328] Hence the subordination of logic to ethics.

However, when the analytical psychologist James probed into the nature of human feeling, he refrained from speculating about any "mode of being," as did Peirce, but recognized the *given*, the objective existence as well as the experiencing individual stream of consciousness as the conditions for feeling or sensation without giving special priority to any one of them. Thus, the so-called given turns out to be a result of both the object and consciousness. In the case of a human being who has once opened its sensory faculties to the first impression, a pure sensation or feeling is a mere theoretical construct.[330] When this approach is adopted in the context where an analysis needs to be made "relative to the perceptions and active powers of human beings,"[331] and not the divine, James is compelled to recognize an important ingredient in consciousness which makes human knowledge and understanding possible, namely, *selectivity*.

If selectivity were to be based upon aesthetics, i.e. the science dealing with "that which is objectively admirable without any ulterior reason," (as Peirce defined it) it would be incumbent upon the ordinary person to consider the decisions of the aesthetician as the ultimate criterion for deciding what is moral and immoral, good and bad, irrespective of whether such decision contributed to his own happiness or the happiness of others. This would be another version of the conception of duty so enthusiastically espoused by Peirce's mentor, Immanuel Kant.

On the contrary, James is willing to recognize the function of *interest* or disposition of the experiencing stream of consciousness in the matter of selecting what is relevant and useful from the "big blooming buzzing confusion" or the "sensible muchness." This seems to be the reason for James' emphasis upon the moral criterion, rather than aesthetic.

The philosophical significance of the Buddha's statement analysing the process of perception could be better appreciated in the light of the above discussion. For the buddha the sense organ (*ajjhattika āyatana*), the object of sense (*bahiddhā āyatana*) and the stream of consciousness (*viññāṇa*) which comes to be conditioned by the sense organ and the object, are the pre-requisites of all knowledge. When all such pre-requisites are available one can speak of contact (*phassa*). For this reason, when examining any metaphysical theory regarding existence, he often remarked that it is dependent upon contact (*phassapaccayā*). Theories that advocate absolute objectivity or absolute subjectivity are abandoned because such theories cannot be formulated independent of contact (*aññatra phassā*).[332]

The recognition of the importance of the stream of consciousness (*viññāṇa*) as a pre-requisite for contact cannot be overemphasized. This would mean that contact is determined by the selective activity of consciousness, this latter being colored by some form of interest (*saṅkhāra*) which is part of that consciousness. Thus, when contact gives rise to feeling or sensation (*vedanā*), that selective activity colored by interest is already operative. In this way, at least a bare element of choice dominated by the most rudimentary form of interest (*saṅkhāra*) enters the scene even before the more explicit emotive or aesthetic judgments could be made. It has already been pointed out how this emotive or aesthetic judgment comes to be determined, not by simple interest, but by a more elaborate and sophisticated self-consciousness or the ego when the act of percepton is completed.

When the Buddha stated that contact (*phassa*) is the foundation of all philosophical theorizing and that one of the factors operative in contact is interest (*saṅkhāra*), he was emphasizing the need to evaluate such philosophical theories, whether they be rational, empirical or metaphysical, in terms of their fruitfulness (*attha*). This seems to be the reason for his emphasizing the primacy of moral considerations over and above aesthetic and logical concerns.

It is this method of deconstruction in the analysis of experience that elminated the belief in the *purity* of any form of experience, feeling, sensation or even knowledge, that is represented by the Buddha's conception of non-substantiality (*anatta*), leaving in its trail, not any form of absolute nothingness or emptiness, but the empirical notions of the "dependent" (*paṭiccasamuppanna*) and "dependence" (*paṭiccasamuppāda*) providing justification for an enlightened form of ethical pragmatism.

Appendix I
Maitreya's *Madhyāntavibhāga*
Lakṣaṇa-pariccheda

(The text is based upon Gadjin M. Nagao's edition, and retains the dialectical pecularities preserved in it.)

Analysis of Characteristics (*Lakṣaṇa-pariccheda*)

1. *Abhūta-parikalpo 'sti dvayan tatra na vidyate,*
   śūnyatā vidyate tv atra tasyām api sa vidyate.

There is unfounded conceptualization. Therein no duality is evident. However, emptiness is evident in that context. That (emptiness) is evident even in relation to itself.

(*MVB* p. 17.)

The duality referred to here is (i) that which is to be grasped or is graspable (*grāhya*) and (ii) the grasper (*grāhaka*). Maitreya begins with the rejection of one of the primary epistemological assertions of the substantialist thinkers, namely, that every act of perception necessarily involves either a transcendental apperception or consciousness of self or a substantial object. With such an assertion of a self, the perception turns out to be something grasped and that something is independent of the grasper. There is here no denial of perception, but merely of the involvement of two independent metaphysical entities in producing such a perception. Vasubandhu is very specific in his explanation of "emptiness." It is related to the unfounded conceptualization (*abhūta-parikalpa*). The emptiness in the unfounded conceptualization is the absence of the grasper and the grasped. It is, therefore, not an absolute emptiness. In fact, such an absoluteness is immediately rejected in the last *pāda* of the quatrain.

Taking the unfounded conceptualization, where what is assumed to exist is not existent (*yad yatra nāsti*) and, therefore, is empty of *it* (*tat tena śūnyaṃ*), one perceives it (i.e., the conceptualization) as it "has come to be" (*yathābhūtaṃ*). Whatever is left over (*avaśiṣṭaṃ*) in that context, namely, conceptualization, that indeed is present (*tat sad ihāsti*). This, undoubtedly, is the recognition of the inevitability of conceptualization in any act of knowing (i.e. *prajānana*). It is a rejection of the view that the so-called emptiness is beyond any form of conceptualization. It is the non-perverse (*aviparīta*) characteristic of emptiness.

In other words, emptiness (*śūnyatā*) is a conceptualization (*parikalpa*) founded upon the perception of "the empty" (*śūnya*). As such, it is not unfounded (*abhūta*), but founded on the stream of experience upon which no metaphysical subject or object is superimposed.

It may be noted that *parikalpa* need not necessarily be imagination, for it is used synonymously with *kalpa* (see I.5, *abhūta-kalpa*). What makes it an imagination is the fact that it is *abhūta* (unfounded). Thus, both *parikalpa* and *kalpa* can be translated as conception, and it turns out to be an imagination only when that concept is assumed to be of *something* that belongs to *someone*, this latter being a "perfectly wanton assumption" (James, *PP*. I.274).

In spite of Vasubandhu's above analysis, the most recent examination of this treatise begins with a basic pre-supposition that he recognizes two levels of reality: the phenomenal and the absolute (see Thomas A. Kochumuttom, *A Buddhist Doctrine of Experience*, p. 29), a supposition that is popular among most modern interpreters of Buddhism. For this reason, we propose to ignore all modern commentaries (except when it becomes necessary to point out continuing misinterpretations), both on Maitreya and Vasubandhu and analyse their treatment of the Buddhist notion of experience in the light of the tradition starting with the Buddha as preserved in the early discourses where no *such* doctrine of two realities is to be found.

2. *Na śūnyaṃ nāpi cāśūnyaṃ tasmāt sarvvaṃ vidhīyate,*
satvād asatvād satvāc ca madhyamā pratipac ca sā.

Being neither empty nor non-empty, everything is, therefore, defined in terms of existence, non-existence and existence. That itself is the middle path.

(*MVB* p. 18.)

If there is any reality, it is not empty in the way the Sautrāntikas explained emptiness, that is, as momentary destruction (*kṣaṇa-bhaṅga*). Nor is it non-empty in the manner in which the Sarvāstivādins envisaged change and impermanence, that is by assuming a permanent and eternal substance. The metaphysical speculations of these two schools created innumerable difficulties for Buddhist discourse. Their forms of conceptualization left no room for the explanation of change and continuity. If something were to change, that change had to be absolute change. If something were to continue, that continuity should be in terms of something that is permanent and eternal.

While the metaphysics of permanence was adequately dealt with by the Buddha, as it was the predominant view of the *Upaniṣads*, the notion of momentary destruction (*kṣaṇa-bhaṅga*) was unknown to him. Interestingly, in rejecting permanence, the Buddha did not resort to an equally metaphysical theory of momentary destruction. Even though he criticized the Upaniṣadic notions of existence (*astitva*) and identity (*ekatva*), as well as the materialist conception of non-existence (*nāstitva*) and difference (*nānatva*), he did not insist upon a theory of momentary destruction either of phenomena or of the experience of such phenomena. The Sautrāntika failure to understand this position led them to a nihilistic view, compelling some of the later Buddhists, like the authors of the early *Prajñāpāramitā* literature, to adopt a discourse that is slightly different from that of the Buddha, yet retaining the spirit of the Buddha's doctrine of non-substantiality. Thus, Vasubandhu quotes the *Prajñāpāramitā* statement: "All this is neither empty nor non-empty," as the motivation for Maitreya's explanation. In fact, the language utilized in the *Prajñāpāramitā* is summarized here as "existence (*sat*), non-existence (*asat*) and existence (*sat*)." When reading this statement, one cannot ignore the constant refrain in the *Prajñāpāramitā*, especially the *Vajracchedikā*, (p. 36) which reads:

"Personal existence, personal existence," as no personal existence . . . that has been taught by the Tathāgata.
Therefore, it is called "personal existence!"

According to Vasubandhu, the first *sat* refers to the existence of the unfounded conceptualization (*abhūta-parikalpa*); *asat* implies the non-existence of the metaphysical twins (*dvayasya*, i.e., the graspable and the grasper). The second *sat* signifies the Buddha's own understanding of existence, namely, the middle path (*madhyamā pratipat*) of emptiness in relation to the unfounded conceptualization (*abhūtaparikalpe śūnyatayā*).

The first pair of *sat* and *asat* cancels each other, leaving the second *sat*. The first *sat* being an unfounded conceptualization, the second *sat* is regarded as a well-founded conceptualization (*yathābhūta-parikalpa*). This distinction would be made clear later on. Having explained what sort of existence and non-existence are involved in the unfounded conceptualizations, Maitreya proceeds to examine its "own characteristics" (*svalakṣaṇa*).

3. *Artha-satvātma-vijñapti-pratibhāsam prajāyate,*
vijñānaṃ nāsti cāsyarthas tad abhāvāt tad apy asat.

Consciousness arises reflecting the object, being, self and concept. However, its object does not exist. Because that [object] does not exist, that [i.e., the perceiving consciousness] too is non-existent.

(*MVB* pp. 18–19.)

Why certain conceptualizations are unfounded (*abhūta*) is explained in this verse. They are assumed to have their own characteristics (*svalakṣaṇa*) which are not founded in experience. Four such conceptualizations are mentioned:

i *artha* (real self-existing object),
ii *sattva* (real self-existing being),
iii *ātma* (real self-existing self), and
iv *vijñapti* (ultimately real concepts).

None of them, in truth, are self-existing entities. (i) The experience that appears (*pratibhāsate*) in the form of material elements give rise to the appearance of a real object (*artha*) that exists independent of experience. (ii) The appearance of a real being (*sattva*) is occasioned by the existence of the five sensory faculties on the basis of which a real distinction is made between one's own stream of existence (*sva-saṃtāna*) and that of another (*para-saṃtāna*). It is interesting to note that Vasubandhu utilizes the five sensory faculties, instead of the sixth (i.e., the mind) to identify one's own personality and that of another. This may be taken to imply that the sharp dichotomy between oneself and another is generally made on the basis of the perception of the physical personality, rather than the psychic personality. (iii) The appearance of self (*ātma*) is the activity of the defiled mind (*kliṣṭaṃ manaḥ*). It is the mind defiled by self-love, self-esteem, etc. (see *Triṃś* 6) that gives rise to the unfounded conceptualization relating to a metaphysical self existing independently of the flux of experience. (iv) Finally, all the concepts (*vijñapti*) are based upon the six types of consciousness (*ṣaḍ-vijñānāni*). However, they do not represent any substantial objects existing independently.

Thus, what is denied is not any and every form of consciousness. Vasubandhu's commentary makes this very clear. The denial pertains to four types of entities envisaged. In the absence of four such graspable objects (*grāhyasyārthasya*), the grasping consciousness (*grāhakaṃ vijñānaṃ*) that is supposed to perceive such entities, namely, the exaggerated function of *manas*, also becomes meaningless.

4. *Abhūtaparikalpatvaṃ siddham asya bhavaty ataḥ,*
na tathā sarvvathā 'bhāvāt tat kṣayān muktir iṣyate

Such is the manner in which its [i.e., the concept's] unfounded nature comes to be established. Because such absence is not universal, through its cessation release is expected.

(*MVB* p. 19.)

The unfounded conceptualizations do occur, giving rise to false impressions about the existence of metaphysical entities. Yet such unfounded conceptualizations are not universal phenomena, for if they were to be universal, then, as Vasubandhu insists, there would be "mere illusion" (*bhrānti-mātra*). If all conceptualizations are unfounded, there would be no way in which one can attain release. It is only through the waning of unfounded conceptualizations that one can attain release.

This is a clear recognition of the fact that a person who has attained freedom (*nirvṛta*) can continue to perceive and conceptualize without having to fall away from freedom. He can not only have experience, but also can engage in intellectual activity without being involved in any notion of self or other, grasper and the graspable. He does not use a different kind of language. While utilizing the same language, he refrains from all metaphysical involvements or assumptions.

5. *Kalpitaḥ paratantraś ca parinispanna eva ca,*
arthād abhūtakalpāc ca dvayābhāvāc ca deśitaḥ.

The conceptualized, the dependent and also the achieved are spoken of in relation to the real object, the unfounded conceptualization and the absence of the twofold [respectively].

(*MVB* p. 19.)

Vasubandhu takes *kalpita* as *parikalpita*, distinguishing it from *abhūtaparikalpa*. What is conceptualized is the object. Unless it is assumed that all conceptualizations are false, which would contradict the statement in the previous verse, it is possible to recognize that a concept is a translation of the thought relating to the object and, therefore, its nature. However, when unjustified assertions are made, as in the case of the "psychologist's fallacy," (see section on "Selfless Self"), the nature of the object as *the* thought disappears, making it the object of thought. The thought thus becomes the cognizer of the object. This, in its turn, leads to a further complication.

When thought becomes the cognizer *of* the object, the object could be independent of the thought. But thought itself changes and, even if the unity of the object is preserved by its independence, there is no unity on the part of the thought that is supposed to cognize it. This function of uniting the thought or thoughts is performed by the so-called self, adding one more metaphysical entity to the one that was previously posited, namely, the object. For the Buddhist psychologist, the *parikalpita*, through the assumption of an independent object (which makes it an *abhūtaparikalpa*), leads to the assertion of an equally independent subject, and the thought process that is dependently arisen (*paratantra*) thus produces a doubly unfounded conceptualization. The absence of the conceptualization of a metaphysical object (*grāhya*) and an equally metaphysical subject (*grāhaka*) constitutes the achievement or accomplishment in freedom (*parinispanna*).

This is an explanation of how the unfounded conceptualization (*abhūta-parikalpa*), whose own nature (*svalakṣaṇa*) was examined previously, comes to be treated under the three natures. These are not mutually distinct natures, but merely the manner in which the stream of experience comes to be dichotomized and trichotomized contributing to unfounded conceptualizations.

6. *Upalabdhiṃ samāśritya nopalabdhiḥ prajāyate,*
   nopalabdhiṃ samāśritya nopalabdhiḥ prajāyate.

Perception does not necessarily arise depending upon perception. Perception does not necessarily arise depending upon non-perception.

(*MVB* p. 20.)

Upalabdhi can mean "perception" in the sense of "grasping of an object." Whether it means perception or grasping, the argument presented here is that our perception or grasping does not necessarily imply the independent existence of an object that is perceived or grasped. There is always the possibility of perceiving or grasping after what is non-existent (*asat*). However, if the latter possibility is universalized, one can easily end up with the view that all perceptions are mere illusions (*bhrānti-mātra*). Vasubandhu had already rejected such a position (p. 19). For this reason, perception does not necessarily depend upon non-perception.

Vasubandhu's explanation makes this point very clear. "Depending upon the perception of or grasping after what is a mere concept (*vijñapti-mātra*), the perception of an object can arise." It means that where there is a mere conceptualization one can assume the existence of an independent object. However, "depending upon the non-perception of the object, there is the non-perception of the mere concept," (*arthānupalabdhiṃ samāśritya vijñap-timātrasyāpy anupalabdhir jāyate*). This means that "mere concept" *cannot* occur unless there is an experience of an object, even though the belief in a substantial object can arise depending upon a "mere concept."

7. *Upalabdhes tataḥ siddhā nopalabdhi-svabhāvatā,*
tasmāc ca samatā jñeyā nopalambhopalambhayoḥ.

Of the perception so established, there is no perceptual self-nature. Through this the similarity of perception and non-perception should be known.

(*MVB* p. 20.)

The most important aspect of perceptual experience that is highlighted by the previous analysis is dependence. Maitreya is, therefore, insisting that the experience so established possesses no self-nature or substance (*svabhāva*). Perceptual experience translated into conceptualization can be either founded (*bhūta*) or unfounded (*abhūta*). The common denominator is that they are both concepts (*vijñapti-mātra*) conditioned by various factors, hence empty of any substance.

8. *Abhutaparikalpaś ca citta-caittās tridhātukāḥ,*
tatrārtha-dṛṣṭir vijñānaṃ tad viśeṣe tu caitasāḥ.

The unfounded conceptualization as well as thought and elements of thought belong to the three spheres. Herein, the perception of the object is consciousness, and its distinctions constitute the elements of thought.

(*MVB* p. 20.)

Kochumuttom takes both *citta* (thought) and *caitta* (elements of thought) as being "the imagination of the unreal" (*abhūtaparikalpa*) (p. 64). This would contradict everything that has been said in *MV* I.6–7. Neither Maitreya nor Vasubandhu are drawing any such implication. Even though Vasubandhu, in introducing this section, says: "Now the varigated character of the unfounded conceptualization is explained," (*tasyaivedānīm abhūtaparikalpasya prabheda-lakṣaṇaṃ khyāpayati*), this should not be taken to mean that both *citta* and *caittas* are necessarily unfounded conceptualizations. If they are to be taken as such, then his explanation of I.5 which is preceded by a similar statement: *abhūtaparikalpaysa . . . saṃgraha-lakṣaṇaṃ khyāpayati*, would make both *paratantra* and *pariniṣpanna* varieties of *abhūtaparikalpa*.

Furthermore, *citta* is here defined as *vijñāna*, and to consider it as an *abhūtaparikalpa* would be to undermine the very foundation of the psychology he was attempting to explicate. It is one thing to assume that a variety of unfounded conceptualizations can occur in relation to *citta* and *caittas*, and completely another to maintain that *citta* and *caitta are* unfounded conceptualizations. Indeed, it is the transcendentalist Sthiramati who reads *ca* as *tu* (*MVB* p. 20, note 5) and identifies the *abhūtaparikalpa* with *citta* and *caittas*. As pointed out by Maitreya himself, it is not impossible for someone to interpret a perception (*upalabdhi*) or thought (*citta*) in a metaphysical way. That does not mean that it is the only way.

Vijñāna is defined as the perception of "mere object" (*artha-mātra*), i.e., an object without any substantial existence (*svabhāva*). The distinction (*viśeṣa*) relating to that "mere object" gives rise to the elements of thought (*caitta*) and these are further defined as sensation, etc.

The recognition of varieties of thought (*citta*) represented by the elements of thought (*caitta*) need not be unfounded (*abhūta*), so long as they are not distinguished in an absolute way (see section on "Perception"). Thought and its elements become metaphysical when they are analysed into exclusive categories, the former representing the container and the latter the contained. However, thought considered as the stream or the flux and elements as the fluctuations can constitute a non-substantialist explanation of the stream of experience. It is only the search for an Absolute that could render all forms of distinction meaningless, whether they be metaphysical or non-metaphysical.

9. *Ekaṃ pratyaya-vijñānaṃ dvitīyam aupabhogikaṃ,*
upabhoga-pariccheda-prerakās tatra caitasāḥ.

One is consciousness that serves as condition. The second represents the function of enjoyment. Therein, the functions of enjoyment, determination and motivation are the elements of thought.

(*MVB* p. 21.)

Citta and *caittas* are not independent entities. Nor are they comparable to the two birds referred to in the *Upaniṣads* (see section on "Indian

Background"), one representing the eternal and permanent self with no function, and the other enjoying the fruit. *Citta* is not known without the *caittas* and the *caittas* are not known without the *citta*. *Citta*, as mentioned earlier, is the stream of experience with flights and perchings. Hence Vasubandhu identifies it with *ālaya-vijñāna*. The *caittas* are specific activities (*pravṛtti*) that occur in the *ālaya-vijñāna* such as sensation, perception and dispositions (*MVB* p. 21, compare *Triṃś* 3, *sadā sparśa-manaskāra-vit-samjña-cetanānvitaṃ*).

Sthiramati's interpretation of the nature of the causal process in this context reintroduces the metaphysics that Vasubandhu abandoned when he renounced his Sautrāntika leanings. Neither the *ālaya-vijñāna* nor the various elements operative there imply any causation where momentary succession is involved (*MVBT* 1.10). Kochumuttom's explanation of this verse based upon Sthiramati seems completely inappropriate (see section on "Psychology in the Yogācāra").

10. *Chādanād ropanāc caiva nayanāt saṃparigrahāt,*
pūraṇāt tri-paricchedād upabhogāc ca karṣaṇāt.

11. *nibandhanād ābhimukhyād duḥkhanāt kliśyate jagat,*
tredhā dvedhā ca saṃkleśaḥ saptadhā 'bhūtakalpanāt.

Through the functions of concealing, implanting, leading, receiving, fulfilling, trichotomizing, enjoying and attracting, through binding, confronting and suffering the universe is defiled. As a result of unfounded conceptualizations arise the threefold, twofold and sevenfold defilements.

(*MVB* p. 21)

These represent an explanation of the twelvefold factors constituting the human personality as it continues to wander along from existence to existence. Interestingly, instead of the normal twelve factors, we have a description of the functions relating to each factor, and how the so-called universe (*jagat*) comes to be defiled as a result of such activity. This being an explanation of the normal life process, it is also the *ālaya-vijñāna* with the operation of the various transformations that produce bondage. the twofold, threefold and sevenfold defiling tendencies that emerge in this life process are the results of unfounded conceptualization (*abhūta-parikalpa*), namely, the recognition of real objects and self.

12. *Lakṣaṇaṃ cātha paryāyas tad artho bheda eva ca,*
sādhanaṃ ceti vijñeyaṃ śūnyatāyāḥ samāsataḥ.

The characteristic, synonym, meaning, variety and establishment of emptiness should be known in brief.

(*MVB*, p. 22.)

Maitreya here proposes five aspects through which emptiness could be properly understood.

13. *Dvayābhāvo hy abhāvasya bhāvaḥ śūnyasya lakṣaṇaṃ,*
na bhāvo nāpi cābhāvaḥ na pṛthaktvaika-lakṣaṇaṃ.

The absence of the [metaphysical] duo is indeed the nature of non-existence, the characteristic of emptiness. It is neither existence nor non-existence. Neither has it the characteristic of difference nor of identity.

(*MVB* pp. 22–23.)

As at 1–2, Maitreya was emphasizing the fact that emptiness is not spoken of in a vacuum. It is merely the denial of the metaphysical object and its perceiving self. Even though emptiness implies the *absence* of the metaphysical entities, it could be interpreted as "pure emptiness or negation." Such an interpretation is countered by Maitreya when he insists that it is neither pure existence nor pure non-existence.

Vasubandhu takes up for elaboration the statement that emptiness is neither difference nor identity. If there were to be difference, then one has to recognize "the nature of the elements of existence" (*dharmatā*) as being different from the elements of existence (*dharma*). This is not appropriate because such natures as impermanence and unsatisfactoriness are not found independently of things that are impermanent and unsatisfactory. The universal is not independent of the particular. If there were to be identity, there could not be knowledge pertaining to purity, for that knowledge would be identical with defiled knowledge. Furthermore, even the universal would not be evident, as it would be identical with the particular.

Vasubandhu utilizes a phrase employed by Nāgārjuna in order to reject the metaphysics of identity and difference, namely, *tattvānyatva* (*Kārikā* XXII.8), implying that this is an explanation free from the metaphysical notions of "difference or change of identity."

14. *Tathatā bhūta-koṭiś cānimittaṃ paramārthatā,*
dharmma-dhātuś ca paryāyāḥ śūnyatāyāḥ samāsataḥ.

In brief, suchness, the limit of existence, absence of a mysterious cause, ultimate fruit and the constitution of elements are synonyms for emptiness.

(*MVB* p. 23.)

This verse undoubtedly would enthuse the Absolutist to read all his ideas into the philosphical and psychological speculations of Maitreya and Vasubandhu, and from there to the Buddha himself. In many ways, it is comparable to Nāgārjuna's statement at *Kārikā* XVIII.9 which, when analysed independent of the Buddha's discourse to Kaccāyana (*S* 2.16–17), provided a way of reading the metaphysics of Absolutism in Nāgārjuna's philosophy. Our reading of Nāgārjuna's statement in the light of the Buddha's discourse has, in fact, enabled us to present Nāgārjuna as a non-Absolutist and a non-substantialist who faithfully followed his teacher, the Buddha (of the Nikāyas and the Āgamas) without being led by his Brahmanical counterparts. The same can be done with the present verse of Maitreya and Vasubandhu's commentary upon it. Maitreya's definition of each one of these synonyms that appear in the following verse can be traced back to early Buddhism.

15. *Ananyathā 'viparyāsa-tan-nirodhārya-gocaraiḥ,*
hetutvāc cārya-dharmmāṇāṃ paryāyārtho yathākramaṃ.

Not otherwise, non-perverse, cessation of it [i.e., *nimitta*], being the sphere of the noble ones, the cause of the noble doctrine—such, respectively, are the meaning of the synonyms.

(*MVB* pp. 23–24.)

Keeping in mind that these are five synonyms for emptiness which was defined earlier as "the absence of metaphysical entities" and not pure negation, it is possible to trace all these concepts in the teaching of early Buddhism.

Tathatā: This term occurs for the first time in the Buddha's discourse on "Conditions" (*Paccaya, S* 2.25). It appears in that context along with three other terms: *avitathatā*, *anaññathatā*, and *idappaccayatā*, to explain the causal process. Thus, Maitreya's synonym for *tathatā* as *ananyathā* reflects the Buddha's own *anaññathatā*. The significance of the four characteristics in the Buddha's discourse have been discussed in my *Causality* (pp. 91–94). In that context, the term *tathatā* was understood as "objectivity" primarily because, in the *Upaniṣads* causality or dependent arising had no reality, being completely subordinated to the permanent and immutable ultimate reality, the *ātman*. Causality was a mere imagination on the part of the ignorant, with no objectivity at all. Explaining this in terms of the metaphysic of experience, the Upaniṣadic thinkers perceived whatever causal process that exists involving change as representing the empirical self, the bird enjoying the fruit, in contrast to the pure and "do-nothing" eternal self. The Buddha, on the contrary, made this empirical self, and along with it the stream of experience, the reality (see section on "Selfless Self"). As such, he considered causality as more than a mere mental construct, or according to the terminology of Maitreya and Vasubandhu, more than a "mere unfounded conceptualization" (*abhūtaparikalpa-mātra*). While it is true that experience reveals an objective reality, it is not possible to go beyond that experience and assume that this causal process is permanent and eternal. Hence, the Buddha confined himself to what is already given in experience as a means to the understanding of the future. This is clearly indicated by the Buddha when he confined the *experience* of causality to the past and present saying: "This causal status has remained" (*S* 2. 25, *ṭhitā va sā dhātu; MKV* p. 40 *sthitaivaisā dharmāṇaṃ dharmatā*), and proceeded to recognize its future validity on the basis of conceptualization or inference. Thus, not being enthusiastic in defining it as a permanent and eternal process, he utilized the negative terms *avitathatā* (lit. not-different-such-ness, or not-otherwise-ness, hence "necessity") and *anaññathatā* (Sk. *ananyathā*, lit. not-other-wise, implying "invariability"). The Buddha seems to have been well aware of the fact that moving from the effect to the cause empirically, one can have a better chance of asserting necessity or invariability. However, proceeding from the cause to the effect, that is, in the attempt to predict the effect, one has to be satisfied with sufficiency (cp. Donald Davidson, *The Logic of Grammar*, Encino, California: Dickinson Publishing Company, 1975, pp. 250–251). This latter aspect is clearly expressed by the term *idappaccayatā*. As such, Vasubandhu's use of the term *nitya* (eternal) should be taken rather cautiously as he himself suggests, i.e., "taking it in the sense of such" (*tathā eveti kṛtvā*) implying constancy.

Bhūta-koṭi: The above understanding of *tathatā* leads us directly to the conception of *bhūta-koṭi*, sometimes referred to as *bhūta-tathatā*. The important part of this compound is *bhūta*, which is a past participle like *sthita* or *ṭhita* discussed above. If experience is confined to what is given in the so-called "specious present," then there is a limit (*koṭi*) and this limit should not be transgressed when making knowledge-claims. The belief in a permanent and independent object and an eternal self transcends such limits of experience and is, therefore, negated by emptiness (*śūnyatā*). Thus, *bhūta-koṭi* turns out to be not only a synonym, but a clear explanation of *śūnyatā*.

Maitreya's explanation of *bhūta-koṭi* as *aviparyāsa* is prompted by the statements of both the Buddha and Nāgārjuna. For the Buddha, the belief in permanence (*nicca*) where there is impermanence (*anicca*) is a perversion (*vipallāsa*, *A* 2.52). Similarly for Nāgārjuna, the grasping after permanence in the impermanent is a perversion (*Kārikā* XXIII.13, *anitye nityam ity evaṃ yadi grāho viparyayaḥ*).

Animitta: This is sometimes interpreted to mean the absence of the object in experience, an idea that is supportive of the Absolutist claim regarding a transcendental consciousness free from subject-object duality. Sometimes it is rendered as "signless" (see section on "Emotions and the Foundation of the Moral Life") or as "never admitting a cause" (Kochumuttom, p. 75).

This would mean that *śūnyatā*, for which *animitta* is suggested as a synonym, represents an uncaused, unconditioned and, therefore, absolute reality. These interpretations have no basis in the teachings of the Buddha. As explained earlier, the term *nimitta* has a very specific meaning in the context of early Buddhism. That meaning is compatible with the philosophical speculation of Nāgārjuna, as well as the psychological reflections of Maitreya and Vasubandhu. *Nimitta* is that hidden *something* (*kiñci, kiṃcit*), a substance or a mysterious cause one looks for "having perceived an object with the sense organ" (e.g. *cakkhunā rūpaṃ disvā*). Indeed, here there is no denial of any one of the perceivable objects of sense, but only of a mysterious substance or cause behind such experience of the object. *Animitta* is, therefore, a negation of a substantial entity, which is also the function of emptiness (*śūnyatā*).

Paramārtha: Without doubt this is the most significant term in Buddhism that enabled that Absolutist to confirm his belief in an "ultimate reality" which he attributes to the Buddha. Our analysis of the contexts in which the term occurs in the early discourses as well as in Nāgārjuna's treatise has already brought out its moral sense, rather than a metaphysical implication (see Introduction to *Nāgārjuna. The Philosophy of the Middle Way*). *Paramārtha* as the "ultimate fruit" is what serves as the sphere of the noble wisdom (*ārya-jñāna*), contrasted with that of the ignoble wisdom (*anārya-jñāna*) that makes a person an individualist (*pṛthagjana*). The relation of *paramārtha* to emptiness consists of the fact that this ultimate fruit is the result of not adhering to an absolute moral law thereby relinquishing one's own happiness as well as the happiness of the others. In other words, *paramārtha* is empty of any absoluteness.

Dharma-dhātu: Like many other conceptions discussed above, this too has received the same metaphysical interpretation at the hands of modern scholars. In the eyes of the Absolutist, it represents the *source* of the universe, comparable to the *ātman* of the Brahmanical thinkers or the *tao* of the Taoists. However, for the Buddha, it was "dependent arising" (*paṭiccasamuppāda*), sometimes referred to simply as *dhātu* or more specifically as *dhammaṭṭhitatā* or *dhammaniyāmatā*, providing a foundation for the ultimate fruit of *nibbāna* (see section on "Psychology of Freedom"). Hence, Maitreya's and Vasubandhu's explanation of it as the cause of the "noble way of life" (*ārya-dharma-hetutva*). It is not the source of everything, but only of the noble life, i.e., the moral life that contributes to the happiness of oneself and others. The fact that these five concepts can be interpreted in terms of the Buddha's own teaching, instead of depending upon the metaphysics of the Brahmanical thinkers, of some of the Taoists, or of some modern interpreters, leaves us with the strong encouragement that, like Nāgārjuna, both Maitreya and Vasubandhu are true disciples of the Buddha.

16. *Saṃkiliṣṭā ca viśuddhā ca samalā nirmalā ca sā,*
ābdhātu-kanakākāśa-śuddhivac chuddhir iṣyate.

It is defiled as well as pure, tainted and free from taint. The purity intended is like the purity of the element of light, gold or space.

(*MVB* p. 24.)

This is an extremely important notion in Buddhist psychology treated with utmost care in the early discourses as well as in Nāgārjuna. The *Laṅkāvatāra* as well as the commentaries of Buddhaghosa (as explained in the sections on "Rational Psychology," and "Transcendental Psychology in the *Laṅkāvatāra*") seem to have produced a metaphysical monster out of this notion by formulating it as an "originally pure thought" (*prakṛti-prabhāsvara-citta*, or *pakati-mano*). Both Maitreya and Vasubandhu seem to be avoiding this notion of original purity. They also have realized that such a notion of original purity was made necessary by an equally metaphysical analysis that leaves absolute difference (*pṛthaktva*, see *MV* I.3) requiring the conception of absolute identity as a means of connecting up such differences. The originally pure mind thus turns out to be no more than a substance that provides a unity to the discrete sense impressions.

In the context of such a metaphysical notion of difference, both Maitreya and Vasubandhu are compelled to raise the question as to how a defiled phenomenon (in the present case, *śūnyatā*) becomes purified; how a tainted phenomenon becomes free from taint. The question that is merely implied in Maitreya is openly raised by Vasubandhu. "If something were to be tained and subsequently become taintless, how is it that it [taintlessness], being of the nature of change, remains constant?" In other words, a freed person can fall away from his freedom or a purified mind can once again become defiled.

In the present work, it was pointed out that without going back to absolute origins, the Buddha explained thought as being luminous, even though not absolutely pure, and how it is continuously defiled by adventitious defilements (*āgantukehi upakkilesehi upakkiliṭṭhaṃ*). The term "adventitious" (*āgantuka*) is used, not in the sense of an absolute alien, but defiling tendencies within and which are inspired by objects of experience. For example, desire (*kāma*) or aversion (*dosa*) are not *necessary* parts of experience or thought whereas pleasant and unpleasant sensations are. The pleasant and unpleasant sensations generated by things in the world are not necessarily defilements in the same way as desire and aversion are. It is, indeed, the waning of the latter that constitutes freedom and purity. The change of nature (*svabhāvānyatva*), according to Vasubandhu, is the disappearance of such *un-necessary* taints (*āgantuka-malāpagamana*).

17. *Bhoktṛ-bhojana-tad-deha-pratiṣṭhā-vastu-śūnyatā,*
tac ca yena yathā dṛṣṭaṃ yad arthaṃ tasya śūnyatā.

Emptiness is of the enjoyer, the enjoyed, that personality, that support and that object. Emptiness is also of that by which it is perceived as such and the fruit of that perception.

(*MVB* pp. 24–25.)

Before commenting on Maitreya's statement, Vasubandhu lists sixteen varieties of emptiness. Emptiness pertains to:

1 subjectivity,
2 objectivity,
3 subjectivity-objectivity,
4 the universal,
5 emptiness,
6 ultimate fruit,
7 the dispositionally conditioned,
8 the dispositionally unconditioned,
9 the pervasive,
10 the beginningless,
11 the formless,
12 the primordial nature,
13 the characteristics,
14 all things,
15 non-existence, and
16 the nature of non-existence.

The first three may be taken as a reference to the emptiness of perceptual experience; 4 and 5 include conceptual thinking; 6–8 relate to the moral life; 9–13 pertain to specific metaphysical issues; 14 represents an assertion of the non-substantiality of all phenomena; while 15 and 16 are intended to eliminate the possible assertion of a negation as representing a substantial entity.

After listing these different forms of emptiness, Vasubandhu proceeds to identify the types of emptiness referred to by Maitreya. *Bhoktṛ-śūnyatā* is the emptiness relating to the six internal spheres, namely, eye, ear, nose, tongue, body and mind. These are faculties that function without being "agents of enjoyment" (*bhoktṛ*). Nāgārjuna's treatment of *indriya* clearly demonstrated that though experience takes place depending upon sense organ and sense object (*Kārikā* III.7), it would not be appropriate to assume the existence either of an agent or of a mysterious capacity within them that produces sense experience, as the scholastics did. As pointed out in the present work, there is no need to look for a mysterious substance (*nimitta*) when an object is perceived through the eye (*cakkhunā rūpaṃ disvā*). *Bhojana-śūnyatā* represents the similar absence of metaphysical causes in the objects so perceived, that is, the six external spheres (*bāhyāni āyatanāni*). These consist of material form, sound, smell, taste, tangibles and concepts.

The psychophysical personality (*śarīra*) that serves as the foundation for the beliefs in "the agent as well as the object of enjoyment" (*bhoktṛ-bhojana*) is equally empty. Vasubandhu identifies this with that he previously called the emptiness of both subjectivity and objectivity (*adhyātma-bahirdhā*). The external world (*bhājana-loka*) that serves as the objective support (*pratiṣṭhā vastu*) is rather pervasive (*vistirṇa*); hence emptiness becomes pervasive or great (*mahā-śūnyatā*).

The subjective sense spheres (*adhyātmika-āyatana*), etc. are perceived as "the empty" (*śūnyaṃ*). Knowledge of it is the knowledge of emptiness (*śūnyatā-jñāna*). However, the knowledge of emptiness could provide room for the belief that the content of that knowledge, namely, "emptiness," is itself substantial. The emptiness of emptiness (*śūnyatā-śūnyatā*) is intended to eliminate such a belief.

The realization that everything is empty is said to contribute to the ultimate fruit of the moral life. The career of a *bodhisattva* is directed toward the attainment of that ultimate fruit. However, the recognition of a fruit also can give the wrong impression that, in contrast to all other changing phenomena in the world, the *bodhisattva* is able to achieve *something* (*kiṃcit*) that is permanent and eternal. The *paramārtha-śūnyatā* is, therefore, intended to abandon any transcendentalist or absolutist notion of the ultimate fruit.

The question naturally arises in the ordinary person as to the purpose of leading a moral life if it were not to bring about a fruit that is not totally different from the fruits of ordinary life characterized by emptiness. If the so-called ultimate fruit is also empty, what incentive is there to lead a moral life? Maitreya's answer is embodied in the verse that follows.

18. *Śubha-dvayasya prāpty arthaṃ sadā satva-hitāya ca,*
saṃsārātyajanārthañ ca kuśalasyākṣayāya ca.

For the purpose of attaining the two forms of the auspicious, and also for the sake of the everlasting welfare of beings, for the purpose of not abandoning the life-process as well as for the sake of the non-cessation of the good,

19. *Gotrasya ca viśuddhy arthaṃ lakṣaṇa-vyañjanāptaye,*
śuddhaye buddha-dharmmāṇāṃ bodhisatvaḥ prapadyate.

For the purity of lineage and also for the attainment of noble qualities and attributes, and [finally] for maintaining the purity of the Buddha's teachings—does a *bodhisattva* conduct himself.

(*MVB* pp. 25–26.)

Maitreya sets up a sevenfold goal for the *bodhisattva:*

1. The two types of the auspicious (*śubha*) consists of (a) the conventional forms of good, referred to by Nāgārjuna as *vyavahāra* (*Kārikā* XVII.24; XXIV.10), which Vasubandhu defines as the good that is dispositionally conditioned (*saṃskṛta-kuśala*), and (b) the ultimate form of good, comparable to the "ultimate fruit" (*paramārtha*), defined by Vasubandhu as the "dispositionally unconditioned good" (*asaṃskṛta-kuśala*). These are the conventional notions of good as well as the ultimate moral ideal.
2. The twofold auspicious activities mentioned above contribute to the lasting happiness of beings. The absence of any specific reference to "the welfare of others" (*para-hita*) is

significant. Maitreya is not inculcating a life of self-immolation. It is a life devoted to the welfare of beings (*satt-va*), oneself not excluded.

3. *Saṃsāra*, if understood as the life-process, is not one to be abandoned. The metaphysical notions of *saṃsāra* and *nirvāṇa* resulting from the metaphysics of the scholastics were explained in our analysis of Nāgārjuna's famous chapter on "The Examination of Freedom" (*Nirvāṇa-parīkṣā, Kārikā* XXV). Concluding the chapter on "Bondage and Release" (*Bandhana-mokṣa-parīkṣā*), Nāgārjuna argued:

   "Wherein there is neither the attribution of freedom nor the elimination of the life-process, what is it that is discriminated as life-process or freedom."

   Attribution of freedom (*nirvāṇa-samāropa*) and the elimination of the life-process (*saṃsārāpakarṣaṇa*) are the results of metaphysical assertions regarding bondage and freedom (*Kārikā* XVI.10). Avoiding such metaphysics where *saṃsāra* and *nirvāṇa* come to be considered totally different existences, a *bodhisattva* need not think of eliminating *saṃsāra*.
4. The non-cessation of good (*kuśalasyākṣaya*) takes the nihilistic sting out of the conception of "freedom without substrate" (*nirupādiśeṣa-nirvāṇa*). Buddhism recognizes the inevitability of death, even of a person who is freed. The search for an eternal life on the part of ordinary man was responsible for various questions that he raises regarding a freed one after death (*tathāgato parammaraṇā*). The Buddha left such questions unanswered. Yet, sooner or later, even among the Buddhists, the question as to what happens to a freed one after death continued to be raised. Popular Mahāyāna came up with two solutions, both of which contradict the Buddha's own standpoint. The first is for the *bodhisattva* to abandon the hope of attaining freedom (*nirvāṇa*) until he was able to help every human being to the other shore. This is contradicted by the Buddha's own way of life, as well as by some of his statements (*Dh* 158). The second is the idea that a *Tathāgata* never dies, and that his *parinirvāṇa* is a mere illusion. This, of course, is not justified by what can be read in the *Mahā-parinibbāna-suttanta.*

   Vasubandhu, commenting upon "the non-cessation of good" provides a more appropriate solution when he says that the good achieved by the *bodhisattva* is neither dissipated nor abandoned even if he were to attain *nirvāṇa* without substrate. In other words, the moral impact of such a person does not cease with his death. If the *dharma-kāya* means no more than this "moral scent that pervades even among the gods" (*Dh* 54, 56), the *bodhisattva* need not have any hesitation to attain freedom. Even though it is pervasive, it is not a substantial entity; hence Vasubandhu's attempt to explain it as being empty.

5. The purity of lineage (*gotrasya viśuddhi*) is not intended to justify the purity of a particular caste or race, but of humanity. Rebirth (*punarbhava*) being recognized as a distinct possibility, a person who has not attained freedom could be reborn. In order to improve one's personality in a future life, it would be necessary to see that no evil aspect of one's personality is carried over to the next. Even Nāgārjuna had no difficulty recognizing the possibility of survival when he claimed that "of all the actions, whether similar or dissimilar, belonging to certain realms, only one would arise at the moment of birth [of a being]," (*Kārikā* XVII.17). It is the need to maintain the purity of that surviving thought that is emphasised by Maitreya.
6. The attainment of noble qualities and attributes (*lakṣaṇa-vyañjanāptaye*) include the thirty-two marks of a great person (*mahā-puruṣa*) as well as the minor attributes sometimes counted as eighty (*aśītyanuvyañjana*). The *Lakkhaṇa-suttanta* of the *Dīgha-nikāya* (3.142-179) provides the earliest source for the doctrine of qualities and attributes. The theme emphasized there is that these qualities and attributes, even though physical in nature, are the results of leading a morally good life in the past. It is indeed an incentive to follow the moral life.
7. Finally, one of the most important aspects of a *bodhisattva*'s career consists in perpetuating the purity of the Buddha's teachings, instead of allowing it to degenerate into a system of futile metaphysics.

20. *Pudgalasyātha dharmmāṇām abhāvaḥ śūnyatā 'tra hi,*
tad abhāvasya sadbhāvas tasmin sā śūnyatā 'parā.

Herein the absence of the person as well as elements is, indeed, the emptiness. Another form of emptiness pertains to the presence of that non-existence in that context.

(*MVB* p. 26.)

As stated earlier, the negation could turn out to be absolute if it is left unqualified. Non-existence can replace existence and this non-existence would be considered ultimately real. In order to eliminate such a conceptualization, Maitreya is insisting that emptiness applies even to the presence of that absence. In other words, neither existence nor non-existence should be conceived as absolutes. Thus non-absolutism is highlighted by the doctrine of emptiness.

21. *Saṃkliṣṭā ced bhaven nāsau muktāḥ syuḥ sarvva-dehinaḥ,*
viśuddhā ced bhaven nāsau vyāyāmo niṣphalo bhavet.

If this were not defiled, then in the case of all human beings, these will remain liberated. If this were not purified, then effort would be rendered fruitless.

(*MVB* pp. 26–27.)

The pronoun *asau* refers to "emptiness" (*śūnyatā*). *MV* I.16 mentioned a twofold emptiness: the defiled and the purified. However, a substantialist explanation would imply that they are naturally or inherently (*svabhāvataḥ*) defiled and purified. Maitreya did not want to convey any such impression when he spoke of the two types of emptiness. If it is naturally purified and the adventitious defilements have no influence whatsoever on it, then that emptiness would remain pure and liberated in the case of all beings. If it is not purified, then it can never be purified and any effort in that direction would be in vain. This indeed is an argument that Nāgārjuna himself adduced against any substantialist notion of enlightenment or non-enlightenment (*Kārikā* XXIV.32). Like Nāgārjuna's, Maitreya's argument is a deadly weapon against the assumption of an "inherently pure thought or enlightenment."

22. *Na kliṣṭā nāpi vākliṣṭā śuddhā 'śuddhā na caiva sā,*
prabhāsvaratvāc cittasya kleśasyāgantukatvataḥ.

It is neither defiled nor non-defiled, neither purified nor non-purified because of the luminosity of thought and the adventitiousness of the defilements.

(*MVB* p. 27.)

This is a rather brave attempt on the part of Maitreya to resurrect the Buddha's interpretation of purity and impurity. The *Laṅkāvatāra* fell into the substantialist trap in prefixing the term *prakṛti* to the phrase *prabhāsvara-citta*, thus giving the impression that thought is by *nature* pure and that it is defiled by adventitious elements. Thought in such a context is not different from the *ātman* of the Brahmanical thinkers. Maitreya seems to be implying that luminosity need not be confused with purity. It merely represents the amenability of thought to refinement, unlike the gross and rough matter that is the source of the experience of resistence (*paṭigha-samphassa*). Any thought of its original purity will involve speculation relating to the inconceivable beginning of things. Malleable thought is easily defiled as a result of the sense data that continue to impress upon it. As explained earlier (see section on "Emotion and the Foundation of the Moral Life"), human emotion that can easily convert itself to a defilement is not a mere response of the human organism to external stimulation. It represents the bodily changes that follow directly the perception of the exciting fact and our feeling of the same changes as they occur. With this, the adventitiousness (*āgantukatva*) is better explained.

Appendix II
Vasubandhu's *Vijñaptimātratāsiddhi Viṃśatikā and Triṃśikā*

(The text is based upon Sylvan Levi's edition. Mystery seems to surround the first two paragraphs of Vasubandhu's auto-commentary on the *Viṃsatikā* not only because they contain views that are incompatible with Vasubandhu's interpretation of Yogācāra but also are lost in their original and reconstructed by Levi on the basis of Chinese and Tibetan translations. For these reasons, they are ignored in the present annotation.)

Vijñaptimātratāsiddhi
Viṃsatikā-kārikā

1. *Vijñaptimātram evaitad asad arthāvabhāsanāt,*
   yathā taimirikasyāsat keśa-candrādi-darśanaṃ.

This is a mere concept, because it reflects a substantially non-existent object, like the perception of hair and [double] moon on the part of one afflicated with eye-disease.

The perception of hair floating in space and the perception of double moon are here considered to be of one who is afflicted with eye-disease. Such illusory perceptions are not uncommon, even though they have no basis in ordinary experience. The possibility of having such illusory perceptions indicates the problems relating to one of our most important sources of knowledge. It is conditioned by various factors, and in this particular case of illusory perception, the dominant factor is the eye-disease. Even if one is not afflicted by such eye-disease, one of the most important factors that determine sensory experience is human disposition. The Buddha, who did not recognize the possibility of omniscience (*sarvajñatva*), was compelled to assume the relevance of human dispositions in any act of perception. For him, there is no other way in which human beings can deal with the sensory input, the "big, blooming, buzzing confusion." In such a context, to assume that an object can be known without any distortion, that it can be known "as it is", is to claim too much. It is this over-claim of the metaphysical realist that Vasubandhu criticizes as the "non-existent object" (*asad-artha*).

For Vasubandhu, this "non-existent object" is a "mere concept" (*vijñapti-mātraṃ*). To label it as a mere concept is not to say it is absolutely false or imagined. On the contrary, it is an experience that involves one's dispositional tendencies and which is communicated through a concept. If this concept were to be "reified," it would not be a "mere concept," but a concept that would correspond exactly with the object that is independent (*vijñapty antaram arthaṃ*, see Vasubandhu's comments on *Viṃś* 10 explained below).

For this reason, this singularly important term *vijñapti* is here rendered as "concept," contrary to the available understanding of it as "ideation" or "consciousness." Vasubandhu, as the author of the *Abhidharmakośa*, has already utilized this term and its negative form (*avijñapti*) to explain the varieties of karma discussed in Buddhism (see *Akb* pp. 162, 235–236; also in Nāgārjuna's *Kārikā* XVII. 4–5). In those contexts, it was used in the sense of "intimation." However, where such "intimation" or "communication" cannot be made, what is available is a pure fabrication, a *nirmāṇa*. Thus, according to the scholastics as reported by Vasubandhu, any state that is beyond the first stage of meditation (*prathama-dhyāna*) lacks any means of communication (*vijñapti-samutpādakābhāva*, *Akb* p. 427; *Adv* p. 401) and, therefore, is literally indefinable. This is because they believed that after the first stage of meditation all modes of discrimination and, therefore of conceptualization are abandoned. These cannot be spoken of except through fabrications (*nirmita, Akb* p. 427). Our analysis of the four preliminary states of meditation (see "Analytic Yoga") leaves no room for such ineffability. Therefore, in the present context, when Vasubandhu maintains that truth or reality is a "mere concept," he is not insisting that it is beyond conceptualization or description. On the contrary, he is following the Buddha's own explanation that there are no eternal truths (*saccāni . . . niccāni*) apart from sense experience (*aññatra saññāya, Sn* 886) and which are communicated through concepts. As sense experience is dispositionally conditioned and, therefore, liable to change (*sabbe saṅkhārā aniccā, Dh* 277) depending upon conditions, the concepts by means of which such experience is communicated could not be incorruptible nor can they represent an object that is completely independent (see William James, *Some Problems of Philosophy*, pp. 33–34; *Principles of Psychology*, II.78–79).

A metaphysical realist will undoubtedly be shaken up by a statement like Vasubandhu's. Therefore, he will raise questions that worry him most. In the next verse, Vasubandhu anticipates such questions.

2. *Yadi vijñaptir anarthā niyamo deśa-kālayoḥ,*
saṃtānasyāniyamaś ca yuktā kṛtya-kriyā na ca.

If a concept were to be without a real object, neither the determination of space and time, nor the non-determination of the [perceptual] stream nor fruitful activity would be proper.

The denial of a "real object" represented by a concept throws the metaphysical realist into a quandry. He cannot account for four events which he has tried to justify on the basis of the existence of such a real object. The first two are space and time. For a philosopher like Immanual Kant, these were transcendental forms of sensation. For him, non-spatial and non-temporal events are not known through sense experience. Whether one can develop a non-sensuous "intutition" on the basis of which such real objects can be known is an open question in Kant. At least for the present moment, Vasubandhu is not ready to deal with that question.

The denial of a real object also deprives the metaphysical realist of any means of explaining the problem of verification, for two different individuals would not be able to perceive the same object.

Worst of all, such a denial will leave any response to sensory stimuli, any form of uniformity of behavior, without an explanation. Not only a life of morality, but even the ordinary day-to-day life of fruitful activity would be rendered meaningless.

The claims of the metaphysical realists like the Sarvāstivādins were well known to Vasubandhu, who wrote a treatise like the *Abhidharmakośa* long before he embarked upon the present venture. Unlike the Vaiśeṣikas, they asserted that even though individual atoms (*paramāṇu*) constituting an object cannot be grasped, the collocation of atoms (*paramāṇu-saṃcaya*) can be known and that when such harmony of atomic causes of elements (*dharmānām*) exist, there comes to be the capacity for action (*kriyā-sāmarthya* = *kṛtya-kriyā*, see *Adv.* p. 277).

3. *Deśādi-niyamaḥ siddhaḥ svapnavat pretavat punaḥ,*
saṃtānāniyamaḥ sarvaiḥ pūya-nadyādi-darśane.

As in dreams, the determination of space, etc., is established. Furthermore, as in the case of departed spirits, the non-determination of the [perceptual] stream is established by the perception of the stream of puss, etc., by all of them.

Vasabandhu seems to be least interested in discovering a special intuitive faculty through which a "real object," whether it is eternal or not, could be perceived. Instead of looking for any transcendence, he prefers to deal with the problem of sense experience itself. If the determinations of space and time are possible in dream experience even without the so-called "real object," why it is necessary to posit such an object when one is called upon to explain sense experience?

However, the problem of explaining similar perceptions of different individuals is not so easily resolved by utilizing dream experience. Therefore, Vasubandhu resorts to the experience of the "departed spirits" (*preta*), not with a view to establishing the reality of a "spirit world" existing unseen by the ordinary means of cognition, but with the intention of laying bare the over-claims of the metaphysical realists in asserting a "real object."

The Buddha's discourse on "Pātāla" (*S* 4.206–207), indeed, becomes very relevant here. To the question as to whether there is a real "hell" beneath the ocean where human beings are reborn as a result of leading immoral lives, the Buddha responded by saying that such a "hell" is no more than the "painful feelings" (*dukkhā vedanā*) one experiences. Whether it is heaven or hell, it is within this fathom-long conscious body (*S* 1.62). It is what one makes of one's life. And in that process one is guided by one's sensory experiences that are determined on the basis of one's dispositions. To use the terminology of a pragmatist, it is not a ready-made world; rather one that is "being made" all the time.

Thus, it is not impossible for human beings to encounter similar "hellish" experiences and these require no ultimately real objects. On the contrary, they are produced by a variety of conditions among which the so-called "real object" may play a much less significant role than even human dispositions.

4. *Svapnopaghātavat kṛtya-kriyā narakavat punaḥ,*
sarvaṃ narakapālādi-darśane taiś ca bādhane.

Fruitful activity is comparable to affliction in dreams. Again, all of them are similar to experiences in hell involving the perception of the guardians of hell as well as persecution by them.

Fruitful human activity is easily explained through a comparison with dream experience. However, Vasubandhu is keen on continuing his explanation based upon "hellish" experiences, especially because by these means he could explain how such things as fear of punishment serve as useful deterrants against immoral behavior. How the belief in a supreme being as a dispenser of justice, even though not acceptable to Vasubandhu, can be the cause of fruitful activity needs no explanation. What is being emphasized by Vasubandhu is the fact that the positing of a "real object" is not a necessary condition for such activity.

5. *Tiraścāṃ saṃbhavaḥ svarge yathā na narake tathā,*
na pretānāṃ yatas tajjaṃ duḥkhaṃ nānubhavanti te.

The appearance of animals in heaven is not comparable to that of the departed spirits in hell, for [some of them, like the guardians] do not experience suffering produced in that context.

Before proceeding to question the "real existence" of even states such as "hell" and the "world of spirits," Vasubandhu seems to be interested in explaining the difference between the guardians of hell and those undergoing suffering in such states. The former, even though living in hell, do not undergo suffering in the same way as others do. This may be a rather insignificant problem to be given such prominence in a rather concise treatist like the *Viṃśatikā*. Yet, Vasubandhu's desire to explain this difference reveals that he is as interested in the questions regarding moral responsibility as he is with the problem of epistemology.

6. *Yadi tat karmabhis tatra bhūtānāṃ saṃbhavas tathā,*
isyate pariṇāmaś ca kiṃ vijñānasya nesyate.

If it were to be assumed that through their actions the appearance and evolution of beings occur in that context [i.e., in hell], why is it not assumed in the context of consciousness?

This represents Vasubandhu's reaction to the moral implications of the atomistic theory of action which he himself espoused as a Sautrāntika. During the time he was a Sautrāntika, Vasubandhu spared no pains in explaining how seeds of action could produce fruits (*phala*) in different states of existence (*Akb* p. 254). However, placing this doctrine of moral retribution in the context of the theory of moments that was popular with the Sautrāntikas, Vasubandhu was compelled to devise various ingenious methods to account for the continuity of the momentary stream of personal existence (ibid., p. 250). Having realized the unsatisfactoriness of that explanation which would not solve the metaphysical problem of "difference," Vasubandhu is here raising the question as to why such fruits could not be considered part of the stream of consciousness without being located in an altogether different sphere. In other words, he is insisting that moral responsibility be explained on the basis of the continuity in a life process (*saṃsāra*) explicated in terms of dependence without breaking it up into discrete segments and then looking for "real objects" in order to account for that continuity. His reference to the evolution of consciousness (*vijñāna*) is significant, especially in the context in which the "identification" of a personality is considered. While the physical body is a necessary component in such identification, it is not a sufficient condition. He was probably aware that the Buddha himself recognized the importance of conscious life (*vijñāna*) in explaining the process of "re-identification" (*satānusāri viññāṇaṃ, D* 3.134). This doctrine of re-identification was an important part of Vasubandhu's explanation of action in his treatise called *Karmasiddhiprakaraṇa*.

7. *Karmaṇo vāsanānyatra phalam anyatra kalpyate,*
tatraiva nesyate yatra vāsanā kiṃ nu kāraṇaṃ.

The dispositional basis of action is conceived in one context and the fruit in another. For what reason is it [the fruit] not assumed to be in the same place as the seed?

Vāsanā, though generally referred to a seed (*bīja*) is a dispositional tendency (*saṃskāra*) that dominates one's behavior (*karma*). Vasubandhu who abandoned the metaphysics of the Sautrāntikas is here insisting that dispositions as well as their effects are manifested in a conscious personality whose continuity through space and time is to be explained on the basis of consciousness (*vijñāna*). The Sautrāntika metaphysics that emphasized difference involves an explanation that leaves the seed of action in one place and the fruit or consequence in another. He seems to have realized that his former credo was not very different from the view that the Buddha had rejected, namely, external causation (*paraṃkataṃ*) of action.

8. *Rūpādy āyatanāstitvaṃ tad vineya-janaṃ prati,*
abhiprāyavaśād uktam upapāduka-sattvavat.

Considering the people who are to be disciplined, the existence of spheres such as material form is spoken of for a very specific purpose. It is comparable to the [reference to] beings of spontaneous birth.

If it is consciousness itself that reflects spheres such as material form (*rūpa*) and that there are no such objects of perception, then the Buddha could not have spoken of such spheres of existence. Vasubandhu rejects such an argument (*akāraṇam etat*), insisting that the Buddha has spoken of these for the benefit of those who are to be disciplined (*vineya-jana*).

However, before leaping in to the conclusion that this refers to the "skill-in-means" (*upāya-kauśalya*) on the part of the Buddha who would speak of non-existent events as existent merely for pragmatic purposes, it would be necessary to examine the metaphysical implications of the realist position that militates against any discourse on discipline (*vinaya*).

A metaphysical realist would recognize a persistent object having its own substantial form (*svabhāva*). For him, the perceiving stream of consciousness (*vijñāna*) is a mere passive *tabula rasa* on which the object leaves its series of disconnected impressions. As such, that stream of consciousness lacks not only any continuity, but also the capacity to change its course on its own initiative. Discipline (*vinaya*) of a human being makes no sense in such a context. Neither moral action nor moral responsibility can be accounted for satisfactorily. A radical empiricist approach is required to correct this position. Indeed, this is what Vasubandhu is suggesting when he, in his auto-commentary, explains "specific purpose (*abhiprāya*)" as the intention of acknowledging the unbroken continuity (*anucchedaṃ*) of the stream (*saṃtati*) in the future (*āyatyāṃ*). In other words, Vasubandhu seems to take the object as an experience on the basis of which the continuity in consciousness is established. The meaning of the word "object" is thus confined to its practical results, not any metaphysical existence apart from experience. The recognition of continuity in consciousness based upon an experience of an object provides for an opportunity for moral progress as well as responsibility.

Vasubandhu sees the best illustration of this sort of solution in the Buddha's recognition of "beings of spontaneous birth" (*upapāduka-sattva*, Pali *opapātika*).

9. *Yatah svabījād vijñaptir yad ābhāsā pravartate,*
dvividhāyatanatvena te tasyā munir abravīt.

The sage has described how a concept, reflecting the twofold spheres, proceeds from its own seed.

The reference here is to *vijñapti* rather than *vijñāna*. *Vijñapti* can mean that by which a certain awareness of consciousness (*vijñāna*) is communicated; hence a concept. In order to refute the claims of the metaphysical realist, who assumes the object to have its own nature independently of the perceiving consciousness, Vasubandhu insists upon the concept of the twofold spheres, namely, the visual organ and the visible object, as arising from its own seed. This seed, as explained earlier, is none other than the dispositions (*vāsanā*) (see *Viṃś* 7). In the verse that follows, Vasubandhu considers this explanation as a way of establishing or penetrating into the non-substantiality of the human person (*pudgala-nairātmya*). This fact is very significant, for having rejected the realist conception of a self-existent object, Vasubandhu wants to avoid positing consciousness (*vijñāna*) as an ultimately real entity. In fact, he seems to understand the concept (*vijñapti*), not simply as a projection of consciousness, as a metaphysical idealist would assume, but rather as a product of the twofold spheres that are determined by dispositions (*vāsanā*). This, in a way, is not too far removed from the explanation provided by the Buddha. Only the terminology used is different. In the case of the Buddha, however, the causal account of perception and, therefore, of conception was intended to eliminate the belief in a metaphysical self (*ātman*). Vasubandhu, of course, has an additional problem to deal with, namely, the view of the metaphysical realist. Hence, after presenting a way of penetrating into the non-substantiality of the human person, Vasubandhu immediately proceeds to reject the substantialist notions of real elements (*dharma*).

10. *Yathā pudgala-nairātmya-praveśo hy anyathā punaḥ,*
deśanā dharma-nairātmya-praveśaḥ kalpitātmanā.

This, indeed, is the way of penetrating into the non-substantiality of a person. However, the discourse on the penetration into the non-substantiality of elements is different in elucidating self as being imagined.

The manner in which the understanding of the non-substantiality of a person (*pudgala-nairātmya*) is achieved is explained in the previous verse. That involved the recognition of a concept generated by dispositions without having to deny perceptual activity. The realization of the non-substantiality of the elements is to be achieved through considering the self (*ātman*) in phenomena as a mere imagination (*parikalpita*). The self (*ātman*) referred to here is substance (*svabhāva*) admitted by the foolish people (*bāla*) (*Viṃś* 6). Vasubandhu's commentary provides ample information regarding the nature of percepts and concepts that he is expounding. Through the establishment of a "mere-concept" (*vijñapti-mātra*), Vasubandhu perceives a way of penetrating into the non-substantiality of all things (*vijñaptimātra-vyavasthāpanayā sarva-dharmāṇām nairātmya-praveśo bhavati*), and not by its annulment (*na tad apavādāt*). Indeed, what is denied is a concept of an object that stands independent or apart from a concept (*vijñapty antaram arthaḥ*). On the contrary, even while recognizing a plurality of concepts (hence the use of the plural term *vijñaptīnāṃ*), Vasubandhu admits their meaningfulness (*arthavatītva*).

Thus, Vasubandhu is compelled to look for a "middle standpoint" from which a concept (*vijñapti*) can be understood. The Buddha's statement that "spheres such as material form exists," needs to be salvaged from the metaphysical interpretations, not only of the "soul-theorists" (*ātma-vādin*), but also of the substantialists (*svabhāva-vādin*). The verses that follow are, therefore, devoted to a critical analysis of the realist interpretation of the nature of the object.

11. *Na tad ekaṃ na cānekaṃ viṣayah paramānuśaḥ,*
na ca te saṃhatā yasmāt paramāṇur na sidhyati.

Atom-wise, an object is neither one nor many. Neither is it a conglomeration of them. For that reason, an atom is not established.

Before he became disillusioned with the Sautrāntika (and Sarvāstivāda) treatment of the object of perception, Vasubandhu was involved in an extensive study of the conception of atoms (*paramāṇu*), for that was the very basis of the explanations of perception in these two schools. His *Abhidharmakośabhāsya* abounds in speculations regarding the nature of atoms and how they constitute an object (see *Ak* pp. 32–33). Indeed, the atoms were even considered as the "ultimate reality" (*paramārtha*) by some of these schools (*Akb* p. 334). Vasubandhu's fascination with such speculation at that time may have blinded him to the fact that it was not very different from the philosophical enterprize of the Vaiśeṣikas. Abandoning his Sautrāntika leanings, Vasubandhu now realizes the authorship of the theory of atoms. Therefore, in the present treatise he specifically attributes the theory of atoms to the Vaiśeṣikas.

In this auto-commentary, Vasubandhu explains the implications of the theory of atoms, as it emerged in the Vaiśeṣika school. According to him, the Vaiśeṣikas believed that spheres like material form (*rūpa*), which holds one-to-one correspondence with the concepts of material form, represent a unity (*eka*) in terms of a molecule, i.e., an entity that consists of parts (*avayavīrūpa*). However, in terms of atoms it is a plurality (*aneka*).

Vasubandhu argues that a whole is not perceived apart from its parts. Even so, a molecule is nowhere perceived independent of its constituents.

Similarly, the object is not a unity of atoms or parts. Neither is it a plurality, for the atoms that go to constitute a molecule are also not perceived, either as individual units (*pratyeka*) or as an aggregate (*saṃhata*).

12. *Saṭkena yugapad yogāt paramāṇoḥ ṣad-aṃsatā,*
ṣaṇṇāṃ samāna-deśatvāt piṇḍaḥ syād aṇu-mātrakaḥ.

Because of the necessity of joining with six others, an atom will have six facets. Since the six atoms occupy equal space, even the aggregate would be a mere atom.

An atom, by definition, is without parts (*niravayavaś ca paramāṇavah, Akb* p. 32). If so, how one atom could join with other atoms to produce a molecule, turned out to be a source of controversy among the different teachers of the Sarvāstivāda and Sautrāntika schools (ibid., pp. 32–33). Compared with such varying views, Vasubandhu preferred a theory presented by Vaśumitra, who maintained that one atom does not touch another, but that the idea of touching one another represents merely the absence of any space between them (*nirantare tu spṛṣṭa-saṃjñeti*, ibid., p. 33). In that context, Vasubandhu was not abandoning the very conception of atoms. He was simply favoring one theory over another. However, in the present context, Vasubandhu is looking for arguments to abandon the whole theory.

Vasubandhu's realization that as a Buddhist he could not argue for an empirical foundation of a theory of atoms, as the Vaiśeṣikas did, compelled him to resort to rational arguments to deny its validity. Therefore, he argues: When an atom has to combine with six others from six directions, it has to possess six facets. For one atom cannot occupy the space of another.

However, if each atom were to occupy an identical space and, by definition an atom has no magnitude, then the aggregate itself would be a mere atom. In fact, an aggregate would not be perceived if the parts are separate from one another (*paraspara-vyatirekād*).

13. *Paramāṇor asaṃyoge tat saṃghāte 'sti kasya saḥ,*
na cānavayavatvena tat saṃyogo na sidhyati.

When the coalesence of an atom is not possible, whose coalesence will there be at the time of aggregation. By not admitting the absence of parts, the coalescence of an atom is not established.

Saṃghāta refers to the combination or aggregation of atoms, while *saṃyoga* implies coalesence. As mentioned earlier, for an atom to aggregate with other atoms, it should possess at least six different facets or sides. This means that it has parts, and such an assertion would go against the very definition of an atom. To avoid this contradiction, the Kāśmīra Vaibhāṣikas insisted that atoms do not aggregate or do not touch one another (*na spṛśatīti, Akb* p. 32). If the atoms do not touch one another, then there is no way in which they could coalese, for in the case of this latter process, not only would they touch one another with parts, but will have to mingle with another completely (*sarvam ātmana*, ibid.). This is impossible if the atoms were to have parts (*avayavatva*). Thus, aggregation and coalesence involve two anti-nomial processes. Without parts there could be no aggregation. With parts there cannot be coalesence. Yet, in order to coalese, the atoms should come together and they cannot come together because, by definition, they have no parts.

14. *Dig-bhāga-bhedo yasyāsti tasyaikatvaṃ na yujyate,*
chāyāvṛtī kathaṃ vānyo na piṇḍaś cen na tasya te.

The unity of one that possesses spatial distinctions is not proper. [If there were to be no spatial distinctions,] how can there be an enveloping shadow? If an aggregate were to be different [from the atoms], those charcteristics would not be part of it.

For Vasubandhu, the conception of unity and plurality are as metaphysical as are the conceptions of atoms and aggregates to which they are applied. In the context of a theory of atoms, unity would imply the absence of any spatial distinctions such as front and back, lighted and shaded segments, etc. If an aggregate were to be different from the atoms, the characteristics that are not part of the atoms could not appear in the aggregate of which they are parts. The conceptions of unity and plurality are, therefore, the same as the metaphysical ideas of identity and difference.

15. *Ekatve na kramenetir yugapan na grahāgrahau,*
vicchinnāneka-vṛttiś ca sūkṣmānīkṣā ca no bhavet.

When there is unity, there is no progressive movement nor simultaneous perception and non-perception. Neither is there interrupted and diversified activity nor perception of subtle things.

The criticism presented here is based upon the assumption that unity is the same as identity perceived in the form of substance (*svabhāva*). A few centuries earlier, Nāgārjuna had amply demonstrated the difficulties involved in explaining movement (*gati* = *eti*) and change in the context of a theory of substance. Vasubandhu is here reiterating the same arguments. Candrakīrti, who was explaining Nāgārjuna's arguments, utilized the example of a 'foot' (*caraṇa*), considered as an aggregate of atoms (*paramānu-saṃghāta*), to illustrate the difficulties in explaining movement (*MKV* p. 93).

Furthermore, Vasubandhu argues that the conception of a unitary substance would create problems regarding the perception of an object. No object is perceived in its entirety. Certain parts or facets are perceived and, at the same time, certain other parts remain unperceived. Unity, implying a substance, should make it possible to see all parts by seeing one part. The front and back of an object could be seen at the same time, and this is empirically impossible.

The same applies to interrupted and diversified activity. If the perceived object consists of one unitary substance, it would be perceived in an identical form all the time. There cannot be variation in the perception even though that perception may be interrupted due to other circumstances.

Finally, any process of discovery will be rendered meaningless, for very often what is claimed to have been discovered is some subtle thing that has escaped one's attention previously. Perception of such subtle differences would not be possible if things continue as identities or substances.

16. *Pratyakṣa-buddhiḥ svapnādau yathā sā ca yadā tadā,*
na so 'rtho dṛśyate tasya pratyakṣatvaṃ kathaṃ mataṃ.

Immediate knowledge is as in dream, etc. When that occurs, then that object is not perceived. How, then, can immediacy be conceived.

This is an extremely important epistemological observation. There is no doubt that human beings perceive and continue to perceive objects. However, at the time of perception of the object, there certainly is no awareness that one is perceiving that object. When awareness arises that one is perceiving an object, then at that very moment the object is no more perceived. Vasubandhu is here making an extremely subtle epistemological distinction between "perceiving an object" and "being aware of the perceiving of an object." For him, what is generally understood as immediate perception (*pratyakṣa*) is the former, not the latter. Thus, by the time the awareness of perception arises, the object perceived is already in the past and is non-existent.

Vasubandhu's analysis of perception represents a veiled rejection of a metaphysical *cogito*, i.e., one who is conscious of himself before an object is perceived. It is a different way of expressing what Nāgājuna intended to say in Chapter III of his *Kārikā*. In any act of experience, one does not start with the awareness of oneself (*svam ātmānaṃ darśanaṃ, Kārikā III.2*). Instead, self-consciousness (*vijñāna*) is what emerges depending upon the sense organ and the object of sense (*cakkhuñ ca paṭicca rūpe ca uppajjati cakkhuviññāṇaṃ, M* 1.111). This causal account of perception, which can be traced back to the Buddha himself and which is re-stated by Nāgārjuna (*Kārikā III.7; MKV* p. 118) is utilized by Vasubandhu who was keen on rejecting the naive realism of the Sarvāstivādins that an object that impinges on the senses can be perceived in its "real form" without distortions. Instead of assuming that one can perceive a real object, Vasubandhu is emphasizing the variety of conditions that affects every act of perception. Dream experience (*svapna*) turns out to be a valuable means by which he could inculcate this idea.

17. *Uktaṃ yathā tad-ābhāsā vijñapitiḥ smaraṇaṃ tataḥ,*
svapne dṛg-viṣayābhāvaṃ nāprabuddho 'vagacchati.

As such, a concept is said to reflect that [experience]. Memory arises therefrom. One who is not awakened does not realize the absence of the object of perception in dream.

The immediate experience (*pratyakṣa*), discussed in the previous verse, receives further explanation here. There is no denial that such an immediate experience occurs. The question is whether that experience reflects a "real and substantial object" (*sad-artha*). Vasubandhu's answer seems to be clearly in the negative. What then is that immediate experience? Is it a "big blooming buzzing confusion?" Vasubandhu's auto-commentary seems to confirm that this is the case. With the emergence of memory (*smṛty utpādāt*), the experience of the object (*arthānubhava*) is interrupted and a "mental concept" (*mano-vijñapti*) arises, reflecting that experience but mixed up with one's memory. It is this latter that is referred to as the "thought of material form, etc." (*rūpādivikalpika*).

Thus, the object as "conceived" is not identical with the experience, even though it has a basis in experience. This does not mean that Vasubandhu was recognizing a "pre-cognitive" or "pre-conceptual" reality, which is beyond all forms of discrimination and description. He does not refer to it as *vijñapti-mātra*, for *vijñapti* is the conceptualized. Such conceptualization involving memory (*smṛti*) brings in many other elements such as the exercise of thought (*vikalpābhyāsa*) and dispositional tendencies (*vāsanā*). The "sensible muchness" receives its form through such exercise and tendencies. These, however, are not comparable to the eternal and transcendental categories recognized by Kant. They are as changeable and impermanent as the flux of sensible muchness.

This is the same as the epistemological position adopted by the Buddha when he explained dispositions (*saṅkhāra*) (see section on "The Buddha's Conception of Personhood").

In other words, a "concept" is a substitute for a completed sensory process, no part of which can be arbitrarily picked up and shown to be the "ultimate reality." Without such a concept, no intellectual activity relating to sense experience is at all possible. To awaken to this realization, which is what is implied by *prabuddha*, does not mean the development of an altogether different "intuition." It is a realization that in any act of cognition, we are involved in conceptualization based upon experience as well as our dispositional tendencies, and that there is no "ultimate reality" or "substance" involved in such experience. This is the radical non-substantialist position of the Buddha.

18. *Anyonyādhipatitvena vijñapti-niyamo mithaḥ,*
middhenopahṛtaṃ cittaṃ svapne tenāsamaṃ phalaṃ.

The determination of mutually related concepts is based upon mutual domination. In dream experience, thought is overwhelmed by torpor. Hence the difference in fruit.

At this stage, Vasubandhu anticipates an objection from the realist. If the evolution of the individual stream of consciousness (*svasaṃtāna*) in terms of dispositional tendencies (*vāsanā*) were to dominate the concepts (*vijñapti*) that are formed on the basis of sense experience (*arthapratibhāsa*), and not the objects themselves (*na arthaviśeṣāt*), how can the determination of concepts take place as a result of contact with good or bad friends or the hearing of the true or false doctrines? In other words, our conceptual thinking can be changed by our associations with good or bad people, with true or false ideas. Such changes would be meaningless if concepts were to simply evolve out of our own stream of consciousness, rather than external objects.

Vasubandhu's treatment of concepts (*vijñapti*) is not different from Nāgārjuna's exposition of convention (*saṃvṛti, vyavahāra* or *prajñapti*). For the former, a concept is not a mere linguistic symbol. A concept is also a convention based upon experience as well as dispositions (*vāsanā*). These, therefore, have fruits (*phala*) on the basis of which their goodness or badness, reality or unreality is determined. The fruits of dream experience are different from the fruits of waking experience, not merely because the former has no external basis and the latter is founded on real external objects, but because of the degree to which the thought process is dominated by torpor or sluggishness. In the waking state, the thought process, being less sluggish, can be dominated by the "concepts" (*vijñapti*) of others as well. Hence the human response to varying conventions of the society in which they live, as well as of the societies that they come to associate with. Understanding Vasubandhu's notion of *vijñapti* in this manner, one avoids attributing any solipsism to him.

19. *Maraṇaṃ para-vijñapti-viśeṣād vikriyā yathā,*
smṛti-lopādikānyeṣāṃ piśācādi-manovaśat.

Death is a transformation [of the personality] produced by a specific concept of another. It is comparable to the loss of other's memory through being overwhelmed by demonaic thoughts, etc.

A metaphyical realist believes that the material body has its own nature (*svabhāva*) and, as such, its termination occurs primarily on the basis of material causes. He assumes that Vasubandhu's philosophy makes death or termination of life (*maraṇa*) meaningless. It is interesting to note that Vasubandhu is not actually denying the phenomenon of death. Instead he is emphasizing an aspect of the life-process (*saṃsāra*) that the metaphysical realist has completely ignored or cannot explain on the basis of his conception of self-nature. This is the influence of the concepts of others in bringing about a person's death. Conventions of society often bring about the death, not only of criminals, but also of large numbers of innocent people. Hitler's conception of the purity of the Aryan race brought death to millions of Jews. One word from a so-called spiritual leader can cause havoc on the lives of millions of people.

Furthermore, for Vasubandhu, who was a faithful Buddhist, death in this life is not the end of the life-process (*saṃsāra*). It is only a brief interruption, like the interruption of a person's memory through being possessed by demonaic thoughts.

20. *Kathaṃ vā daṇḍakāraṇya-śūnyatvaṃ ṛṣī-kopataḥ,*
mano-daṇdo mahā-vadyaḥ kathaṃ vā tena sidhyati.

How can the devastation of the Daṇḍaka forest resulting from the anger of a sage be established. Or, how can it be established that mental punishment is more blameworthy.

Whether the fire that devastated the Daṇḍaka forest was generated by the anger on the part of a sage, or whether he initiated the fire because of his anger is not clear from the above statement. The ability to develop psychokinetic powers (*ṛddhi*) is not discounted in Buddhism. Only its value as a means of attaining spiritiual progress is abandoned.

The Buddha certainly recognized the overwhelming power of the human mind, either in the perpetuation of evil or the promotion of good. Hence his emphasis on the need to cleanse one's thought (*citta-pariyodapana*). Vasubandhu is utilizing the Buddha's discourse to Upāli, a disciple of Mahāvīra. where the Buddha emphasized the importance attached to mental action (*mano-kamma*, instead of *mano-daṇḍa*) in his teachings (*M* 1.371–387). Furthermore, the Buddha's statement: "The world is led by thought" (*cittena niyyati loko, S* 1.39) would make no sense if the mind were to be given a secondary place in explaining human behavior. He would want to maintain that even the substantialist theories, which can in the long run be destructive of human life as well as institutions, are the results of concepts.

21. *Para-citta-vidāṃ jñānam ayathārthaṃ kathaṃ yathā,*
sva-citta-jñānam ajñānād yathā buddhasya gocaraḥ.

The knowledge of those who are telepathic is without a real object. How? It is like the knowledge of one's own thought. It is due to ignorance. Such is the sphere of the enlightened one.

The present verse is often taken as evidence for the metaphysical idealism of Vasubandhu, comparable to the Vedāntic standpoint where the subject-object discrimination is dissolved in a higher intuition. However, a careful consideration of the terminology used by Vasubandhu may yield an altogether different view. Vasubandhu is not denying telepathic knowledge. He is merely rejecting the view that such knowledge reveals the existence of a real object (*yathārtha*), not a mere object (*artha*). *Yathārtha* is identical with *sad-artha*. The problem relates not only to telepathic knowledge, but also to the knowledge of one's own thought. There is no question that thoughts occur in a conscious human being. Vasubandhu has already indicated how the so-called immediate experience vanishes into thin air when reflection occurs (*Viṃś* 16). Similarly to assume the thinking process of another (*para-citta*) is as metaphysically involved as the recognition of a *cogito*. What remains at the end of both processes is a "mere concept" (*vijñapti-mātra*), and this is the sphere of the enlightened one. It is, indeed, the knowledge that all phenomena (*dharmāḥ*), including one's own personal experience, are non-substantial (*anātman*).

22. *Vijñapti-mātratā-siddhiḥ sva-śakti-sadṛśī mayā,*
kṛteyaṃ sarvathā sā tu na cintyā buddha-gocaraḥ.

The establishment of a "mere concept" has been achieved by me according to my ability, even though it is unthinkable. It is, indeed, the sphere of the enlightened one.

In his commentary, Vasubandhu characterizes the doctrine of "mere concept" (*vijāptimātra*) as one which involves a variety of relative determinations (*ananta-viniścaya-prabheda*) and immeasurable profundity (*agādha-gāmbhīrya*), thus leaving room for some to assume transcendence of *vijñapti-mātratā*. However, considering the statement closely, especially in the light of some of the fundamental teachings of the Buddha as well as the manner in which a disciple of the Buddha would pay reverence to the "true doctrine" (*sad-dharma*), this statement can be explained in a totally different way.

The "middle path" (*madhyamā pratipat*), proposed by the Buddha in his discourse to Kaccāyana was not one that would yield an absolutistic interpretation. The theory of "dependent arising" (*pratītyasamutpāda*) was, indeed, intended to avoid any notion of an absolute ultimate truth or reality. If Vasubandhu's theory of "mere concept" (*vijñaptimātra*) has any affinity to the Buddha's middle way, it could not provide any basis for a "extreme decision or determination" (*anta-niścaya*). Being fully cognisant of this character of the Buddha's teaching, Vasubandhu is emphasizing not only the relativity (*ananta*) but also the variety of contexts (*prabheda*) in which it can be applied.

The statement that it is immeasurable in profundity (*agādha-gāmbhīrya*) can only be properly understood in the context in which Vasubandhu, as a devoted disciple of the Buddha, places himself in relation to the Buddha. The humility with which he treats his own explanation of the Buddha-word and the respect with which he held the Buddha's own insight, is clearly implied in his statements: "It is not possible for one like me to think of it with its manifold implications," (*sarva-prakārā tu sā mādṛśaiś cintayituṃ na śakyate,* p. 11).

It is the sphere of the enlightened ones (*buddhānāṃ*), because it is where the distinction between the knowledge (*jñāna*) and the known (*jñeya*) are completely destroyed. What is destroyed is not the discrimination between the subject and object, but rather the relationship between knowlege and the known. In other words, it is a complete rejection of the discrimination that a metaphysical realist or a substantialist would make between knowledge (*jñāna*) and the object of knowledge (*jñeya*). It is what Nāgārjuna was emphasizing when he wanted to establish the non-substantiality of elements (*dharma-nairātmya*), namely, the appeasement of the object (*draṣṭavyopaśama, Kārikā* V.8). It is not intended as a justification for absolute idealism.

Vijñaptimātratāsiddhi
Triṃśikā-vijñapti-kārikā

1. *Ātma-dharmopacāro hi vividho yaḥ pravartate,*
vijñāna-pariṇāme 'sau pariṇāmaḥ sa ca tridhā.

Whatever, indeed, is the variety of ideas of self and elements that prevails, it occurs in the transformation of consciousness. Such transformation is threefold, [namely,]

Upacāra is a usage or a prevailing idea. Self (*ātman*) was an idea that predominated the Indian philosophical scene before the advent of the Buddha. The notion of elements (*dharma*) possessing substance (*svabhāva*) is an idea that came to prevail as a result of the speculations of the Sarvāstivāda school of Buddhism. In their attempt to get rid of the notion of substantial elements, the Sautrāntika school of Buddhism adhered to the notion of a momentary stream of consciousness (*citta-saṃtāna*), and surreptitiously reintroduced the old Indian notion of a self (*ātman, pudgala*). These are distinct and subtle theories that Vasubandhu had to deal with. As such, if Vasubandhu's explanation is going to be any different, he should avoid the variety of metaphysical theories presented by the Sarvāstivādins and the Sautrāntikas. This would be the most important fact to be borne in mind when evaluating Vasubandhu's explanation of the transformation of consciousness (*vijñāna-pariṇāma*). Any explanation that would involve either the Sarvāstivāda or the Sautrāntika metaphysics would vitiate Vasubandhu's efforts to restore the original teachings of the Buddha, if that was what he had in mind when compiling this treatise.

Therefore, when Vasubandhu declared that the concepts of self (*ātman*) and elements (*dharma*) occur in the process of consciousness (*vijñāna*) that undergoes transformation (*pariṇāma*), he seems to be emphasizing the epistemological issues rather than replacing the self and elements with another equally metaphysical idea that consciousness is the only reality.

Sthiramati explains the motivation for the compilation of the *Triṃsikā* as follows:

> "Or else, some think that, like consciousness (*vijñānavad*), the object of knowledge (*vijñeyaṃ*) exists as a substance (*dravyataḥ*). [Others assume] that like the object of knowledge (*vijñeyavad*),consciousness (*vijñāna*) exists only in terms of convention (*saṃvṛtitaḥ*) and not in an ultimate sense (*paramārthataḥ*). The treatise was compiled for the sake of rejecting these two extreme (*anta*) views."

The implication is that Vasubandhu perceives consciousness (*vijñāna*) as having an ultimate meaning (*paramārtha*). This would mean that he is rejecting the metaphysical realism of Sarvāstivāda as well as the nominalism of the Sautrāntikas. As a philosopher interested in epistemology, he lays great emphasis on psychology, especially the psychology of perception. As such the phenomenon of consciousness (*vijñāna*) was of prime importance. Even though some of his views about the external world compare well with those of George Berkeley, his involvement in human psychology aligns him more with William James. He abandoned his Sautrāntika leanings because of the metaphysical problems in which the Sautrāntikas got involved. Moving from the position of a Sautrāntika to the position of a Vijñānavādin (or Yogācārin), Vasubandhu would not be making any progress in his philosophical position if he were to bring back similar, or even more complicated metaphysical theories into his new philosophy. The drastic changes Vasubandhu brought about in the terminology employed by the classical idealists in the Buddhist tradition as represented by the *Laṅkāvatāra-sūtra* and the *Saṃdhinirmocana-sūtra* would also make no sense if he is considered to be a metaphysical idealist.

Furthermore, there must be some valid reason for Vasubandhu to abandon his Sautrāntika leanings and adopt a Vijñānavāda standpoint. That reason is clearly explained by Vasubandhu in his *Viṃśatikā*, especially when he criticized the theory of atoms (*paramāṇu*). The theory of atoms, though not identical with the theory of moments, is based upon the latter. Yet, Sthiramati brings back the theory of momentariness in his explanation of the transformation of consciousness (*vijñāna-pariṇāma*), even though Vasubandhu never utilized the theory of momentariness in the present treatise. Sthiramati's explanation is almost identical with the Sautrāntika standpoint that Vasubandhu was rejecting. He says:

Transformation is the obtaining of its own identity on the part of the effect simultaneous with the moment of the destruction of the cause and the moment of its abandoning its characteristic, (*kāraṇa-kṣana-nirodha-samakālaḥ kāraṇa-kṣaṇa-nirodha-vilakṣaṇaḥ kāryasyātmalābhaḥ pariṇāmaḥ, p. 16).*

2. *Vipāko mananākhyaś ca vijñaptir viṣayasya ca,*
tatrālayākhyaṃ vijñānaṃ vipakaḥ sarva-bījakaṃ

the resultant, what is called mentation, as well as the concept of the object. Herein, the consciousness called *ālaya*, with all its seeds, is the resultant.

The transformation (*pariṇāma*), as explained here, avoids the notion of an absolute beginning and, therefore, of a temporal sequence as prior and posterior. This is one important reason for Vasubandhu to refer to *ālaya-vijñāna* as a resultant (*vipāka*), which is a semantic equivalent of "dependently arisen" (*pratityasamutpanna*), rather than as seed (*bīja*) or cause (*kāraṇa*) in this initial reference or description of it. Transformation, therefore, is not from a primordial substance, like the *prakṛti-prabhāsvara-citta* of the *Laṅkāvatāra*. It is a transformation of consciousness involving the *ālaya*, the *manas* and *viṣaya-vijñapti* all acting together, and it is this process that gives rise to the beliefs in self and elements (*ātma-dharma-upacāra*).

Instead of assuming them to be actual states in an *inevitable* process of transformation, they are better understood as three occurrences that are intended to explain a variety of issues relating to the problem of perception.

The concept of *ālaya* is, indeed, central to the explanation of the problem of perception in Buddhism. As pointed out earlier, it occurs in the Buddha's discourse on "The Noble Quest" (*Ariyapariyesana*), where he expressed his reluctance to preach the doctrine because human beings are overwhelmed by *ālaya*. Nāgārjuna utilized a similar term *adhilaya* (*Kārikā* XXIV.13) in order to explain the same problem. We have interpreted *ālaya* as "mooring." It is the source of the dispositional tendencies (*saṃskāra*) that are operative in the perceptual process. The relationship between lust (*rāga*) or craving (*taṇhā*) or even hatred (*dosa*) and dispositions (*saṅkhāra*) recognized in the early Buddhist tradition corresponds to the relationship between *ālaya* and *vāsanā* in Vasubandhu's explanation of Buddhist epistemology.

Unfortunately, the term *ālaya* came to be associated with the Sautrāntika concept of *āśraya*, implying a store or location (*sthāna*) of the momentary impressions, a conception that is as metaphysical as the *ātman* of the later Nyāya epistemologists who believed that all knowledge occurs in the *ātman*. Thus, Sthiramati, following the *Laṅkāvatāra* version, defines *ālaya* as "the location of all seeds of the defiled dharmas" (*sarva-saṃkleśika-dharma-bīja-sthāna*). For him, *ālaya* is primarily a synonym for *sthāna* (p. 18), and the original meaning of the term "mooring" in the sense of "attachment" (*alīyante*) is secondary.

Vijñāna is not an entity. It is the act of being conscious (*vijānātīti vijñānaṃ*, p. 18; *vijānātīti viññāṇaṃ*, *S* 3.87; cp. William James, *Essays in Radical Empiricism*, p. 4). *Ālaya-vijñāna* is thus the process of consciousness that gets anchored, resulting in "attachment" or "desire." In that sense it is a resultant (*vipāka*). However, since such consciousness continues to be functional in human behavior, it also serves as the cause (*kāraṇa*) or seed (*bīja*).

In his auto-commentary on the *Viṃśatikā*, Vasubandhu provided an explanation of immediate experience (*pratyakṣa*). For him, an immediate experience evaporates into thin air the moment one tries to identify it. This is because such identification involves reflection and the so-called immediacy is lost in the process. Identification, therefore, involves the activity of *manas* and the process culminates with the conceptualization of the external object (*viṣaya-vijñapti*). It is significant to note that here Vasubandhu is referring not to the conscousness of the object (*viṣaya-vijñāna*), but to the concept of the object (*viṣayasya vijñaptiḥ*), for it is through such concepts that objects of immediate experience are identified. If not so identified, they remain forever unknown.

3. *Asaṃviditakopādi-sthāna-vijñaptikaṃ ca tat,*
sadā sparśa-manaskāra-vit-saṃjñā-cetanānvitaṃ.

It is unidentified in terms of concepts of object and location, and is always possessed of [activities such as] contact, attention, feeling, perception and volition.

The term *asaṃvidita* qualifies only two of the activities and not the rest. This means that most of the activities such as contact (*sparśa*), attention (*manaskāra*), feeling (*vit*), perception (*saṃjñā*) and even volition (*cetanā*) are available. Even though consciousness of the object, etc. is available, these are not yet identified by breaking that consciousness into distinct entities, and substituting concepts (*vijñapti*).

This description of *ālaya-vijñāna* eliminates any possibility of presenting it as the primordial source of all experience. Indeed, what is emphasized is the existence of all forms of experience whenever they take place on the basis of conditions.

4. *Upekṣā vedanā tatrānivṛtāvyākṛtaṃ ca tat,*
tathā sparśādayas tac ca vartate śrotasaughavat.

In that context, the neutral feeling is uninterrupted and is not defined. So are contact, etc. And it proceeds like the current of a stream.

This is the flux of experience where events are not identified or defined. It is similar to what William James called the "plethora of the experienced continuity unbroken into parts." The simile of the stream (*sota*) used by the Buddha to illustrate the process of becoming (*bhava*) is here utilized by Vasubandhu without any metaphysical embellishment in the form of a theory of moments (*kṣaṇavāda*), relished so much by his erstwhile companions, the Sautrāntikas.

5. *Tasya vyāvṛttir arhatve tad āśritya pravartate,*
tad ālambaṃ mano-nāma vijñānaṃ mananātmakam.

Its (i.e. *ālaya's*) dissipation occurs in *arhat*ship. Associated with this process and depending upon it occurs the consciousness called *manas*, which is of the nature of mentation.

Vyāvṛtti means "taking a different direction" and does not involve annihilation or complete cessation (*nivṛtti*). The different direction it takes is dependent upon the appeasement of the dispositions, and this latter is achieved through the elimination of lust (*rāga*), hatred (*dveṣa*) and confusion (*moha*). The elimination of these three roots of evil is considered to be freedom or "worthiness" (*arhatva*). At this stage, the *ālaya-vijñāna*, in a sense gets transformed, and is no more an *ālaya* ("attachment") but simply *vijñāna*. It is cleansed of all defiling tendencies, but not the experiences of contact, attention, feeling, perception or volition.

After describing the normal stream of experiential consciousness, Vasubandhu proceeds to explain how the ideas of self and elements (*ātma-dharma-upacāra*) emerge. As stated in the commentary on the *Viṃśatikā*, the conceptualization of an object, though based upon the experienced flux, involves reflection. Such reflection inevitably brings about the feeling of "I" (*ahaṃ*). The difference between Buddhist and Brahmanical speculation on this issue is that the latter assumed that all experiences begin with the perception of "self," while according to the former, it is merely a product of reflection. This stage, according to Vasubandhu is represented by *manas*.

Subsequent explanations of Vijñānavāda seems to assume that this state of consciousness is different from *mano* in the early Buddhist tradition. Therefore, it is looked upon as the seventh consciousness, the *ālaya-vijñāna* being the eighth. However, Vasubandhu himself makes no such characterization. For him, *manas* serves the same function as *mano* in the early Buddhist tradition (see section on "Yogācāra Psychology"). Vasubandhu also holds an identical position when he insists that the concepts (*vijñapti*) of objects (*viṣaya*) are dependent upon the *manas*. It is the coordinating activity of *manas* that gives rise to the notion of a self. Hence Vasubandhu's description of *manas* as possessing the four defilements, discussed in the verse that follows.

6. *Kleśaiś caturbhiḥ sahitaṃ nivṛtāvyākṛtaiḥ sadā,*
ātma-dṛṣṭy ātma-mohātma-mānātma-sneha-saṃjñitaiḥ.

Endowed with the four types of defilements, constantly concealed and undefined, involving self-view, self-confusion, self-esteem and self-love,

If there is any notion of self (*ātman*), it eludes oneself everytime an attempt is made to identify it. The *avyākṛta* represents this indefinability or unidentifiability of the notion of self, even though this concept of self continues to be part of our view of the world, as well as the confusion, esteem and love that it generates. For Vasubandhu, it is a defiling tendency that is produced with reflection or mentation on occasions of sense experience.

7. *Yatrajas tanmayair anyaiḥ sparśādyaiś cārhato na tat,*
na nirodha-samāpattau mārge lokottare na ca.

And also possessed of other forms of contact, etc. (i.e. attention, feeling, perception and volition) born of such (self-view, etc.) and made of such (self-view, etc.). It is not found in the worthy one, nor in the state of cessation nor in the supra-mundane path.

With the emergence of self-consciousness, all perceptual activities such as contact, attention, feeling, perception and volition, which previously "belonged," now come to be "possessed." What was earlier "dependently arisen" (*pratītyasamutpanna*) in the individual stream of consciousness, now turns out to be part of an ego. The stronger the view, the confusion, the pride and love of this self, the greater is the ego that emerges within the experiencing personality.

This would mean that a perceptual process which was originally a product of various conditions, including dispositions (*vāsanā*), comes to be possessed by the so-called "ghost in the machine." As a result, the dispositions that were part of the perceptual flux are solifidified thereby contributing to further dispositional tendencies and the creation of a sharp dichotomy between the self and other. When this ego reaches its climax, one ends up with the belief in a permanent and eternal self which, unfortunately, remains unidentified through any available means of ordinary experience.

8. *Dvitīyaḥ pariṇāmo 'yaṃ tṛtīyaḥ ṣaḍ-vidhasya yā,*
viṣayasopalabdhiḥ sā kuśalākuśaladvayā.

Such is the second transformation. The third represents the acquisition of the sixfold object, and this is either good, bad or indeterminate.

Even though this is considered to be the third transformation, there is no indication that it is temporally subsequent. Vasubandhus' emphasis is on the "acquisition" (*upalabdhiḥ*), rather than the object itself. In the transformation discussed earlier, the acquisition or grasping is directed at oneself, whereas in the present it is focussed on the object of experience. This acquisitive element that emerges in the process of experience is heightened by the incapacity on the part of the human person to deal with the "big blooming buzzing confusion." Thus, selectivity becomes an inalienable part of the perceptual process. The recognition of this fact by Vasubandhu, as well as many other leading Buddhist thinkers since the time of the Buddha, has prevented them from assuming the possibility of knowing something in "its ultimately real form." Instead of being an ultimate reality, the object becomes a convention (*saṃvṛti*) or something that is "put together" (*saṃskṛta*) in terms of one's interest. As such, it turns out to be either good or bad or indeterminate.

9. *Sarvatragair viniyataiḥ kuśalaiś caitasair asau,*
saṃprayuktā tathā kleśair upa-kleśais tri-vedanā.

That [acquisition of the sixfold object] is associated with wholesome psychological conditions, both universal and particular, and similarly with primary as well as secondary defilements. That includes the threefold feeling.

Verses 9–14 are devoted to an enumeration of the different categories of psychological conditions (*caitta, caitasika*) that occur in human beings resulting form the perceptual process explained earlier. The list undoubtedly is the work of early Ābhidharmikas who attempted to determine, with great precision, the variety of psychological elements that come to be associated with the perceptual process. Vasubandhu, as the author of *Abhidharmakośa*, had dealt with all these psychological conditions and had no difficulty utilizing that list without getting involved in either the Sarvāstivāda or Sautrāntika metaphysics (see *Akb* pp. 54–55). In fact, his predecessor in the Yogācāra tradition, namely Asaṅga, had done so (see *Abhidharma-samuccaya*). The adoption of that list was merely for the sake of being comprehensive in his treatment of consciousness.

10. *Ādyāḥ sparśādayaś chandādhimokṣa-smṛtayaḥ saha,*
samādhidhībhyāṃ niyatāḥ śraddhātha hrīr apatrapā.

The first [i.e., universals] are contact, etc. Yearning, resolve, memory together with concentration and wisdom are particulars. Confidence, shame and remorse,

Contact, attention, feeling, perception and volition are referred to as universals (*sarvatraga*) as they occur with all forms of consciousness. Particulars (*viniyata*) are associated with some and not all acts of being conscious. In this and the next verse, ten good psychological conditions are enumerated.

11. *Alobhādi trayaṃ vīryaṃ praśrabdhiḥ sāpramādikā,*
ahiṃsā kuśalāḥ kleśā rāga-pratigha-mūḍhayaḥ.

The triad consisting of absence of greed, etc., effort, deligence and non-violence are wholesome [psychological conditions]. The [primary] defilements are lust, aversion and confusion,

12. *Māna-dṛg-vicikitsāś ca krodhopanahane punah,*
mrakṣah pradāśa īrsyātha mātsaryaṃ saha māyayā.

pride, view and doubt. Furthermore, anger, enmity, hypocricy, malice, envy, avarice along with deception,

13. *Śāṭhyaṃ mado 'vihiṃsāhrīr atrapā sthyāna-muddhavaḥ,*
aśraddhyam atha kausīdyaṃ pramādo muṣitā smṛtiḥ.

fraudulance, self-esteem, violence, shamelessness, remorselessness, deceitfulness, stupidity, lack of confidence, sluggishness, indolence and forgetfulness,

14. *Vikṣepo 'samprajanyaṃ ca kaukṛtyaṃ middham eva ca,*
vitarkaś ca vicāraś cety upa-kleśā dvaye dvidhā.

distraction, inattentiveness, worry, sloth, reflection and investigation—these are the secondary defilements, the last two being twofold [defiled and non-defiled].

15. *Pañcānāṃ mūla-vijñāne yathāpratyayam udbhavaḥ,*
vijñānānāṃ saha na vā taraṅgāṇāṃ yathā jale.

The arising of the five forms of consciousness, together or separately, within the foundational consciousness is like the waves in the water.

The foundational consciousness (*mūla-vijñāna*) referred to here is the mental consciousness (*mano-vijñāna*), since specific reference is made by Vasubandhu to the five other forms of consciousness which are the visual, auditory, olfactory, gustatory and tactile consciousness. *Manovijñāna* is associated with *manas* which, along with the other five senses, eye (*cakṣu*), ear (*śrota*), nose (*ghrāṇa*), tongue (*jihvā*) and body (*kāya*) constitute the six senses. If, as explained earlier, *manas* occupies a pre-eminent position among the six senses because it is the co-ordinator of the other five senses it can be rightly called the foundational sense, and *mano-vijñāna* then is synonymous with *mūla-vijñāna*. If the foundational consciousness (*mūla-vijñāna*) is the same as *ālaya-vijñāna*, there is no justification for the popular interpretation in Vijñānavāda that *ālaya-vijñāna* is the eighth consciousness and *manas* is the seventh in addition to the six forms of consciousness referred to above. On the contrary, the threefold evolution of consciousness (*vijñāna-pariṇāma*), with *ālaya, manas* and *viṣaya-vijñapti*, will be another way of dealing with or explaining the six types of consciousness recognized by the Buddha as well as the later Buddhists. The recognition of *ālaya-vijñāna* as the *eighth* consciousness and *manas* as the *seventh* followed by yet another six types of consciousness, therefore, seems a colossal mistake made in the interpretation of Vasubandhu. The present verse, indeed, does not allow for such an interpretation of Vasubandhu's treatment of consciousness. Furthermore, the previous analysis of *ālaya-vijñāna* clearly indicated that activities such as contact, attention, feeling, perception and volition occur in that consciousness, except for the fact that they are not identified. *Manana* and *viṣaya-vijñapti* explain the manner in which they come to be identified, leading finally to the emergence of the beliefs in self and elements.

Vasubandhu seems to have introduced the simile of the "waves in the water" (*taraṅgāṇāṃ yathā jale*) in order to avoid the metaphysics of identity and difference that plagued the Sarvāstivāda and Sautrāntika schools. Yet, the literal interpretation of *ālaya-vijñāna* as the location (*sthāna*) seems to have been responsible for the re-introduction of the same metaphysical notions with a substantial consciousness and fluctuating aspects. This is how the simile is mostly understood.

16. *Mano-vijñāna-saṃbhūtiḥ sarvadāsaṃjñikād ṛte,*
samāpatti-dvayān middhān mūrchanād apy acittakāt.

The manifestation of mental consciousness takes place always, except in the sphere of non-perception, in the two attainments and in the state of torpor occasioned by insensibility and absence of thought.

Mental consciousness (*mano-vijñāna*), described in the previous verse as fundamental consciousness (*mūla-vijñāna*) and, therefore, identical with *ālaya-vijñāna*, functions on all occasions, except when the conditions for such activity are removed. Examples of such occasions when mental consciousness is not functional are: (1) the world of dieties (*āsaṃjñika-sattva*), who probably were a class of deities without the normal sensory faculties, (2) the two final stages of *dhyāna*, namely, the state of neither-perception-nor-non-perception (*naiva saṃjña naivāsaṃjñā*) and the state of cessation of perception and what is felt (*saṃjñā-vedayita-nirodha*) and, (3) the clouding of consciousness conditioned by various disorders such as epilepsy and other conditions that prevent the functioning of this fundamental consciousness.

17. *Vijñāna-pariṇmo 'yaṃ vikalpo yad vikalpyate,*
tena tan nāsti tenedaṃ sarvaṃ vijñapti-mātrakaṃ.

Thus, thought involves this transformation of consciousness. For that reason, what has thus been thought of does not exist. Therefore, all this is mere concept.

There is no denial of an object here. What is denied is the existence of a real object that is reflected "as it is" in consciousness. The fact that consciousness, while reflecting the object, has passed through several transformations makes it impossible for the object to be known "as it is." For this reason, all that is available is a "concept" (*vijñapti*), not an ultimate reality or substance, either in oneself or in the world of experience.

18. *Sarva-bījaṃ hi vijñānaṃ pariṇāmas tathā tathā,*
yāty anyonya-vaśād yena vikalpaḥ sa sa jāyate.

Consciousness, indeed, possesses all seeds. Its transformation occurs in a variety of ways. It proceeds on the basis of mutual dependence as a result of which such and such thoughts are born.

The so-called seeds of consciousness are the dispositional tendencies, the *vāsanās*, in terms of which the objects of experience are understood. No object of experience is known or cognized as something that is completely independent of all the previous experiences. Every new occurrence is *understood* in relation to something that has already been experienced. For this reason, consciousness is said to have the seeds of everything, not in the sense that it is a repository of all innate ideas. The transformation of consciousness and the development or advancement of knowledge are thus based upon dependence (*anyonyavaśād*), not in isolation or as a result of a complete break in the sequence of thinking, that is, with no connection to the past or the existing body of knowledge. Neither the percept nor the concept remains an incorruptible and permanent entity. They are all dependently arisen.

19. *Karmaṇo vāsanā grāha-dvaya-vāsanayā saha,*
kṣīṇe pūrva-vipāke 'nyad vipākaṃ janayanti tat.

Karmic dispositions, together with the two dispositions of grasping, produces another resultant when the previous resultant has waned.

Depending upon one's dispositions, one understands the duality involved in grasping, namely, grasping (*grāha*) and grasped (*grāhya*) or grasping (*grāha*) and grasper (*grāhaka*). The former leads to the wrong impression about substantial elements (*dharma*) that are independent of grasping, and the latter generates the belief in the existence of a substantial self (*ātman*) as the agent of grasping. Such dispositions and understandings, of course, produce consequences (*vipāka*). This is a different way of presenting the pragmatic theory of truth. Of the pragmatic theory that says "truth is what works," the more unpalatable aspect, namely, the psychological process that is involved in the working of that truth, is here emphasized.

The continuous working of the effects or fruits provides a foundation for verification and common acceptance of "mere concept" (*vijñaptimātra*) which, otherwise, would be considered a "mere fabrication," allowing room for all forms of day-dreams and utopias (see William James, *Essays in Radical Empiricism*, p. 32).

20. *Yena yena vikalpena yad yad vastu vikalpyate,*
parikalpita evāsau svabhāvo na sa vidyate.

Whatever thought through which an object is thought of as a substance, that indeed is a fabrication. It is not evident.

In the present context, the object (*vastu*) that is thought of it not an ordinary object of experience, but one that possesses self-nature or substance (*svabhāva*). An ordinary object of experience (as explained earlier as well as in the verse that follows) is one that is "dependently arisen" (*pratītyasamutpanna*). Such dependence is not confined to the various physical conditions that provide a foundation for experience. It also includes the psychological factors involved in such experience. However, an object that has self-nature does not depend upon any such conditions. Vasubandhu, who was the author of the famous *Abhidharmakośa*, could not have been unaware of the implications of the Sarvāstivāda notion of self-nature. Substance (*svabhāva*), as an independent entity, could not be part of experience as understood by the Buddhists who are faithful to the Buddha's epistemological standpoint. If substance were to be thought of or conceptualized in spite of its being not given in experience, it should be a mere fabrication, like a unicorn or a hare's horn. *Parikalpa,* as opposed to *vikalpa*, implies such fabrication with no grounding in experience. It is a mere imagination.

21. *Paratantra-svabhāvas tu vikalpaḥ pratyayodbhavaḥ,*
niṣpannas tasya pūrvena sadā rahitatā tu yā.

A dependent self-nature is a thought that has arisen depending upon conditions. However, the absence of the one prior to it is always the accomplished.

Just as much as one can have the thought of something that is non-existent by simply fabricating or imagining, there also can be a thought that is dependent upon various conditions. Indeed, if there were to be a self-nature that has "come to be" (*bhūta* = *niṣpanna*) or is accomplished (*pariniṣpanna*), it should pertain to the dependent (*paratantra*), rather than the fabricated (*parikalpita*).

Pariniṣpanna is often equated with *paramārtha*. On the basis of a substantialist (both Buddhist and Brahamincal) interpretation of *paramārtha* as "ultimate reality," the term *pariniṣpanna*, in spite of its being a past participle (like the term *bhūta*), is taken to mean an Absolute Reality. Thus, consciousness turns out to be the independent, the non-relative, ultimate reality in the world. There is little doubt that this is a gross misrepresentation of Vasubandhu's view, especially when placed in the context of his philosophical enterprise embodied in the *Viṃśatikā*.

The epistemological investigations in that treatise precludes any possibility of recognizing an ultimate reality that transcends experience. Experience itself involves subjective as well as objective conditions. The search for an ultimate reality in the objective world was criticized by Vasubandhu because it leads to an abandoning of the only epistemological means available, namely, sense experience. Phenomena (*dharmāḥ*), either in the form of substance (*svabhāva*) or as atoms (*paramāṇu*), were rejected because they were not available to any experience. Having abandoned such an attempt, Vasubandhu was not ready to present consciousness (*vijñāna*) as the Absolute Reality, for that would be to reintroduce some aspects of the Brahmanical notion of a self (*ātman*). The epistemological arguments used against the acceptance of an ultimately real object would be as valid against the acceptance of an ultimately real subject. For this reason, the *pariniṣpanna* needs to be understood in a totally different way.

The use of the past participle—*pariniṣpanna*—(comparable to the Buddha's own use of the past participle, *yathābhūta*) is extremely significant. Hsüan Tsang's rendering of this phrase into Chinese retains this meaning. Instead of being an Absolute or Ultimate Reality, it would mean something that is achieved or accomplished. Furthermore, the Buddha's own use of the term *paramattha*, as well as Nāgārjuna's utilization of the term *paramārtha*, in the sense of "ultimate goal or fruit," should prevent any absolutistic interpretation of the conception of *pariniṣpanna*. However, while the Buddha's and Nāgārjuna's use of the term *paramārtha* has a more ethical connotation, Vasubandhu's primary concern in the present treatise being epistemological, one is justified in taking the term *pariniṣpanna* in such an epistemological context. That epistemological implication is clearly brought out in the verse that follows.

22. *Ata eva sa naivānyo nānanyaḥ paratantrataḥ,*
anityatādivad vācyo nādṛṣṭe 'smin sa dṛśyate.

Thus, it [i.e., the accomplished] should be declared to be neither identical nor different from the dependent, like impermanence, etc. When that [i.e., the dependent] is not perceived, this too is not perceived.

This explains the relationship between *paratantra* and *pariniṣpanna*. Vasubandhu provides an important clue to an understanding of this relationship. The *pariniṣpanna* is like impermanence (*anityatā*). For the Buddha, as well as for Nāgārjuna, impermanence makes no sense except in relation to "the impermanent" (*anitya*). For them, the empirical is the impermanent. What then is the status of impermanence (*anityatā*) and how is it known? All the available evidence seems to indicate that "impermanence" (*anityatā*) is an epistemological "achievement" or "accomplishment" based upon the perception of "the impermanent" (*anitya*). There is nothing more that can be known or realized through the perception of the impermanent. Absolutist or substantialist philosophical enterprise has, for centuries, suggested the possibility of knowing the "permanent' (*nitya*) through or on the basis of the impermanent (*anitya*). For the Buddhists, this is something that cannot be accomplished. Buddha's realization is said to consist of penetrating into the *dhammatā* on the basis of an understanding of the *dhamma*. Thus, the characterization of the *parinispanna* as the Absolute Reality is a total misrepresentation of Vasubandhu's thought.

23. *Trividhasya svabhāvasya trividhāṃ niḥsvabhāvatāṃ,*
saṃdhāya sarva-dharmāṇāṃ deśitā niḥsvabhāvatā.

The non-substantiality of all elements has been preached for the sake of [establishing] the threefold non-substantiality of the three types of substances.

Vijñānavāda scholarship has enthusiastically advocated the conception of three substances (*svabhāva*). Yet, Vasubandhu is insisting that there indeed are no substances, but only non-substances (*niḥsvabhāva*). In other words, the three *svabhāvas* are meant to establish *niḥsvabhāva*. How could this be, unless the term *svabhāva* is used in different senses by Vasubandhu?

When Vasubandhu uses the term *svabhāva* in relation to *parikalpita*, *paratantra* and *parinispanna*, he seems to imply types or species, rather than substances that are eternal and immutable. The analysis of the experiential flux into elements (*dharma*) and the substitution of concepts to denote them for the purpose of identification does not mean that this experiential flux is *either* an indistinguishable and, therefore, a non-differentiated substance (*svabhāva*) *or* a series of discrete atomic pulses of sensation, representing atomic events (*paramāṇu*) which are, in themselves, indistinguishable, but which are related by the experiencing consciousness. Both these views are substantialist, even though one emphasizes identity and the other, difference in the form of discreteness. These concepts of identity and difference are, therefore, truly metaphysical, for in both cases the perceived differences and plurality in phenomena can be explained only by assuming the creativity of the perceiving consciousness.

Against these two metaphysical theories of identity and difference, Vasubandhu is insisting that there exists a variety in the experiential flux that can neither be identified nor differentiated at the metaphysical level (*asaṃviditaka . . . sparśa-manaskāra-vit-saṃjñā-cetanānvitaṃ* = *ālaya-vijñāna*, *Triṃś* 3 = *mano- or mūla-vijñāna*, ibid 15), but which is identified at the conceptual level (*vijñapti*). Thus, the identification of difference at the conceptual level is not entirely due to the function of imagination; it is grounded in the fundamental consciousness (*mūla-vijñāna*). For this reason, while some concepts are merely imagined (*parikalpita*), others are dependently arisen (*paratantra*). This latter experience serves as a foundation of reality, for it produces effects or consequences (*vipāka*) which can be shared or verified by other experiential processes as well. The knowledge accomplished by understanding the second type of event is uniformity (*dharmatā*), and since this is an extension of the knowledge of the dependently arisen phenomena (*dharma*) to include the obvious past and the yet unknown future, it is still a "mere concept" (*vijñapti-mātra*). Thus, there are three types of activities represented by the different concepts, the pure imagination represented by the *parikalpita*, the experience of the dependent substituted by the *paratantra*, and the rationally accomplished by the formulation of *pariniṣpanna*, all of which are non-substantial (*niḥsvabhāva*).

24. *Prathamo lakṣaṇenaiva niḥsvabhāvo 'paraḥ punaḥ,*
na svayaṃbhāva etasyety aparā niḥsvabhāvatā.

The first is non-substantial in terms of characteristics. The other, again, is one that possesses no self-nature and, as such, is a different [form of] non-substantiality.

Unlike Nāgārjuna, who was primarily interested in getting rid of substantialist metaphysics, Vasubandhu is concerned with explaining experience and knowledge, while at the same time getting rid of the metaphysical assumptions. Dealing with the problems of concept and reality, he is interested in explaining how different types of concepts are formed. As such, his is a more detailed examination of the psychological foundations of concepts and, therefore, of language, in relation to experience. In the present context, the two types of concepts, the imagined (*parikalpita*) and the dependent (*paratantra*), are examined in relation to what they do *not* represent.

As a Sautrāntika, he dealt with the problem of characteristics (*lakṣaṇa*) in great detail. The Sautrāntikas defined a characteristic in terms of causal efficacy (*kāritra*), which in turn is explained literally as "the receiving of the gift of fruit" (*phala-dāna-pratigrahaṇa, Akb* p. 267), i.e., fruitfulness. However, the Sautrāntikas were not satisfied with an ordinary analysis of characteristics. Their extreme analysis of phenomena (*dharma*) into momentary entities, compelled them to speak of own-characteristics (*sva-lakṣaṇa*). This latter introduces the substantialist metaphysics. Therefore, avoiding such substantialist metaphysics, Vasubandhu confines himself to the more pragmatic notion of *lakṣaṇa* in order to distinguish between imaginary and real concepts. The imaginary are, therefore, empty of characteristic (*lakṣaṇa*) or causal efficacy that is shared with or experienced by others as well, like those of dream experience (*Viṃś* 18). They are sometimes referred to as *abhūta-parikalpa*, i.e., a mental fabrication about something that has not come to be. Concepts such as eternal self (*ātman*) or substance (*svabhāva*) fall under this category.

The second type of concept is the dependent (*paratantra*). It is empty of self-existence (*svayaṃ-bhāva*). In fact, it is a negation of what is asserted by, and an assertion of what is negated in, the former. Thus, the dependent is empty of a substance (*svabhāva*) that exists on its own (*svayaṃ-bhāva*) and possesses characteristics (*lakṣaṇa*) as a result of its fruitfulness (*kāritra*). It is the type of concept explained at *Triṃś* 18.

Sthiramati's interpretation of dependence as "the non-substantiality pertaining to arising" (*utpatti-niḥsvabhāvatā*, p. 41) can be misleading, unless such arising is specified as "self-arising" (*svatotpatti*), which is the implication of self-existence (*svayaṃ-bhāva*). It would be the same sort of arising that was negated by Nāgārjuna.

25. *Dharmānāṃ paramārthaś ca yatas tathatāpi saḥ,*
sarva-kālaṃ tathābhāvāt saiva vijñapti-mātratā.

[The third is] the ultimate meaning of events, because it is also suchness. Since it remains such all the time, it, indeed, is a mere concept.

The present statement is most susceptible to an absolutistic interpretation unless it is examined in the background of the most disturbing controversy within the Buddhist philosophical tradition, and which brought back all the metaphysics that the Buddha himself wanted to get rid of. It is the controversy regarding the existence of "everything" (*sarvaṃ*) during the three periods of time, past, present and future. It is the theory advocated by the Sarvāstivādins and which continued to plague the Buddhist philosophical tradition for centuries, eliciting responses from outstanding philosophers like Moggalīputtatissa and Nāgārjuna. With the analysis provided in the present verse, Vasubandhu joins the band of distinguished philosophers who attempted to preserve the Buddha's anti-metaphysical stance by rejecting such a theory.

The term *paramārtha* has a variety of meanings. In the first instance, it can mean "ultimate reality." This is the sense in which the metaphysicians used the term most often. Secondly, in a predominantly ethical context, it implies "ultimate purpose, goal or fruit." Thirdly, in a purely epistemological investigation, it would stand for "ultimate meaning."

The Buddha who abandoned any metaphysical or substantialist speculation, avoided, and sometimes, denounced the first of these meanings. As a full-fledged pragmatist, he recognized the second and third even though, as one who was most interested in morals, he emphasized the second. In our previous study of Nāgārjuna, we have indicated how faithful he was to the teachings of the Buddha. Vasubandhu, however, was more concerned with the epistemological implications of the term.

Therefore, in the present verse, we have rendered the term *paramārtha* as "ultimate meaning." This ultimate meaning pertains to *dharmas*. True *dharmas*, in contrast to the imagined ones, are said to have characteristics (*lakṣaṇa, Triṃś* 24). Thus, the term *dharma*, in the present context is translated as "events."

Yet, the moment the two characteristics—*tathatā* ("suchness") and *sarvakālaṃ tathābhāva* ("remaining such all the time")—are applied to *paramārtha*, one can easily get caught in the metaphysical trap, even though these two characteristics are indispensable in formulating an acceptable account of experience as well as reason. A superficial interpretation of these two characteristics would easily throw Vasubandhu into the metaphysicians' camp, with the Sarvāstivādins and Sāṅkhyans as his companions. However, Vasubandhu has already embarked on a lengthy controversy with some of them, especially with regard to the famous Sarvāstivāda theory of *sarvam asti* (*Akb* pp. 266–267). Indeed, his criticism of that theory seems to have infuriated the Sarvāstivādins to such an extent that they were willing to respond to him with a whole treatise, the *Abhidharmadīpa*.

Vasubandhu's ingenious response to the metaphysician and his solution to their problem is contained in one phrase—*saiva vijñapti-mātratā*.

Keeping this in mind, it is possible to explain *tathatā* as "objectivity," that is, the sense in which the term occurs even in the early discourses of the Buddha (*S* 2.25, also Kalupahana, *Causality*, pp. 92–93). It is this objectivity that Vasubandhu attempted to explain by recognizing the characteristics (*lakṣaṇa*) that distinguish the imagined (*parikalpita*) from the dependent (*paratantra, Triṃś* 24).

Sarvakālaṃ tathābhāva need not necessarily imply permanence (*nityatā*). In fact, it expresses the same sense in which the Buddha utilized the terms *avitatathā* and *anaññathatā* (*S* 2.25; Kalupahana, *Causality*, pp. 93–94). For this reason, the phrase expresses the notion of "regularity" or "uniformity."

Vasubandhu was still aware that in the Buddha's discourse, regularity or uniformity, though based upon experience of related or dependently arisen (*pratītyasamutpanna*) events, was still an inductive inference. Without such inductive inferences and conceptualizations about the future in terms of the past and the present experiences, man would be like a mere "sessile sea-anemone," with no possibility of any intellectual activity. This intellectual exercise, whether it pertains to the substitution of concepts, either in the explanation of the flux of experience (see *Triṃś* 18) or in expressing uniformity (as in the present verse), is what Vasubandhu admits when he claimed that all this is "mere concept" (*vijñapti-mātra*). This, indeed, is the relationship between the *paratantra* and *pariniṣpanna* that he expressed at *Triṃś* 21.

26. *Yāvad vijñapti-mātratve vijñānaṃ nāvatiṣṭhati,*
grāha-dvayasyānuśayas tāvan na vinivartate.

As long as consciousness does not terminate in mere concept, so long will the dispositions for the twofold grasping not cease.

The twofold grasping was mentioned earlier (*Triṃś* 19). "Grasping" (*grāha*) also can mean "knowing." The *Viṃśatikā* was devoted to a refutation of the two metaphysical extremes that one reaches on occasions of sense experience. Sensory knowledge, when carried beyond its confines can lead to the belief either in a metaphysical self (*ātman*) or in substantial elements (*dharma-svabhāva*). Such transgressions are the results of dispositional tendencies. The Buddha's discourse on "Everything" (*Sabba-sutta*) wherein he refused to go beyond sense experience in order to speculate regarding existence was known to all the Buddhists. This does not mean that either knowledge (*grāha*) and the known (*grāhya*) or knowledge (*grāha*) and the knower (*grāhaka*) have to be denied. What is denied is a knower that is independent of knowing, a metaphysical *cogito*, or an object that is independent of knowing, which is implied in substantial elements. These metaphysical beliefs are determined, not by the available experiences, but by one's dispositions. Hence Vasubandhu's reference to the "inclination toward the twofold grasping" (*grāhadvyasya anuśayaḥ*), rather than the twofold grasping itself.

Following upon his analysis in the previous verse, Vasubandhu maintains that so long as one does not realize that any such speculation going beyond the immediate flux of experience confines oneself to mere concepts (*vijñapti-mātra*), one cannot overcome one's inclination toward metaphysical beliefs.

27. *Vijñapti-mātram evedam ity api hy upalambhataḥ,*
sthāpayann agrataḥ kiṃcit tan-mātre nāvatiṣṭhate.

Indeed, one who, on account of one's grasping, were to place some thing before himself [saying]: "This is mere concept," will not stop at "mere-ness."

In terms of its implications, this statement is not at all different from Nāgārjuna's statement regarding emptiness (*śūnyatā*) at *Kārikā* XIII.8: "Those who are possessed of the view of emptiness are said to be incorrigible." Vasubandhu's statement is not so abrasive as Nāgārjuna's. In a more restrained form, Vasubandhu is insisting that the idea of "mere concept" (*vijñapti-mātra*) should not be reified as an ultimate "some thing" (*kiṃcit*), a hidden truth. This, indeed, is similar to Nāgārjuna's own refusal to recognize either the life-process (*saṃsāra*) or freedom (*nirvāṇa*) as "some thing" (*kiṃcit, Kārikā* XXV.20). It is an attempt to prevent the re-introduction of metaphysics into the explanation of *vijñaptimātra*.

28. *Yadā tv ālambanaṃ vijñānaṃ naivopalabhate tadā,*
sthitaṃ vijñapti-mātratve grāhyābhāve tad agrahāt.

When consciousness with object is not obtained, then there being no object, one is established in the state of mere concept, for there is no grasping for it.

One is established in the state of mere concept when the search for an independent object of experience is abandoned. Being established in such a state of awareness, there cannot be any grasping. This is similar to the view expressed by Nāgārjuna regarding views. For Nāgārjuna, the middle path is a view. Yet, because this view provides no absolute truth, there is nothing to grasp on to. Thus, the relinquishing of views is the result of adopting a non-metaphysical view. Similarly, the adoption of the view that the so-called real object is a mere concept enables one to abandon grasping for *vijñaptimātratā*, for there is nothing in the *vijñapti-mātra* that one can grasp on to. It may be noted that the distinction Vasubandhu makes between *vijñapti-mātra* and *vijñapti-mātratā* is similar to the distinction. Nāgārjuna makes between *śūnya* and *śūnyatā*.

29. *Acitto 'nupalambho 'sau jñanaṃ lokottaraṃ ca tat,*
āśrayasya parāvṛttir dvidhā dauṣṭhulya-hānitaḥ.

It is without thought and without object. It is also the supramundane knowledge. Through the destruction of the twofold depravities, there is reversion of the source [of such depravities].

30. *Sa evānāśravo dhātur acintyaḥ kuśalo dhruvaḥ,*
sukho vimukti-kāyo 'sau dharmākhyo 'yaṃ mahā-muneḥ.

This, indeed, is the realm free from influxes. It is unthinkable,

wholesome and stable. It is the serene body of release. This is called the doctrine of the Great Sage.

While Nāgārjuna concluded his famous treatise extolling the virtues of the Buddha's doctrine in eliminating the mass of suffering (*duḥkha-skandha*), Vasubandhu strikes a more positive note when he refers to the state of freedom, namely, the serene body or state of release.

This state is said to be without thought, not because all consciousness is gone, but because there is no thinking in terms of substantial entities. Hence there is nothing to grasp on to as a real object.

It is supramundane knowledge, not because it constitutes a transcendent intuition, but because the dispositional tendencies (*vāsanā*) are appeased. With the appeasement of the dispositional tendencies, the character of the fundamental consciousness (*mūla-vijñāna*) is transformed. Instead of constantly looking for an ultimately real subject (*ātman*) or an absolutely real object (*dharma*), a person deals with the world of experience as it has come to be (*yathābhūta*). Such knowledge reveals things as they have come to be (*bhūta-tathatā*).

Unperturbed by any mystery, not looking for the hidden something, a sage leads a life free from influxes. It is unthinkable, not because such a state is beyond all conceptual thinking, but because it cannot be appreciated by those who are constantly thinking of something mysterious. It is a state of happiness not punctuated by suffering. Hence it is stable. It is the highest state of release enjoyed by the enlightened ones. The doctrine of the Great Sage pertains to this state of freedom and happiness.

Notes

1. *The Central Philosophy of Buddhism*, London: Allen & Unwim, 1959, pp. 49–50.

2. *Nāgārjuna. The Philosophy of the Middle Way*, Albany: The State University of New York Press, 1986.

3. See S. N. Dube, *Cross Currents in Early Buddhism*, New Delhi: Manohar, 1980, the only available detailed study of the *Kathāvatthu*.

4. Second revised edition, Delhi: Motilal Banarsidass, 1975.

5. "Origin and Doctrines of the Early Buddhist Schools," (A Translation of the Hsuan-Chwang Version of Vasumitra's Treatise) translated with annotation by Jiryo Masuda, *Asia Major*, 2(1925):1–78.

6. *Yogācāra Idealism*, p. 2; see also note 4.

7. See *Causality. The Central Philosophy of Buddhism*, Honolulu: The University Press of Hawaii, 1975, Chapter 4.

8. *M* 2.170.

9. *Immanuel Kant's Critique of Pure Reason*, tr. N. K. Smith, London: Macmillan, 1963, p. 136.

10. ibid., emphasis added.

11. J. H. Paton, *Kant's Metaphysics of Experience*, London: Allen & Unwin, 1970, I.403.

12. Kant, *Critique of Pure Reason*, p. 34.

13. ibid.

14. *Collected Papers of Charles Sanders Peirce*, edited by Charles Hartshorne and Paul Weiss, Cambridge, Mass.: Harvard University Press, 1963, 5.12.

15. Bertrand Russell, *The Principles of Mathematics*, New York: W. W. Norton & Company, paperback, no date, p. 11, note 1.

16. *Collected Papers* 5.474.

17. ibid., 5.12.

18. Richard Rorty, "Pragmatism, Relativism, and Irrationalism," in *Proceedings and Addresses of the American Philosophical Association*, 53 (1980):719–738.

19. *VRE* pp. 512–513.

20. *Bṛhadāraṇyaka Upaniṣad*, 1.4.1.

21. *Muṇḍaka Upaniṣad* 3.1.1.

22. *Bṛhadāraṇyaka Upaniṣad*, 1.4.11, 14.

23. William James, *PP* p. 138 (I.134).

24. ibid.

25. *D* 2.62.

26. *M* 1.136.

27. James, *PP* p. 142 (I.139).
28. *S* 3.86.
29. ibid.
30. ibid., 3.87, *rūpaṃ rūpattāya, . . . vedanaṃ vedanattāya, . . . saññaṃ saññattāya, . . . saṅkhāraṃ saṅkhārattāya, . . . viññāṇaṃ viññāṇattāya abhisankhataṃ abhisankharotīti saṅkhāro.*
31. *PP* p. 144 (I.141).
32. *M* 1.265 which refers to *gandhabba*, which is another name for the combination of *saṅkhārā and viññāṇa.*
33. Karl R. Popper and John C. Eccles, *The Self and Its Brain*, New York: Springer International, 1977, pp. 36–47.
34. *D* 2.198.
35. James, *SPP* p. 36.
36. *PP* p. 177 (I.177).
37. *S* 3.86.
38. *ERE* p. 4.
39. *PP* p. 182 (I.182).
40. S. Radhakrishnan, *2500 Years of Buddhism*, ed. P. B. Bapat, New Delhi: Ministry of Information and Broadcasting, Government of India, 1956, p. xii.
41. See discussion of the problem by Rune Johansson, *Psychology of Nirvana*, London: Allen & Unwin, 1969, pp. 67 ff.
42. *Atmatattvaviveka* (of Udayana), Calcutta: Bibliotheca Indica, 1939, p. 5.
43. *S* 2.77.
44. *D* 3.105.
45. *S* 1.15.
46. *D* 3.134.
47. *PP* p. 233 (I.239).
48. *PP* p. 238 (I.245).
49. *Ud* 1.
50. *PP* p. 239–240 (I.247–248).
51. *D* 4.105.
52. *S* 2.25
53. *M* 1.256ff.
54. See *SPP* pp. 97–117.
55. *PP* p. 236 ff.(I.243ff.).
56. ibid., p. 232 (I.238).
57. ibid., pp. 232–233 (I.238–239).
58. *A* 1.10.
59. ibid., 1.254.
60. *S* 3.66.
61. ibid., 2.72; 4.15, etc.
62. ibid., 5.218.
63. ibid., 2.94.
64. *D* 3.105.
65. *M* 1.1 ff.
66. *Dh* 1–2.
67. *S* 4.15.

68. *M* 1.256.
69. ibid., 1.259.
70. ibid., 1.111-112.
71. *S* 3.87.
72. *M* 1.111.
73. ibid.
74. *S* 2.53.
75. *PP* p. 725 (II.79).
76. *Concept and Reality in Early Buddhist Thought*, Kandy: Buddhist Publication Society, 1971, p. 5.
77. *It* 38.
78. *SPP* p. 36.
79. *M* 1.482.
80. ibid.
81. *PP* p. 195 (I.196).
82. ibid., p. 264 (I. 274).
83. ibid.
84. ibid., pp. 654–655 (II.5).
85. ibid., p. 653 (II.13).
86. *Sn* 916.
87. *PP* p. 280 (I.292).
88. *S* 5.421.
89. ibid., 3.76 ff.
90. ibid.
91. *M* 1.395.
92. *S* 2.20; also 1.170.
93. *Dh* 129–130.
94. *A* 1.147–148.
95. *PP* p. 283 (I.296).
96. *ERM* p. 160.
97. *PP* p. 281 (I.293).
98. ibid., p. 282 (I.294).
99. *Vin* 1.44 ff.
100. *D* 3.260; *Sn* 268.
101. *D* 1.91–92.
102. *A* 1.149.
103. *PP* p. 283 (I.296).
104. *Sn* 68.
105. *It* 38.
106. *D* 2.130–131.
107. ibid., 3.230.
108. *PP* pp. 1065–1066 (II.449–450).
109. ibid., p. 1065 (II.449).
110. ibid., p. 1066 (II.450).
111. *S* 3.142.
112. *PP* p. 1067 (II.451).
113. ibid., pp. 10681069 (II.453).

114. ibid., p. 1069 (II.454).
115. *D* 2.36; *M* 1.167; *S* 1.136, etc.
116. *M* 1.174, see also section on Analytical Yoga."
117. *D* 1.70; *M* 1.180 ff.
118. I. B. Horner, *The Middle Length Sayings*, London: PTS, 1967, 1.226.
119. Ñāṇananda, *Concept and Reality*, pp. 53, n.1, 65, 82.
120. *S* 4.295.
121. Ñāṇananda, *loc. cit.*
122. *S* 4.295.
123. *M* 1.167.
124. See *Thera- and Therī-gāthās*, ed. H. Oldenberg and R. Pischel, London: PTS, 1966.
125. *Dh* 99.
126. *S* 1.22.
127. *PP* pp. 1084–1085 (II.470–471).
128. *Dh* 129, *attānaṃ upamaṃ katvā na haneyya na ghātaye.*
129. *M* 1.135, . . .*dhammā pi bhikkhave pahātabbā pageva adhammā*; also *Vajra* p. 32.
130. *WB* p. 153.
131. *D* 3.232; *M* 1.341, *neva attantapo na parantapo*; *M* 1.369, *na attabyābādhāya saṃvatteyya na parabyābādhāya saṃvatteyya.*
132. *Dh* 166.
133. *PP* p. 435 (I.459).
134. ibid., p. 216 (I.221).
135. ibid., p. 434 (I.459).
136. ibid.
137. Murti, *Central Philosophy of Buddhism*, pp. 49–50.
138. See Kalupahana, *Causality*, p. 80.
139. *D* 1.13.
140. *S* 2.25.
141. ibid.
142. *Buddhist Philosophy. A Historical Analysis*, Honolulu: The University Press of Hawaii, 1976, p. 229.
143. *PP* p. 435 (I.460).
144. *S* 2.34.
145. *PP* p. 435 (I.460).
146. ibid., p. 436 (I.461).
147. *D* 1.202; *M* 1.190.
148. *D* 1.202.
149. *Sn* 874.
150. *SPP* p. 35.
151. ibid., p. 37.
152. ibid.
153. *M* 3.234 ff.
154. ibid., 1.1 ff.
155. see Nāṇananda, *Concept and Reality*, p. 50, note. 1.
156. Most Sinhalese editions contain the above reading. The editor of the PTS

edition, who could not believe in this lone exception, seems to have changed the expression to read: *Attamanā te bhikkhū bhagavato bhāsitaṃ abhinandun ti*, *M* 1.6.

157. *SPP* pp. 33–34.
158. *S* 1.14–15.
159. *SPP* p. 34, quoted earlier.
160. *Śvetāśvatara Upaniṣad*, 1.14.
161. *D* 1.13 ff.
162. ibid.
163. ibid., 1.63 ff.
164. *Dialogues of the Buddha*, London: PTS, 1899, 1.84.
165. *M* 1.163–166.
166. *S* 4.295.
167. *D* 3.261–262.
168. ibid., 3.230.
169. *M* 1.296.
170. ibid., 1.175, *paññāya c'assa disvā āsavā parikkhīṇā honti.*
171. *D* 1.76.
172. ibid., 1.157.
173. ibid., 1.77.
174. *M* 1.408–409.
175. *D* 3.230.
176. ibid., 1.84; *M* 2.39, etc.
177. *A* 2.52.
178. *PP* p. 574 (1.609).
179. *M* 1.79.
180. *ERE* p. 22.
181. *VRE* p. 317.
182. ibid., p. 392, note 1.
183. ibid., p. 391.
184. *ERM* pp. 129–146.
185. ibid., pp. 137–138.
186. ibid., p. 139.
187. ibid., p. 143 (emphasis mine).
188. ibid., p. 145.
189. *Collected Papers* 5.474.
190. ibid., 5.414.
191. *ERM* p. 145.
192. *Akb* p. 331.
193. ibid.
194. ibid., p. 329.
195. *Ātmatattvaviveka*, p. 3, *sarvaṃ janasaṃvedanāsiddhaṃ duḥkhaṃ*, meaning "all human experiences are suffering."
196. *VRE* pp. 114–115.
197. *The Soul; its Sorrows and its Aspirations*, 1852, pp. 89, 92, quoted by James, *VRE* p. 73.
198. *VRE* pp. 73.

199. ibid., p. 114, emphasis mine.
200. *M* 2.215.
201. ibid., 2.219–222.
202. ibid., 2.222.
203. Quoted from Oedipus in Colonus, 1225; see *VRE* p. 120, note 9.
204. *VRE* pp. 130.
205. *M* 3.94–99.
206. *S* 3.94–99.
207. *VRE* p. 130.
208. *S* 5.421.
209. *M* 1.265.
210. ibid., 1.85.
211. *S* 4.172.
212. *Pragmatism*, ed. Frederick Burkhardt, Cambridge, Mass.: Harvard University Press, 1968, p. 136.
213. *Tragedy and Philosophy*, Princeton: Princeton University Press, 1968, p. 339.
214. *Freedom and the Moral Life. The Ethics of William James,* Philadelphia: The Westminster Press, 1969, p. 42.
215. *S* 1.135.
216. p. 39.
217. *WB* p. 153.
218. See Kenneth K. Inada, *Nāgārjuna*, Tokyo: Hokuseido Press, 1970, p. 73.
219. *WB* p. 153.
220. ibid.
221. p. 57.
222. *S* 4.15.
223. See K. N. Jayatilleke, *The Early Buddhist Theory of Knowledge*, London: Allen & Unwin, 1963, which makes no reference whatsoever to this discourse.
224. *Concept and Reality*, p. 55.
225. See *Psychology of Nirvana.*
226. *Concept and Reality*, p. 55.
227. See Kalupahana, *Buddhist Philosophy*, pp. 69–88.
228. *Concept and Reality*, p. 53.
229. *D* 3.230.
230. *Ud* 8.
231. *Concept and Reality* pp. 29–30.
232. *M* 3.44–45.
233. *Kārikā* XXV.24.
234. *D* 1.193.
235. *Ud* 1–2.
236. *M* 1.341; *S* 4.172.
237. *Sn* 530; see also 516, 521, 526, 527, 532 referred to by N̄āṇananda, *Concept and Reality*, pp. 32–33.
238. *S* 1.22.
239. *M* 1.167.
240. *D* 2.310; *S* 3.26, 158.
241. *D* 2.100.

242. *S* 1.11.
243. *M* 1.416. This statement is repeated with regard to deeds of speech and thought.
244. *VRE* p. 383, emphasis mine.
245. *ERM* p. 6.
246. *VRE* p. 210.
247. ibid., pp. 249 ff.
248. ibid, pp. 250–251.
249. ibid., p. 253.
250. See C. B. MacPherson, *The Political Theory of Possessive Individualism. Hobbes to Locke*, Oxford: Oxford University Press, 1962.
251. See *VRE* p. 256; compare chapter on "Brāhmaṇa" in the *Dhammapada.*
252. *VRE* p. 256.
253. ibid., p. 257.
254. ibid., p. 383, italics mine.
255. ibid., p. 384.
256. *ERM* p. xvi.
257. *VRE* pp. 350–351.
258. ibid., p. 263.
259. *D* 2.156.
260. *M* 3.202 ff.
261. *Guide Through the Abhidhamma Piṭaka*, Kandy: Buddhist Publication Society, 1971, p. 12.
262. ibid., pp. 2–3,
263. Colombo: The University of Ceylon Press, 1958, pp. 25–41.
264. *DhsA* p. 6.
265. *Kathāvatthuppakaraṇa-aṭṭhakathā*, p. xv.
266. *Abhidhamma Studies. Researches in Buddhist Psychology*, revised and enlarged edition, Kandy: Buddhist Publication Society, 1965, p. 9.
267. John Locke, *An Essay Concerning Human Understanding*, ed. Alexander Campbell Fraser, Oxford: The Clarendon Press, 1894, vol. 1, p. 392.
268. pp. 25 ff.
269. *VbhA* p. 321, *pañcahi viññāṇehi na kañci dhammaṃ paṭivijānāti.*
270. *Adv* p. 32.
271. p. 27.
272. See Saratchandra, p. 34.
273. *Vism* p. 444.
274. See Saratchandra, pp. 82–88.
275. *DhsA* 212.
276. ibid., 421.
277. *Kārikā* III.2.
278. *M* 1.137–138.
279. *Kārikā* XVIII.2.
280. ibid., XVIII.7.
281. ibid., XVIII.17.
282. *A* 2.52.
283. *Kārikā* XXIII.15.

284. *Adv* pp. 259 ff.
285. *Akb* p. 79.
286. *Kārikā* XXIV.18.
287. *The Laṅkāvatāra Sūtra*, Translation, by D. T. Suzuki, London: Routledge & Kegan Paul, 1966, pp., xlii–xliii.
288. *The Laṅkāvatāra Sūtra*, ed. B. Nanjio, Kyoto: The Otani University Press, 1956, p. 375.
289. *Kārikā* XXIV.32.
290. ibid., XVII.1.
291. *S* 1.39; *A* 2.177.
292. *Dh* 1-2.
293. *Nāgārjuna. The Philosophy of the Middle Way*, p. 63.
294. *J* 1.52.
295. *A* 1.254.
296. *Laṅkāvatāra* (Nanjio) p. 358.
297. ibid.
298. ibid.
299. ibid., p. 46.
300. ibid., p. 282.
301. ibid., p. 310.
302. *Kārikā* XVII.1.
303. See *anyathā-bhāva, Kārikā* XV.8.
304. *Yogācāra Idealism*, pp. 145–146.
305. *PP* p. 262 (I.271-272).
306. ibid.
307. *Viṃś* 18.
308. *PP* p. 756 (II.112).
309. *Viṃś* 22.
310. *Triṃś* 2.
311. *Kārikā* XXIV. 13.
312. See Ninian Smart, *Doctrine and Argument in Indian Philosophy*, London: Allen & Unwin, 1964, p. 58.
313. *PP* p. 108 (I.323-324).
314. *A Treatise of Human Nature*, ed. L. A. Selby-Bigge, Oxford: The Clarendon Press, 1968, p. 252.
315. *PP* p. 287 (I.300).
316. *Triṃś* 6.
317. *D* 1.193.
318. See *PP* p. 311 (I.327).
319. *Triṃś* 9–14.
320. *ERE* p. 4.
321. *Triṃś* 15.
322. *S* 2.40.
323. *CP* 5.416.
324. ibid., 1.304 (emphasis added).
325. ibid.
326. ibid., 1.302.

327. ibid., 1.191.
328. ibid., 1.26.
330. *PP* p. 657.
331. *CP* 6.406.
332. *D* 1.43–45.

Index of Sanskrit Terms

Index of Pali Terms

General Index

A priori assumption 144; categories or structures 8, 18, 26; condition 35; fact and value 12; theological system 102
Abhidhamma Piṭaka, 105, 106, 108
Abhidharma (Abhidhamma), 4, 5, 23, 105, 107, 109, 110, 116, 127; Abhidharmikas 199
Abhidharmadīpa, 109, 112, 211
Abhidharmakośa, 5, 107, 109, 141, 174, 175, 199, 205
Absolute, 75, 93, 123, 124, 127
absolute, alien 165; beauty 56; beginning 136, 194; certainty 71; change 151; dependence 134; dichotomy 85; difference 23, 164; distinction 112; emptiness 39, 150; existence 130; fiction 27; freedom 88; idealism 192; idealist 141; identity 23; knowledge 78; laws 50, 51, 99, 163; negation 40, 42, 117, 169; nothingness 39, 147; objectivity 146; origin 164; reality 150, 191, 205–207; self-assertion 40, 42; self-denial 40, 42, 91; sense 107; statement 80; subjectivity 146; surrender 101; truth 13, 191
Absolutism, 39, 60, 119, 123, 128, 130, 160, 170; non- 51, 170
Absolutist, 67, 127, 162, 163, 166; non- 78; 128, 160
absolutist, implication 80; notion of ultimate fruit 166; philosophical enterprise 207; system 10; ways of thinking 79
aesthetics, 6, 144–146
Āgamas, 13, 54, 116, 119, 122, 160
aggregates, 15, 17, 20–22, 29, 31, 32, 38 39, 84, 87, 184
Ajanta, 48
Ālara Kālama, 66, 67
altruism, 39, 40; altruistic, 50
Aṅguttara-nikāya, 90
annihilation, 125, 197; of dispositional tendencies 86; of emotions 46; of the sensory process and conception 67; of self 38, 78, 117
annihilationism, 53, 61, 84
anxiety, 16, 84, 85
appeasement, 62; the yoga of 143; the body 98; of dispositions 16, 43, 86, 97, 129, 197, 214; of grasping 119; of the modes of self and selfhood 117; of object 192; of obsession 95; of reasoning and investigation 65; of thought 63
apperception, transcendental, (Kantian version) 7, 8, 22; (Jamesean critique) 40, 53; (Indian version) 12; (Buddha's critique) 15, 29, 37, 38, 58, 59, 70, 95, 112; (Nāgārjuna's critique) 117; (Maitreya's critique) 149
Araṇavibhanga-sutta, 99
Ariyapariyesana-sutta, 66, 94, 97
Arjuna, 13, 41
Asanga, 126, 131, 200
Asoka, 116
atoms (theory of) 175, 182–185, 193; atomic, causes 176; events 207; impressions 18, 22; particles 132; atomism 132
Avadānas, 128

Berkeley, George, 193
Bhagavadgītā, 13, 41, 91
body (physical) 15, 17, 18, 29–31, 44, 74, 94, 166, 178, 201; conscious 176; deed of 99; experience of 44, 94; material self 38, 95; materialist conception 69, 189; mind and 20, 124, 137; reflection on 69; serene body of release 214; tranquillity of 68, 98
bondage, 15, 18, 75, 119; *ālaya* as the seed of 139, 158; Brahmanical notion of 24, 28; dispositions in 89; metaphysical assertions regarding 168; *papañca* as the